Prelude to Civil 1642

Mr. Justice Malet and the Kentish Petitions

T. P. S. Woods

with an Introduction by
IVAN ROOTS

MICHAEL RUSSELL

& R Print 054 -

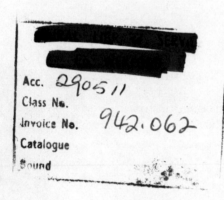

First published in Great Britain 1980
by Michael Russell (Publishing) Ltd.,
The Chantry, Wilton, Salisbury

Filmset in Monophoto Bembo
by Santype International Ltd., Salisbury, Wilts
Printed in Great Britain by
Hillman Printers (Frome) Ltd.

Contents

List of Illustrations

(between pages 116 & 117)

Plan of the Palace of Westminster 1641–42.
Adapted from Plan III, *The History of the King's Works*, H. M. Colvin (1963ff.)I, and reproduced by courtesy of the Controller of Her Majesty's Stationery Office.

Westminster Hall, west end [actually south], with the Courts of Chancery and King's Bench in session.
Anonymous (17th century). Reproduced by courtesy of the British Library.

The Site of the Maidstone Assizes 1641–42.
From a sketch made in 1623 and in the possession of J. H. Baverstock in 1832.

Gilt badge depicting head of Charles I.

Mr. Justice Malet, aged about sixty.
Anonymous caricature. Reproduced by courtesy of the British Library.

Mr. Justice Malet, aged about seventy-nine.
Anonymous (1661). Reproduced by courtesy of Colonel Sir Edward Malet Bt., OBE.

The Commons Chamber during the Long Parliament.
Anonymous (1641). Reproduced by permission of the Secretary and Keeper of the Records of the Duchy of Cornwall.

Lady Malet.
Anonymous (c. 1661). Reproduced by courtesy of Colonel Sir Edward Malet Bt., OBE.

Hatchments of Baldwin and Sir Thomas Malet in All Saints Church, Poyntington.

Acknowledgements

First and foremost I am indebted to Professor Ivan Roots, a specialist in this period of English history who has given me a wealth of helpful advice and encouragement. Colonel Sir Edward Malet and Dr. Hugh Malet have put their extensive knowledge of their family at my disposal, they have read various drafts and made valuable suggestions. Others have also read the whole book in draft and have made me free of their knowledge: Dr. R. F. Hunnisett of the Public Record Office, whose work sorting and indexing the assize records made possible a full account of assizes at Maidstone and elsewhere; Professor J. S. Cockburn of Maryland University, the greatest living expert on the English assizes of the sixteenth and seventeenth centuries; Mr. Maurice Bond, Clerk of the Records at the House of Lords, who is *the* authority on the role of its assistants, and his Deputy, Mr. H. S. Cobb, to whose patience, courtesy and practical help I owe a great deal; Dr. John Baker of St. Catharine's College, Cambridge, who was a never-failing source of information about judges, serjeants and their portraits. A number of people have made substantial contributions to various parts of this book: Miss E. McNeill of the Middle Temple Library, Dr. M. Blacksell of the Geography Department, Exeter University, and Mrs. Blacksell, Mr. Denys Spittle of the Royal Commission on Ancient and Historic Monuments and Constructions, Mr. H. M. Colvin, Reader in Architectural History at Oxford University, Mr. Graham Jones, and various county archivists—especially Mr. H. L. Douch of Cornwall, Miss M. E. Holmes of Dorset, Dr. Felix Hull of Kent, Mr. I. P. Collis and Mr. D. M. M. Shorrocks of Somerset and Mr. M. W. Farr of Warwick. I am particularly grateful to Mr. Shorrocks whose inspired research and detection helped me sort out the houses at Poyntington where Sir Thomas Malet and his uncle Michael lived. Mr. Simon Hughes MSc (Statistics) advised me on the compilation of Appendix III and checked the results. Mr. Hugh Montgomery-Massingberd, a former editor of *Burke's Peerage*, checked the citing of peerages. Mrs. D. M. Clarke and Miss M. J. O. Kennedy were able to find and transcribe for me a mass of seventeenth-century manuscripts in the Public Record Office, British Library and elsewhere. Mrs. G. Carter, Mrs. P. Royal, Mrs. J. Willbourn and Miss M. Christopher typed drafts of the book not once but many times. There were a host of others who assisted in various ways: archivists, directors, keepers and librarians, but especially the staffs of the London Library in St. James's Square and the Somerset Library in Street. Last, and by no means least, I owe a very special debt to Mr. A. P. Detsicas and the Council of the Kent Archaeological Society for their financial and moral support. With so many people to help, the book almost wrote itself. I am grateful for an opportunity to thank them once more.

Poyntington   TOM WOODS

Note on Transcription

In quoting from seventeenth-century sources I have generally retained the original spelling, but have modernized capitalization, extended contemporary contractions and sometimes modified punctuation. Occasionally I have modernized the quotation completely where it appears as words spoken in the text. I have used modern place names where I could identify them. For my authority on the correct spelling of surnames, I have used Keeler, *DNB*, Foss and Everitt in that order.

I have departed from these principles in Appendices II, IV and V, where I have stuck more closely to the typography of the originals, in order to convey a truer impression of the time.

Dates are given in the Old Style, but with the year regarded as beginning on 1 January.

T. P. S. W.

Introduction

Historians are still trying to establish the long-term causes of the English Civil War which began in 1642. Some have emphasized deep-seated economic and social issues traced back even to the first Tudors and beyond. A crisis was perhaps unavoidable. But a civil war within two years of the summoning of the Long Parliament in 1640 was unexpected by contemporaries and should be a matter of surprise to us. For nearly a year of that Parliament Charles I, bereft of his most experienced and confident ministers, faced an almost unanimous hostility to his policies. That fact alone suggests that a shooting war—which demands at least two sides in arms—was the most unlikely outcome of all. Delving into the more distant past will not explain it.[1] The answer lies more in the peculiar circumstances of 1642 and what is required—and fortunately is gradually being provided by historians ready to break out of the comfortable grip of S. R. Gardiner's great narrative—is a close, even microscopic, study of events, moves and personalities, not only at Westminster and in the organs of central government, but within the whole range of provincial communities.

We need to rake among the grass roots in order to understand how King Charles came to raise his standard at Nottingham on 22 August 1642, in the assurance that he had a party and armed forces sufficient to match the political and military machine of King Pym. Only a few were closely involved in the affairs and attitudes of Whitehall and Westminster and when men came to decide whether to fight or at least to support one side or the other, it was in the localities mostly that they did it.[2] If they steered clear of a commitment, it was chiefly at home they did that, too. We must never forget the neuters nor the men who changed sides, some several times over, responding mostly to local rather than national developments.[3] Some of the most vital personal decisions came between the failure of Charles I's attempted *coup* against the Five Members in January 1642 and the battle that never was at Turnham Green in the following autumn. These are months that call for particular attention in 'the local dimension' of the drift towards civil war.

It is within this context that we should look at Tom Woods's study of Mr. Justice Malet and the Kentish Petitions. As each evil counsellor, subverted institution and abused financial expedient fell, so underlying rifts among MPs and within the political nation were exposed and, once exposed, widened. Discontent is a powerful cement to bring together the disparate—conservatives and radicals, pragmatists and ideologues—but it seldom sets fast. Cohesion was already weakening when the Irish Rebellion (October 1641), followed by the Grand Remonstrance, raised in an acute and practical form the question of who should control the military power, that ultimate guarantor of sovereignty in state and society, which enables the effective pursuit of policy by other and peremptory means. To introduce a militia bill at all was a radical measure, to contemplate enacting it without the King's assent by making it an ordinance enforceable by contempt seemed to many revolutionary, especially as it was associated wtih further claims in religion and government. Moreover there were widespread symptoms of a breakdown in law and order as 'the meaner sort of people', encouraged by some of their betters, sought a role in politics. Sir Edward Dering was prepared to offer his 'hearty thanks for those excellent laws' lately passed, but he and others were beginning to see in the actions of John Pym and his associates a threat to the 'well ordered chain of government' which for moderate men was essential both at the centre and the periphery.[4]

The petition which Dering proposed at the Maidstone assizes in March 1642 gave expression to this concern and sought the renewal of a 'good understanding' between the King and his two Houses of Parliament. The petition was by no means unique. In the spring and summer of that year petitions and counter-petitions proliferated in the localities, interlarding the manifestos and propositions which made first for 'paper skirmishes' and then for a paper war between King and Parliament. The real significance of this particular petition was the strong reaction it provoked. The two Houses of Parliament were 'transcendently incenced'. Some saw it as 'a desperate design to put not only Kent, but, for aught is known, all Christendom too into combustion'.[5] There was almost panic. Revenge on the leading petitioners made for a quickening of pace. For Gardiner the petition was a signal of civil war, impending and inevitable—a firebell in the night. Its sentiments stirred radical views and widened gaps in opinion. For these reasons the petition and its context demand detailed attention. That is what Tom Woods has generously given—and in doing so he has thrown light on much else besides.

Tom Woods was by profession a business man, and a successful one. By inclination he became a historian, and, in my judgement, an able one. When he served on the University of Exeter Appointments Board, he told me of his interest in Sir Thomas Malet, whose house, Poyntington Manor, near Sherborne, he lived in and loved. He had already begun so intelligently to establish the facts and assess the significance of Malet's career that I had no hesitation in encouraging him to write it up. Thereafter he read everything relevant, sought out fresh sources and asked new questions of the well-known, consulted the best authorities, listened to them and, as he judged it appropriate, acted upon advice.

The result is a perceptive and extremely well-informed contribution to knowledge and understanding of the immediate circumstances in which civil war broke out. It is also a finely drawn portrait of a notable seventeenth-century lawyer. Very much more than a work of piety, it is written in an appealing blend of scholarly meticulousness and natural vigour. In it Tom Woods has more than realized my prognostications. The pity of it is that he died bravely of cancer before his book could be published. To the last he was devoting attention to each detail, trying to ensure that the work should be exact, polished and professional. I am honoured to have been associated with him in the making of this book and to have been invited to write this Introduction.

In *Prelude to Civil War 1642* Tom Woods has provided his own memorial. I commend this learned, elegant book without cavil to everyone, serious student or general reader, for whom the Stuart era has its own compelling appeal.

The University of Exeter   IVAN ROOTS

I

The Hour and the Man

'He is a learned man of good report. God give him joy.'

SIR RICHARD HUTTON
Judge of the Court of Common Pleas
(written in 1635).[1]

When he dissolved his third Parliament in 1629 Charles I won the agreement of the majority of his judges to proceedings in Star Chamber against the leaders of the Country opposition who had opposed his policies in the Commons. Only Sir John Walter, his Chief Baron of the Exchequer, objected. Charles tried to make him resign, in the end simply forbidding him to sit on the bench and suspending him for the rest of his life. It was a small but significant incident in a long Stuart campaign to intimidate the judges and ensure their continued subservience to the Crown;[2] and it preceded eleven years of 'personal rule', with no Parliament to check abuses of power by Charles and his servants or to vote him the money he needed.

Abuses of power there certainly were. Some of the worst were committed by William Laud, who became Archbishop of Canterbury in 1633. He persecuted the Puritans, who wanted to 'purify the usages of the established church from the taint of popery or to worship separately by forms so purified'.[3] Laud, who was dedicated to uniformity of worship, disciplined Puritan clergy and withdrew the licences of preachers who held Puritan views. He introduced a number of 'innovations' aimed at securing a greater measure of reverence in church. He used the Courts of Star Chamber and High Commission (he was a member of both) to enforce his social and ecclesiastical policies and to punish offenders.[4] In order to preserve their freedom of worship, the Puritans became involved in colonizing ventures. When these failed or only partly succeeded, some of them fell back on their only practical alternative. They used their overseas ventures as a cloak for secret activity designed to secure a new Parliament and the removal of those who threatened their liberty.[5]

The King himself, without Parliament to vote him the funds he needed, had still to try to balance his budget. Of his various money-raising schemes, it was the issue of ship money (though arguably not the most dubious form of royal taxation) which was to have the most far-reaching repercussions. In 1634, following the ancient custom of English kings, Charles addressed writs to the seaports requiring them to furnish either ships or money instead. In the following year he extended the tax to inland towns as well as those on the coast. To this there was some opposition but his judges endorsed the measure by a majority of ten to two. When he issued his third writ, the judges once more lent their authority. Charles did in fact use the money to strengthen his fleet, but he used his fleet to assist the armies of Catholic Spain against the Protestant Dutch. It was this that the Protestant English resented. Two men determined that the case against ship money should be heard in open court. One was Lord Saye and Sele, a leader of the opposition in the Lords for the last sixteen years. The other was John Hampden, who was prosecuted for not paying the tax. Hampden was found guilty by the votes of seven judges to five. Charles could claim to have won, but in the eyes of his subjects he had lost. For them the ship-money levy was now an abuse simply because it lacked the support of the English people.[6] The issue had become one not of law but of politics.

Charles's alienation of the Scots was more emphatic. He and Laud tried to impose on them a prayer book based on the English pattern. The Scots rebelled. In June 1639, without money and popular backing, the King was forced to make a treaty, by which he undertook to leave Scottish affairs to the Scots.[7] Early in 1640, in order to get funds for a futher expedition against the Scots, Charles called a Parliament, but the Commons were obdurate and unhelpful. John Pym, the member for Tavistock in Devon, recited the accumulated grievances of the last eleven years. When Charles heard that Pym was in communication with the Scots and about to introduce a motion declaring the Commons on the side of the rebels, he dissolved the Short Parliament, attempted to invade Scotland without adequate funds or forces and was driven back to the Tees. In October 1640 by the Treaty of Ripon the Scots forced Charles to agree to pay an indemnity for as long as they remained upon English soil. Unless he summoned another Parliament he could not find the money.[8] In the ensuing elections there was a major victory for 'the Country'—those who claimed to seek the good of their local communities and to oppose the ways of 'the Court', represented by the privy councillors and their adherents, who supported the royal policies. There was no 'Country party', indeed there were no parties in the sense in which we talk of political parties today. The word 'party' in this context was applied only in a pejorative sense, meaning 'faction'. Those who were of 'the Country' acknowledged no party whip, no party programme and no party leader. There was, it is true, a determined core of Puritans, whose unanimity of purpose and action gave them influence out of all proportion to their numbers.[9]

John Pym was the architect of this great electoral victory and the leader of the Puritan core in the Commons. As Secretary of the Providence Island Company he had earned the support and respect of its twenty-six participants ('adventurers'), of whom more than half now assumed key opposition roles in one or other of the two Houses. Though he was an impressive speaker, it was behind the scenes that he was at his most effective. They called him 'the Ox', but this did less than justice to his intelligence, his organizing ability and his political instinct.[10]

The Long Parliament met in November 1640. The overwhelming majority of members were united in their desire to remove abuses and the King's 'evil counsellors' who had caused them. At once Pym's Puritan core consolidated its position and began to neutralize the King's supporters in both Houses. Within days the Commons brought to the Lords a charge of high treason against Thomas Wentworth, Earl of Strafford, the strongest and most ruthless of all the King's servants, and secured his imprisonment in the Tower. In due course they accused Archbishop Laud of high treason and sent him also to the Tower. They drove overseas John Finch, Baron Finch of Fordwich, who as Lord Keeper of the Great Seal had bullied the judges over ship money, and Secretary Windebank who liked the Catholics too much. They accused the judges who supported the King at Hampden's trial and two who supported Hampden on technical grounds. And they harried many of the minor courtiers. For four long months, while the Puritans strengthened their machine, not one of the King's 'evil counsellors' was brought to trial. At last Strafford was arraigned in Westminster Hall by the Commons of England while the Lords acted as judges. When the Lords were unwilling to convict, the Commons dropped the impeachment and in May 1641 passed a Bill of Attainder which was intended to pronounce Strafford a traitor without the need for proving it.[11]

From the start of the Long Parliament there had been a massive propaganda campaign in support of the Puritan programme for reform. There were fiery sermons from the pulpit, printed pamphlets and above all circulating petitions.[12] At first the petitions listed general grievances including 'evil counsellors', ship-money, monopolies and the levying of troops. Then there was a petition signed by some ten to twenty thousand Londoners to abolish the whole bench of bishops 'root and branch'. This was presented to the Commons backed by some 400 orderly, well-dressed, supporters. It shocked many in the House that day, who deprecated especially the canvassing of ordinary people, for the King's Council and the City government held it illegal and seditious to canvas support for petitions by getting signatures. Some feared that tumultuous assemblies of people might try to overthrow Parliament.[13]

The London petition became a signal for a flood of others from all over England. Most were for or against bishops. Those demanding the abolition of bishops were better organized, more actively canvassed and more numerous. Pro-forma petitions were sent out from London to Puritan activists in the provinces and Puritans were everywhere busy soliciting hands. It was not uncommon to get signatures from people who could not read and to trick others by reading to them a moderate petition and getting them to sign something more extreme. Some petitions were actually forged. On 25 January 1641, in a coordinated effort, the knights of the shire for eleven different counties all handed in petitions with thousands of signatures demanding the abolition of the bishops.[14] One petition signed by 2,500 Puritans in Kent came before Sir Edward Dering, one of the two knights of the shire for that county, as chairman of the Commons committee on religion. This also demanded the abolition of episcopacy 'root and branch'. Dering saw at once that it was a parrot version of a copy sent down to Kent from London. He modified its language before presenting it to the Commons for it was not bishops that he minded, but what he called 'lordly prelacy'.[15]

So far Pym's role had been one of restraint so that the moderates in Parliament did not react against his policies. But when Strafford's fate was still undecided, when Pym had played every trick he could muster, and when it still seemed as if the King and the Lords might reject the attainder, restraint seemed no longer opportune. On 21 April 10,000 citizens had marched on Westminster led by three City trained-band captains. They came peaceably enough, but they brought with them another monster petition demanding the death of Strafford and the reform of the Church. A fortnight later they returned with swords and staves demanding an answer. By now they had been incensed to fever heat by rumours of popish plots and of Royalist attempts to seize power by force. Between five and ten thousand shopkeepers, craftsmen, apprentices and citizens filled the Palace of Westminster and lined the approaches to the two Houses so that members and peers had to run the gauntlet of cries for Strafford's death. On 8 May the Lords had become so frightened and depleted in numbers that the Puritans got their majority and the mob switched its attention to the Palace of Whitehall. Two nights of riot were enough. On 10 May Charles agreed to Strafford's execution. Within a week William Juxon, Lord High Treasurer of England, resigned the white staff of his office to the King. It was clear that the King could no longer protect his officers of state.[16]

After Strafford's death, the Puritan attacks switched back to the bishops. Pym's aim was to remove them from the House of Lords, where, royally appointed, they supported royal policies. He got a Bishops' Exclusion Bill along these lines approved by the Commons and sent to the Lords, who rejected it. In the meantime his more extreme supporters drafted another bill based on the root and branch petition, seeking to abolish bishops altogether, and got Sir Edward Dering to present it. Dering was flattered and moved by the opportunity to become the centre of attention, although he eventually regretted his action. The Root-and-Branch Bill was unlikely to succeed where the more moderate measure had failed.[17]

Reforming legislation followed in the wake of retribution against counsellors, judges and bishops. Two bills were going through their stages in the two Houses that would deprive most of the prerogative courts, both spiritual and temporal, of their jurisdiction. And then Pym heard of a proposed visit by the King to Scotland. At once he scented intrigue and feared that Charles would march on London at the head of an army. He had to make peace with the Lords. On 24 June he carried to them the Ten Propositions asking (among other things) that the army might be disbanded as soon as the troops were paid, that the King's journey might be delayed, that evil counsellors might be removed and replaced by 'such officers and counsellors as his people and Parliament may have just cause to confide in'; that 'trusty' lord lieutenants might be appointed and that the ports might be placed in 'good hands'. Pym wanted the command of the armed forces taken away from men who might be loyal to the King and given to those whom he and his supporters could trust. The Houses reunited and Charles was once more isolated. He agreed to disband the army and was again pressed to delay his journey to Scotland.[18]

With the sole exception of Sir George Croke, one of the justices of the King's Bench, all the judges who had been involved in the ship-money business were now either dead or threatened with impeachment. Poor, senile, principled Croke was now in his eighty-first year. He was one of two judges of the King's Bench to be exempted by the House of Commons from the charge of having delayed justice to its members imprisoned in 1629 for words spoken in Parliament. Only he and Sir Richard Hutton of the Common Pleas had come down flatly and unequivocally against the King and the majority of the judges in Hampden's case. He did these things because he believed he was right, but at his age championing his principles against intense opposition was an exhausting business. The struggle wore him out and in the summer of 1641 he was allowed to retire and to keep his salary, allowances and title.[19] On 1 July 1641 Serjeant Thomas Malet was appointed to succeed Croke in the King's Bench.[20]

The Malets were great landowners in Normandy long before the Conquest. One of them took a well-born Saxon wife, whose sister, the Lady Godiva, was the grandmother of King Harold of England. Another fought with William at Hastings and after the battle buried Harold in a cairn overlooking the sea. A Malet was Lord Great Chamberlain of England and held vast tracts of land from Henry I, the King whom they called the 'Lion of Justice'. A Baron Malet of Curry Malet was a guarantor of Magna Carta. Thomas Malet's great-grandfather was solicitor to Henry VIII. By 1641 they were something of a clan, not universally rich, but conscious of their lineage and proud of their service to King and kingdom.[21] Thomas himself was born about 1582, but we do not know where. His father, Malachi Malet, a third son, lived in a modest way at Luxulyan in Cornwall. His mother came from the same county and was a daughter of Richard Trevanion. Beyond that we know almost nothing of Malet's father and mother or the place where they lived.[22] In 1600 Malet was admitted to the Middle Temple and in 1606 he was called to the bar by Sir Henry Montagu, who was reader in that year, responsible for the training of the young students.[23]

Probably through family connections Malet was elected to James I's

Parliaments of 1614 and 1621 as member for Tregony in Cornwall.[24] In the first he took little part in the proceedings.[25] In the second he spoke on at least fifty-four occasions, was named to eleven committees for bills and helped to prepare charges against Sir Giles Mompesson, the most flagrant of the monopolists, and Sir John Bennett, a corrupt judge of the Prerogative Court at Canterbury.[26]

In both these Parliaments Malet was an active supporter of the Country opposition to the Court group in the Commons. In committee and in full session of the House he spoke out again and again against unparliamentary taxation, patents and monopolies.[27] He made himself master of parliamentary procedure. He studied old records and quoted his authorities to the House.[28] Members came to respect his precedents, found themselves supporting his speeches and gradually gave him their confidence.[29]

Malet was not a member of James I's 1624 Parliament, perhaps because his practice was growing at the bar or because he could not reconcile his past political views with the work he had begun to do for Lord Conway, one of the principal secretaries of state. This was not solely legal or advisory. He conducted negotiations on Conway's behalf. For instance, he helped to resolve the marriage settlement of Conway's second daughter, Brilliana, to Sir Robert Harley and had the difficult task of interrogating him about the worth of his properties and the encumbrances upon them.[30]

Through Conway's patronage Malet secured a seat in the first two Parliaments of Charles I as member for Newtown, Isle of Wight. Whether from respect for his patron, concern for his livelihood or for some other reason, Malet the zealous, painstaking reformer of 1621 had become Malet the casual, half-hearted courtier of 1625 and 1626. He spoke hardly at all. When he did, it was mainly to urge moderation. This sort of seeming inconsistency was not unusual at the time. There were then no sharp divisions upon party lines as there are today and men were very pragmatic in their approach.[31]

In 1628 Charles had to summon his third Parliament, like the others because of the need to raise money. Once more, Conway commended four of his clients to boroughs on the Isle of Wight. Malet was among them. But the old magic failed. None of Conway's nominations succeeded. This exemplifies a shift in power that had been taking place over a period of thirty years. Queen Elizabeth had kept a tight hold on the House of Commons through the prestige and power of her privy councillors there and through the patronage of her great lords. By now patronage was recoiling in the face of local opposition. The Council had been shorn of its prestige.[32]

Conway died in 1631 and Malet lost his patron. However, Malet had a solid practice at the bar and his name appears again and again in the law reports as pleading in the King's Bench.[33] And then at the beginning of Trinity Term in 1635 he was at last created serjeant-at-law and admitted to the ancient and honourable Order of the Coif.[34] Serjeants were not appointed; they were *created*, like peers of the realm. None but they might practise in the Court of Common Pleas. They alone might wear the coif, the distinctive dress of their order, a white lawn cap, fitting tightly round the head. The judges called them 'brother' and they might remain covered even in the presence of the King himself.[35]

Malet's patrons at the time were the Queen, whom he had served as Solicitor General since 1626, and Henry Montagu, now Earl of Manchester, who had called him to the bar in 1606. Following the custom of newly created serjeants Malet presented the judges with rings: the motto he chose for the inscription was 'Deo, Regi, Regine, Legi'. He believed that the rule of law was compatible with the prerogative of kings.[36]

In an atmosphere of mounting political tension, Malet conducted his legal practice at Westminster, building up a solid reputation in the courts. Between November 1637 and October 1639 he was Treasurer of Serjeants' Inn, Chancery Lane[37] and sometime before 1639 he acquired a house in the parish of St. Clement Dane Westminster in addition to his chamber in Serjeants' Inn, and an estate in Somerset.[38] He always had difficulty in making ends meet. On vacation in Somerset he worried about the safety of his house and chamber which lay locked and uninhabited during his absence and about his clerk who was slow to remit his fees. When the plague came to London and Westminster in the latter part of 1639, he was glad to let his town house for most of the following year.[39]

Malet's promotion to the bench in July 1641 was the climax of his legal career. It came at a climax in English history. The hour called for courage and wisdom and strength. In 1637 it had been Judges Hutton and Croke who stood out against the majority of the judges in resisting the arbitrary acts of the King. In 1642 it was to be Malet who stood out from the majority of the judges in resisting the arbitrary acts of the two Houses of Parliament. Malet had been held in high esteem by Hutton, he was to be a worthy successor to Croke and to show himself as principled as either.[40] Within a week he was knighted by the King at Whitehall.[41]

2

Woolsack and Bench

'For I did think, and still shall think a great difference betweene
the words of a judge sitting judicially in a court of judgement
... and his speech in any other place.'

MR. NICHOLAS FULLER
in the House of Commons, 12 April 1606.[1]

After his promotion Malet went to Westminster in state, wearing his
scarlet robes.[2] His new life had begun. Henceforth, he would be addressed
as 'My Lord' while he sat at assizes (and at other times by those who
sought to flatter him),[3] he would be 'Mr. Justice Malet' when he was
acting as assistant to the House of Lords (though the Clerk of the Parliaments
more often spelled him 'Mallett' in the manuscript journals of the House),[4]
and to the world at large 'Sir Thomas Malet'; if they wanted to be
pedantic they might add 'Knight, one of the Justices of His Majesty's
Court of King's Bench at Westminster'.[5]

By 1641 the Palace of Westminster had been the centre of England's
life since before the Conquest and of Malet's for four decades. He had
known its courts of law as student, barrister, Solicitor General to the Queen
and serjeant-at-law. He had known it as a member of the House of Commons
in four different Parliaments.

The centre of this palace, indeed the heart of England itself, was Westminster Hall. Two hundred and fifty feet long and seventy in width, it was
the greatest building in a palace of kings. Rufus built it to be a monument
to his might. Richard Plantagenet raised the hammer-beamed roof, so
high that you could only dimly discern it in the shadow of the great
ribs and timber arches on which it rested. There in the vaulted gloom
flew the carved angels that bore his coat.[6] At the upper end of the Hall
below the great south window was a wooden platform that supported
two courts of law.[7] On this spot and under an open sky English kings
did justice before ever the Conqueror came.[8] In 1641 this was still the
stage where the state trials of the great were played. Here, three months

before Malet's promotion, the Lords sat as judges to try the Earl of Strafford. Now the wooden screens and scaffolding were gone. The Lord High Steward had relinquished his office. The peers had returned to their chamber and put off their robes. Strafford was dead, condemned by Act of Parliament, because they could not convict him by process of law.[9]

On the platform in the south-east corner of the Hall was the Court of King's Bench which took the Sovereign's title for its name. Its jurisdiction was partly criminal and partly civil. The judges sat on a dais raised above the body of the court and facing the arched entrance door at the northern end.[10] The Chief Justice of King's Bench on Malet's promotion was Sir John Bramston, one of the six judges bailed for £10,000 each while they awaited impeachment proceedings for their part in the ship-money business.[11] Besides Bramston and Malet the only other judge of King's Bench permitted to sit was Sir Robert Heath, for the fourth judge of the court, Sir Robert Berkeley, another ship-money judge, had been accused of high treason and arrested while actually sitting in court.[12]

In the south west corner of the Hall and divided from the King's Bench by a narrow passage was the Court of Chancery where the Lord Keeper of the Great Seal of England, supported by the Master of the Rolls and the masters in chancery, presided upon his marble seat. He fulfilled the office of Lord Chancellor without his higher-sounding title. In his court a man could sometimes obtain redress that he could not obtain through the courts of common law. The Lord Keeper in July 1641, Lord Littleton of Mounslow, had held his office for less than six months. His predecessor, Lord Keeper Finch, had fled overseas to avoid impeachment by the Commons for supporting the King and coercing the judges over the ship-money issue.[13]

In front of the Courts of Chancery and King's Bench there was an oak partition that kept the crowd at a distance and yet allowed the judges to see and hear over the top all that happened beyond. If Malet looked down the length of Westminster Hall from his seat in the King's Bench, he could see the Court of Common Pleas almost at the far end on the left. It heard civil suits, cases between subject and subject. It, too, was fenced in by wooden planks. In term time and with Parliament in session, the crowd that stood or milled between the courts in Westminster Hall could be so thick that, to quote a contemporary observer, 'you might without offence shoulder a lord to get through the press.' There were barristers and clients discussing cases, solicitors touting for work. There were the 'men of straw' with a telltale wisp in their shoe to say their witness could be bought; servants waiting for masters who were engaged in the courts or sitting in one of the two Houses; vendors of pens, ink, parchment, paper and food; people using the hall as a short cut to the warren of buildings beyond the Commons steps; and the idlers who had merely come to see the play.[14]

The patent of Malet's appointment described him as 'one of our justices assigned to hold pleas before us'. The King was, in fact, never present in court. Yet his disembodied presence was more awful than the King himself. The patent continued 'as long as he shall well behave him selfe in the execution thereof'. This was important, for the majority of earlier appointments to the bench had been made during the King's pleasure and sometimes the King had removed his judges from office because he disapproved of their judicial decisions. If the new wording gave some protection to the judges against the use of arbitrary power by the King it was clear that it did not protect them from the wrath of the Commons. They had simply exchanged one arbitrary master for another.[15]

Trinity term was three weeks in length. While it lasted the Court of King's Bench sat six days a week in the mornings only. The judges sat *en banc*, hearing each case together. The court was first and foremost the supreme criminal court of England. Primarily it heard pleas of the Crown—criminal cases. Usually these were removed from inferior courts by writ; very rarely did it hear cases in the ordinary way. Yet it was still on occasion a court of first instance for great men and great causes. King's Bench could also exercise a measure of control over illegal acts or omissions by other courts and by persons and bodies entrusted with the government of the country, both at local and national level.[16]

The court's procedure for civil actions was complicated, protracted and costly. When men resorted to law they prepared to spend months in London or Westminster. For suits over trifling sums there could be ten or fifteen adjournments before the business was done. In the end it was often only the lawyers who won. There was a story of two men who went to law over a hive of bees and each spent £500 on the case. And yet men respected the law; it was the lawyers they disliked.[17]

When he received his patent as justice of King's Bench, Malet also had from the office of the Clerk of the Crown in Chancery a writ of assistance signed by the King and sealed with the Great Seal of England. By this he was commanded, 'all other things laid aside', to be personally present in Parliament to treat and give his advice. It was in the House of Lords and not on the bench that his superior duty lay.[18]

Let us re-create the House as it was in July 1641.

Symbolically, the doors of the Upper House stand open, for as old as Parliament itself is the tradition that the King in Parliament receives petitions from his subjects and there must be no physical impediment to the access of petitioners.[19] (By contrast, the doors of the Commons were usually closed and sometimes—dramatically—locked.)[20] The House has difficulty in keeping the lobby clear of servants, supplicants and onlookers. From time to time their Lordships have to order ushers and doorkeepers to deal with the crowd that impedes their entrance.[21] Their servants are expected to wait in the Court of Requests and their visitors in the Painted Chamber.[22]

The House of Lords is in reality the upper chamber of a hall built four hundred years ago by Henry III for his wife, Queen Eleanor of

Provence. On the ground floor below it there is now a coal store where once a queen housed her wardrobe. Fawkes used it for his gunpowder.[23] The two Houses still give thanks for their deliverance and the judges wear scarlet to mark it each year on 5 November.[24] The chamber itself is dominated by the Chair of Estate, an elaborate throne raised three carpeted steps above the black and white chequered floor of the House. It faces the entrance. Over it are the royal arms and behind and on either side are curtains to protect the occupant from the draughts. A richly pelmeted canopy, the Cloth of Estate, is suspended above the arms and curtain and throne.[25] The whole magnificent pavilion remains empty, unoccupied, except for occasions of special ceremony and importance, the opening and dissolution of Parliament, the royal assent to bills and sometimes addresses to the two Houses. The vacant throne is a constant reminder of the unseen presence of the King-in-Parliament.[26]

Edward Littleton, Lord Littleton of Mounslow, Lord Keeper of the Great Seal of England, sits as Speaker of the House below and in front of the Cloth of Estate, for only the Sovereign may sit upon the throne. Standing he is impressive, for he is a tall man with broad shoulders. But hunched uncomfortably upon the broad expanse of the woolsack, lacking confidence in himself and faith in his royal master, he seems to have shrunk. He wears a black silk gown braided with gold. There is a white ruff at his throat and white lace at his wrists. On his head he carries the round hat of the period. Before him lie the Great Seal of England in its embroidered bag and the mace, a symbol of royal authority.[27] His seat, the upper woolsack, is a mattress covered in red and stuffed with wool to keep him in mind of the origin of so much of England's prosperity.[28]

Actually, there is not one woolsack, but four, set about the Clerk's table in the centre of the chamber. The other three are like that of the Lord Keeper, made of red sage and stuffed with wool. On the inside of the two sacks running down the chamber away from the Chair of Estate sit the judges of King's Bench and Common Pleas and the barons of the Exchequer. Their robes are black or violet faced with taffeta (for it is summer). They wear stoles and scarlet casting hoods over the right shoulder. Amongst them sits Sir Charles Caesar, the Master of the Rolls, dressed in black. On the outside of the sack on the Lord Keeper's left sits Sir Edward Herbert, the Attorney General, in damasked silk. Next to Sir Edward sit those of the King's serjeants who have no seat in the Commons. One of them, Sir John Glanville, was once Speaker of the Commons. All these are called to Parliament by writ of assistance. None but the judges may wear their headdress in the presence of the Lords and they may only do so when the Lord Keeper has given them permission.[29]

At the bottom end of the sack on the Lord Keeper's right are the masters in chancery, wearing black gowns sombrely braided in black. They sit two on one side of the sack and two on the other, back to back. They are not summoned by writ like the assistants. They are mere attendants, acting on the instructions of the Lord Keeper. And on the bottom woolsack facing the Lord Keeper across the table sit the Clerk of the Parliaments and the Clerk of the Crown in Chancery, dressed in barristers' gowns. Behind them the two assistants of the Clerk of the Parliaments kneel on the floor of the House. They write the journals in draft and copy out bills (for peers, at a price), using the woolsack as a desk.[30]

In the front row on the Lord Keeper's left sit the great officers of state. To their left and on a cross bench, which they share with the viscounts, facing the Clerk's woolsack, sit the remaining earls. The barons sit in the second row on the Lord Keeper's left and on cross benches behind the viscounts. The temporal lords wear their everyday clothes. The broad-brimmed hat is almost universal. White turndown collars are replacing ruffs. Cloaks brush the black and white stone floor and sword scabbards project behind their skirts. Some of the cloaks are lined with velvet and daubed over with gold lace two fingers broad; these make a striking contrast with the austere dress of the Puritans.[31] On the right of the Lord Keeper sit the bishops, or rather, as many of the bishops as are not in prison or too infirm to attend. Like the temporal lords the majority have well-trimmed, pointed moustaches and beards.[32]

This is the stage that Malet will grace as a privileged spectator and as a minor actor during the course of the next thirteen months.

The Lords normally began their work at nine o'clock in the morning and rose for their midday meal. Often there was an afternoon sitting as well. It usually began at four and continued into the evening.[33] In theory they expected the assistants to attend their House when it was sitting and to get permission when they wanted to be absent,[34] but in term time there had to be a compromise if the business of the House was not to bring the business of the courts to a standstill. In that term the judges did not usually attend the Lords in the mornings when the courts were sitting, although two or more, who were not threatened with impeachment, were usually present during the afternoon sessions when the courts were risen.[35]

The judges were expected to act as assistants to select committees for bills, to carry important messages to the Commons[36] and occasionally to take depositions from witnesses and prisoners in and about London in cases of treason, riot and similar crimes.[37] After they were accused by the Commons, the ship-money judges were never required to take messages to the Commons, nor did they normally act as assistants to select committees for bills.[38] On days when the House did not sit they had to appear before the Chief Justice of Common Pleas to show they were there.[39] Exceptionally a Chief could be appointed assistant to a committee when his special knowledge was critical to the issue.[40]

If the House requested it, the judges gave their opinions on points of law or procedure.[41] But in the Lords the judges gave no judgements. Decision was a matter for the peers themselves. There was no greater contrast than the role of the judges in court compared with their role as assistants to committees. In King's Bench the judges sat while the greatest peer in the land must stand before them uncovered; their judgements were respected as the embodiment of law itself. As assistants to committees of the Lords the judges must stand uncovered while the peers sat bareheaded; there the opinions of the judges could be ignored and set aside.[42]

If the Lords had a message to send to the Commons they would use as their messengers the judges and law officers of the Crown on matters of major importance and the masters in chancery for minor occasions. They must always send two messengers, but need not send more. It was essential for the honour of the Lords that the traditional procedure be followed in minutest detail. Malet shared these duties with all the other judges who had not been impeached, except Chief Justice Bankes who was sometimes elected in the Lord Keeper's absence to take his place on the upper woolsack.[43]

On Monday 5 July, while the peers wore their robes and the judges wore scarlet, the King came to the Lords and gave the royal assent to two bills which represented the high water mark of reforming legislation in the Long Parliament. No other acts were to surpass them in importance and general consent. The first took from the King's Council the major part of its judicial function. It abolished the Court of Star Chamber, the Council of the North, the Council of Wales and the Marches, and a number of other bill courts. The second abolished the Court of High Commission and deprived the other church courts of power to punish. Both gave to the subject and his property specific protection against the arbitrary use of prerogative power. Both had been presented to the King on the previous Saturday. It had taken him two anxious days to come to a decision. Now the tension was gone.[44]

After those two acts came a mass of legislative consolidation that had been initiated and developed in the Commons over the previous few months. Pym and his supporters had to pick carefully those measures which were sure of support in the Lords. They chose as their primary targets unparliamentary taxation and the remaining courts that upheld it. Systematically they cut off the sources of revenue which Charles had tapped in the eleven years of personal rule and they removed the few remaining offshoots of conciliar coercion. In this they worked closely with their colleagues in the Lords, leaving them to initiate measures that mostly concerned the peers.[45]

Malet was closely associated with this programme. On five occasions that summer he was appointed assistant to the select committee for some reforming bill. Always he shared the duty with one or more brother judges.[46] Committees met in the Painted Chamber either at eight o'clock in the morning or at some time in the afternoon. There was usually an hour or so for discussion before the full House sat in the morning but in the afternoons the pattern varied.[47] There was work for the judges both in and out of committee, for there were precedents to be found,

points of law to be interpreted, passages to be drafted.[48] There were
the bills for quieting[49] and for certainty of forests,[50] both designed to
prevent the Crown mulcting those who had enjoyed ownership for some
substantial period.[51] There was the bill to quash the ship-money proceedings
and to declare the tax unlawful.[52] There was a 'tidying up' bill to free
four border counties of England from the jurisdiction of the Council of
Wales and the Marches.[53] The last of these five bills was directed against
encroachments and oppressions in the Stannary courts which heard civil
actions relating to mining matters in Devon and Cornwall.[54] Three of
these bills eventually became law.[55]

All through that summer the attack upon the King's supporters continued.
On the day that Malet was promoted to the bench Edward Hyde reported
the charges against the last four ship-money judges to the Commons.[56]
Within a week they had taken up to the Lords impeachments against
Judge Berkeley of King's Bench for high treason and Sir John Bramston,
Chief Justice of the King's Bench, Sir Humphrey Davenport, the Chief
Baron of the Exchequer, Justice Crawley, Baron Trevor and Baron Weston
for 'divers crimes and misdemeanours'. In a colourful speech Denzil Holles
represented to the Lords 'the sad object of justice perverted, liberty
oppressed, of judgement turned into wormwood'.[57] At the same time
the Commons began to assail the position of judges in general. They
sent a deputation to ask the Lord Keeper that the judges might not travel
on Sunday because it was a bad example to others.[58] They heard complaints
about the gifts and entertainment lavished on judges at assizes. Without
consulting the Lords they issued a declaration which they sent to the
sheriffs of counties ordering them neither to give nor demand gifts and
entertainment for the King's officers or his judges or the country gentlemen
gathered for the assizes.[59] They brought in a bill to prevent judges and
others from exacting 'unjust and unlawful fees'.[60] They passed a resolution
that previous court decisions were against the law and they claimed reparation against the Council, the judges of the King's Bench and the law
officers of the crown. They sent Lawrence Whitaker to the Tower for
searching Sir John Eliot's trunks on the orders of the Council in 1629.[61]
On 5 August Sir John Colepeper and Edward Hyde represented the Commons at a conference with the Lords and asked them to speed the impeachments of the ship-money judges and to ensure that they were not put
in commission for the coming assizes because 'their names will be unacceptable, and their persons unwelcome.' They wanted to make certain that
judges with Royalist leanings were incapable of exerting pressure in the
counties while the counterbalancing influence of the Country members
of Parliament remained at Westminster.[62]

On 8 July the Commons persuaded the peers to make an approach
to the King on behalf of both Houses, asking especially that he remove
evil counsellors and replace them with officers and counsellors in whom
Parliament could have confidence. The King was angry. The two Houses
had removed all his effective ministers and in a conciliatory gesture he

had already appointed to his Council members of the Country alliance. He summoned the two Houses to meet him in the banqueting house that Inigo Jones had built for his father. There he told them roundly that he knew of no evil counsellors.[63]

Having drastically reduced the royal revenue the two Houses were now responsible for meeting the debts of the kingdom. The Scots must have their indemnity and the armies must be paid before they could be disbanded. The King's proclaimed intention to visit Scotland gave the Puritans a pressing reason for paying off the two armies and for disbanding the English army before he arrived. That session the two Houses had voted six subsidies and a poll tax to balance the exchequer, but even this unprecedented demand was not enough.[64] Time after time Malet found himself dispatched to the Commons to ask for joint conferences of both Houses to arrange for an ending of hostilities with the Scots or about the disbandment of the armies.[65] Meanwhile, the money from the taxes was coming in very slowly indeed.

Inevitably, Pym began to search for guarantees against the use of force by the King. In May he established a powerful committee of six to combat any Royalist resort to arms. It began to initiate and plan the measures it wanted the House to adopt. In mid July the Commons as a whole started to consider whether those in command of forts and castles throughout the country could be trusted for the task. On 23 July they revived the proposal to present the King with a Grand Remonstrance tabling all the misdoings of his reign. In August they began to consider seriously how to put the kingdom into a state of defence.[66]

King Charles and King Pym (as they were shortly to call him) both recognized the vital importance of the Lords in the growing struggle. If Charles had the support of the Lords he could block the constitutional changes that Pym was intent on making. If Pym had it, he had a lever to gain Charles's unwilling assent. The key to the struggle lay in the two royalist groups in the Lords, the bishops who were royal nominees and the Roman Catholics who enjoyed royal protection. As long as they sat in the Lords the King could count upon both for support. Pym was determined to deprive them of their votes.[67]

Since the Bishops' Exclusion Bill had been blocked by the Lords, Pym switched his attention to the Roman Catholic peers. All through that summer there was a mounting campaign against them. The Protestant peers had already voluntarily taken the Protestation devised by the London Puritans to sort out the Protestants from the Catholics. The Commons now sent up to the Lords a bill which made it compulsory for all Englishmen to take the Protestation. Peers who refused were to lose their seats in the Lords. On 29 July the Lords rejected the bill. Pym had to make some kind of headway to cheer his own extremists and to restore the confidence of the Scottish covenanters. The next day the Commons decided to impeach the thirteen bishops who had helped to make unpopular canons in 1640 and they declared that anyone who would not take the Protestation was unfit to bear office in the Church or Commonwealth. They ordered their declaration to be printed and sent down to the constituencies. The majority of peers were angry because they regarded the publication as a breach of privilege. The right to hold office was governed by law and not by any declaration of the Commons. They saw it as having grave constitutional implications and would have defended the constitution against the orders of the Commons. But the King asked them privately to drop the issue until his return from Scotland. A dangerous precedent was created.[68]

When it became clear that the English army could not be disbanded before the King reached it, the two Houses waited upon him and asked him to postpone his journey by fourteen days. The King refused. He gave his assent to a treaty with the Scots on 10 August and told the two Houses he would do what he could to return before Michaelmas. The Scottish commissioners were looking forward to his visit. It seemed as if he would win them to his cause and away from their association with the Puritans. As he mounted his horse a crowd gathered round him in Old Palace Yard, begging him to stay. But he shook them off and rode north. Behind him he left an unhappy majority in both Houses. In the Commons they were fearful of his purpose, fearful for themselves, and determined, if necessary, to arrogate to themselves the essential powers in the state. In the Lords they would have rallied to his support but the King had discouraged them from doing so.[69]

3

Assize Cycle

'That justice may twice every year be derived to the people
in their several countries for their great ease and benefit.'

The Office of the Clerk of Assize (1682).[1]

Twice a year, during vacation in Lent and high summer, the King's judges
rode forth into the counties of England. Armed escorts protected them.
Trumpets sounded at their arrival and at their departing. The authority
of King and Council sat upon their shoulders. Their role was executive
as well as judicial, for they called the justices of the peace to account
for their administration and gave them directions for the ensuing half
year. Powerful, yet never dictators, they were partners with the justices
of the peace in the government of their counties. The justices sat with
the judges on the bench. The justices derived prestige from the reflected
glory of the judges and the judges drew strength from the physical presence
of the justices. During the long period of personal rule the judges had been
an essential channel of communication between the Council and local government in the counties; they were respected as the instruments of power
and for their knowledge and understanding of happenings at the centre.
With Parliament sitting, and in the main a Parliament hostile to conciliar
rule, their position had sensibly changed. The power had shifted, but the
judges, as assistants to the Lords, still saw more of the game than the
great mass of country justices of the peace. Events were moving fast and
people were avid for news of what was happening. The judges had wisdom
and knowledge of central policy to give to the justices; the justices had
understanding of local sentiment and conditions to impart to the judges.
It was a working partnership in which there was still room for friendship.
In the past it had been the occasion of great entertainment justified by
the stature of the visitors and the desire of their hosts to do them honour.
But recent decisions in the courts and edicts of the Council had alienated
the justices and strained the links with the centre. When royal policies
commanded an overwhelming support in the counties, there had been
no need for a separation of powers. Now the role of the judges as administrators had helped to undermine their judicial authority. Their judgements

in judicial matters were suspect because they supported royal policies that were not politically acceptable. Men were asserting their right to withhold from the judges the respect and courtesy they had accorded so willingly in the past.[2]

The English counties, all except Cheshire, London and Middlesex, were divided into six circuits and in normal times there were two judges to each circuit. They were drawn from the King's Bench, Common Pleas and Exchequer. When these courts were unable to provide two judges for each circuit, the deficiency was filled in whole or in part from the ranks of the serjeants. Early that Trinity term the judges gathered together in Serjeants' Inn Hall to pick their circuits. The choice was a fairly free one except that the more senior judges had first pick and no judge might ride the circuit where he lived except with special permission. The Oxford circuit was the longest and the most lucrative. The long, wet journey to the North or the heavy gaol calender and relatively poor financial rewards of the Home circuit were often the fate of the junior puisne, and Malet as most junior judge had no choice at all. In the event Baron Weston and he were allotted the Home circuit, comprising five counties close to London.[3]

It was normal for the judges to wait upon the King and to seek his confirmation of their choice and for the King or the Lord Keeper to give them clear instructions about their conduct of the assizes, what matters they should investigate and what directions they should give. Probably this practice had sunk into disuse.[4] Baron Weston, one of the impeached judges, issued summonses of assize jointly with Malet on 14 July to the sheriff of every county in the circuit.[5] It may have been these and similar summonses which led the Commons to ask the Lords that the ship-money judges might be forbidden to ride circuit. As a result the Lords instructed the Lord Keeper on 5 August to withdraw from the ship-money judges all commissions to go circuit.[6] It was too late to issue fresh commissions under the Great Seal. The ship-money judges did not attend assizes and their names were quietly dropped from every commission on the record. They were not even shown on the checklist of justices submitted by the clerks of the peace to the sheriffs of counties.[7] Only six judges were available for the work of assizes. One by one the Lords gave them permission to go circuit and to some of the impeached judges to go into the country. It was understood that they had to return before the start of Michaelmas term. One of the last to go was Sir John Bankes, the Chief Justice of Common Pleas, who had been acting as Speaker in the Lords. Malet was given leave to prepare himself for circuit on 11 August. He had to open the assizes in Hertford three days later.[8]

For two summers and one winter Malet rode the Home circuit that took in five counties—Hertfordshire, Essex, Kent, Surrey and Sussex. Although it was the least popular, it did have the advantage of being the shortest. Of all the circuit judges Malet would have the longest vacation that summer. Even riding alone, without a brother judge to share the work, he managed to complete it in about nineteen days. Two judges would have taken a little less.[9]

Malet was expected to travel in state as befitted one of His Majesty's justices of assize. He must honour the master whose justice he did. He must wear his serjeant's coat of good broadcloth, faced with velvet and thickly laced at the sleeves. He must have at least six riding attendants and a sumpter in charge of the pack animals. Cavalcades like this were common enough in the streets of London and the villages of Middlesex. The centre was full of great men. But as a judge drew away from Westminster, so his stature increased. In the counties he was the representative of the King himself, must be accorded the honour due to a king. And he was.[10]

The assize towns of the circuit were very nearly constant during Malet's tenure of office. He picked Hertford, Chelmsford, Maidstone and East Grinstead for every circuit he rode. Only in Surrey did the location of assizes vary: in the summer they were at Kingston-upon-Thames and in the winter at Southwark beyond London Bridge. There were no long arduous journeys—at least comparatively speaking. Maidstone was as far as Malet must travel and that was only thirty-five miles from London, an easy day's journey. He never had to spend a night on the way like the judges on other circuits. He avoided the more distant alternatives in order to get through the work single-handed in reasonable time. In Kent he did not go to Canterbury; that was nearly twenty miles further than Maidstone. The state of the Sussex roads made the journey to Lewes quite impracticable in winter. He never attempted to get to Horsham even in summer; it was much further from London than East Grinstead. His itinerary always began with Hertford and took Chelmsford next in order. Maidstone followed on two out of three occasions. That suggests that he travelled direct between one assize town and another, but we do not know that he did. In those days the direct road between London and the assize towns was often the best. There was no horse ferry across the lower reaches of the Thames so that the road between Chelmsford and Maidstone lay over London Bridge.[11]

The journeys he took had an infinite variety of scene, going and climatic conditions, but no contrast was so great as that between the appearance of King Street beyond New Palace Yard and the wilderness of heath, moor, hill and common that occupied most of the distance between the towns of the circuit. 'Champion' country, they called it. Here the going was good over much of the way. But the road was often uncertain. There were no signposts, few definite tracks, maps were primitive and scarce, compasses for land use unknown. A man could get hopelessly lost, even when visibility was good. In fog, travel in such places was a nightmare. These lonely places were often the haunt of highwaymen and footpads. Stamford Hill on the way to Hertford and Shooters Hill on the road to Maidstone were two such notorious places. In summer hooves and wheels churned up a choking, suffocating dust. In winter there were places

where coaches would be brought to a standstill and horses could flounder—
and even drown—in the mud. The King's highway was not a road you
could see; it was simply a right to travel. If a way became an impassable
morass, you took to higher or firmer ground which had not been churned
up by hooves and the wheels of heavy carts. The tracks fanned out as
the going got worse. One such area lay in the valley of Holmedale between
Westerham and Maidstone. It provided reason enough for travel to Maidstone by way of Rochester. In winter, too, snow, biting winds and widespread floods could often add to the rigours of 'travail'.[12]

Malet opened the assizes at Hertford on 14 August, Chelmsford on
the 17th, Maidstone on the 23rd, East Grinstead on the 26th and Kingston-
upon-Thames on the 30th. There was a ritual tradition for the circuit.
Some of it we know. The road to Hertford lay through small disunited
villages, Tottenham Street, Edmonton, Ponders End and Enfield Wash.
In this low-lying land the way was cut by streams, some of them only
provided with footbridges so that the horses had to splash their way across.
It was customary for the sheriff's bailiff to meet the judge on the county
boundary, while the high sheriff of the county waited at some distance
from the assize town with an armed escort, equipped with halberds and
javelins. There would be a following of country gentlemen who counted
it an honour to escort and converse with the judge on his way. There
would be a retinue in the livery of the sheriff, supplied partly by the
servants of the sheriff himself and partly by those of his friends. As the
judge approached, the trumpets sounded, the gentlemen uncovered and
there followed an exchange of speeches. Then they all rode on together
toward Hertford where the assizes were to be held. The pattern was the
same in other counties; sometimes the whole cavalcade would stop at
the house of some magnate for refreshment on the way. At the time
of the judge's arrival the assize town was overflowing with people from
distant parts of the county who put up at the local inns, the houses of
their friends and even lodgings of their own. There were justices of the
peace, mayors of towns, constables and bailiffs of hundreds, coroners, stewards of leets, litigants, lawyers, jurors and witnesses. The half-yearly gathering was also a great social occasion. The judge and his escort would
pass through the crowded streets of the town to the judge's lodgings.
Their approach would be heralded by the sheriff's trumpeters and the town
would answer with a peal of bells.[13]

It was the custom of the principal gentlemen of the county—and particularly those who were joined with him in the commission of oyer and
terminer—to call at the judge's lodgings while he was robing and pay
their respects. Then the judge would proceed in state to church in his
scarlet robes, his hood and his black-cornered cap, accompanied by the
high sheriff and an armed escort. While Malet preferred to ride circuit
on horseback, it is probable that he travelled to the assize service in the
high sheriff's coach. It kept his scarlet robes clean on the journey through
the streets and often provided the only opportunity he had for private

conversation with the sheriff. As they dismounted at the church the trumpets would sound and they would walk up the aisle, under-sheriff, chaplain, high sheriff and judge. The high sheriff sat next to him during the service for he was personally responsible for the safety of the judge. The church would be filled with those who had business at the assizes: the justices of the peace, the mayors of towns in gold chains of office, the burgesses and the commonalty. The chaplain would say the bidding prayer while all the people stood in silence to say 'Amen'.[14]

At Hertford the assize service was held in the parish church of All Saints. The church was filled with a politically conscious congregation, for the householders had been given the vote for the first time in the previous year. The sheriff was Richard Cole, a man of Puritan leanings.[15] His chaplain was a man called Thomas Foxley, who had recently been in prison for expressing extreme Puritan views. The choice was in effect a statement of belief calculated to offend moderate men in the congregation.[16] Although Foxley had become a political symbol, he was in his dotage. His faculties had deteriorated in prison. When he opened his sermon he declared that no man could be saved unless he first became a Puritan. He said he would prove it through the scriptures. His congregation waited expectantly for the proof, but it never came. He was struck dumb. Eventually the congregation was dismissed. Foxley was carried out of the church and Malet left to open the assizes in the timber-framed town house up the road. It was an inauspicious beginning to his first circuit as a judge, doubly a strain because he had no brother judge with whom to share the experience.[17]

In the summer of 1641 the circuit passed uneventfully enough, if you discount the affair of the sermon at Hertford. The judge's charge to the grand juries may have lacked the guidance of the Lord Keeper, but at least it had weight. Malet had to read all the statutes that had become law since Parliament met. At Kingston-upon-Thames the grand jury numbered nineteen, but elsewhere only fifteen grand jurors were sworn. The bulk of grand jurors are described as gentlemen. Amongst them all there was only one esquire and there was a sprinkling of yeomen and burgesses. There were no knights, no baronets and no peers. This is important in view of the events on Malet's next circuit. Many of the indictments were dismissed by the grand jurors. Most of the criminal cases involved stealing and house-breaking. Petty juries of twelve men would be impanelled for five to ten cases according to the availability of jurors. Some of the indicted prisoners seem to have been aquitted, but many pleaded their clergy and were branded and a number appear to have avoided arrest. No one was hanged for stealing sheep (although three were branded for that offence and some were whipped for other stealing offences). Juries were increasingly reluctant to convict when the sentence was death, but a husbandman was convicted in his absence and sentenced to be hanged for killing a man with seven shots from a pistol.[18]

Once the assizes were over, Malet was free from his parliamentary duties

to go to his country estate after the rigours of term and session and circuit. Kingston-upon-Thames was 120 miles from his home at Poyntington in Somerset. Basingstoke and Salisbury lay on the way and provided opportunity for rest and refreshment.[19]

In 1624 Malet had taken a lease of the 'capitall messuage or mannour place of Poyntington in the countie of Somerset' and some of the surrounding land from the then lord of the manor, Fulke Greville, first Baron Brooke of Beauchamp Court in Warwickshire.[20] The house was not the present manor house at Poyntington but one that stood (and stands to this day) hard by the church. It was solidly built of light local stone in the late fourteenth century. It lay near the head of a narrow, beautiful, valley, close to the source of the Yeo. To the north lay green pastures of fuller's earth clay and to the south the bare limestone hills rose steeply from the stream.[21]

Malet was then forty-one, working for Lord Conway, with a growing practice. He must have felt the need for a suitable country house for his wife, Jane, the daughter of Francis Mills. Perhaps, too, he felt that the family they intended to have would grow up healthier in the country than in plague-ridden London or Westminster.[22] He probably heard about Poyntington from his uncle, Michael Malet, who lived in Warwick, was a great friend and man of affairs to Lord Brooke and eventually came himself to retire at Poyntington.[23] It was Michael Malet who obtained the freehold of the present manor house at Poyntington jointly with his nephew Thomas in 1630. This house lay at the bottom of the valley close to the stripling Yeo. It was about 150 years old and it stood foursquare about a stone courtyard, protected on the north by a stone gatehouse, arched and hung with stout doors of iron-studded oak. On occasion the house could be dark, for the hill to the east, a two hundred foot fault-scarp, seemed to close in on dull winter days. But in high summer the stone gave back the warmth of the sun so that the whole building seemed to radiate warmth, to glow in its setting.

In respect of the property he had leased in 1624 Thomas Malet was still a tenant by indenture. He owed a rent to the lord of the manor and suit to his court. By 1641 the lord of the manor was Sir Greville Verney of Compton Verney in Warwickshire, whose brother, John, had once shared lodgings with Malet in the Temple; the estate had descended to Sir Greville through his mother. During his life Malet was, in theory at least, bound to serve Sir Greville in the wars or else find an able man to serve in his place and at his death his best beast must go to his lord as a heriot. Malet had to pay on Lady Day and at Michaelmas a half-yearly rent of £3.8s.4d. Once a year, too, he must render two capons to the steward of the manor. Just as Malet as the King's steward would call the justices of the peace to account at the half-yearly assizes, so the steward of the manor would call Malet and other suitors to account for what happened on the manor of Poyntington—and they must attend upon reasonable notice.[25]

For Malet the house must have been a fortress and a nursery for his family, a source of rest and recreation for himself, a refuge from the strain of life at the centre. He had built a new barn of six bays that was now filling with the harvest. Wheat and oats were being threshed and winnowed on its floor. Straw was stacked under its roof. There were other barns, too, a buttery and milkhouse, courtyards and outbuildings, a garden and an orchard. Part of the demesne farm land was enclosed by walls and blackthorn hedges; part was open. In the bottom of the narrow Poyntington valley he had thirty acres of wet riverside meadow which had already yielded its harvest of hay and was now being grazed by dairy cattle. He had fifty-six acres of arable land that grew the wheat they were in process of harvesting as well as fodder for the cattle. Some of it was fallow. Four hundred sheep ranged the common land on the downs by day and were brought down to be folded on the fallow by night. As the harvest was cut it became possible to allow the cattle to wander over the stubble. It was a happy, purposeful time for those who worked on the demesne and at evening the servants and customary tenants who had toiled during the day would come back to the house for their meal. At Allhallowtide there was a great harvest supper for all who had helped; and afterwards the whole village would go to church and give thanks.[26]

Malet's was a closely knit family. He and Jane hated to be separated from each other and she was later to endure privation and hardship to avoid it.[27] The children were growing up. John, the eldest, had been admitted as a student to the Middle Temple in 1634 at the tender age of eleven or twelve. He matriculated at University College, Oxford in 1638 at the age of fifteen. And now at about eighteen he was one of the youngest ever to be called to the bar in the Middle Temple. He probably reached Poyntington before his father, for he did not stay in the Middle Temple to hear John White's reading in the grand vacation. (White was the Puritan member for Southwark.)[28] Baldwin, the second son, was about fifteen at this time. There were two younger sons, Michael and Thomas, and four daughters, Alice, Katharine, Zenobia and Elizabeth. Last and by no means least there was Malet's uncle, Michael, unmarried and now well advanced in years. He kept his separate establishment in the village. One day Malet would be his heir.[29] It was a good-sized family and it must have been a relief for all of them to relax in the security of their own strength and distance from Westminster in that autumn of 1641.

South from Poyntington, and distant half an hour's ride, lay Sherborne and Sherborne Castle, just over the county border in Dorset. There was a strong link between the Earl of Bristol, who owned Sherborne Castle, and Malet himself. We know that Malet had 'dependence' upon the earl just as he had once been dependent on Secretary Conway. Their relationship was the common one of client and patron that was such a feature of seventeenth-century England. It is not at all certain when they first established a bond. Perhaps their friendship had something to do with the proximity of Poyntington and Sherborne. Bristol was one of the shrewdest statesmen of his age and was now back in the royal favour. He may have been instrumental in Malet's promotion to the bench, for he was certainly behind many recent appointments by the King. He was already at Sherborne when Malet got back to Poyntington. Each had important news for the other. Malet had to tell Bristol of feelings and wants in the counties of his circuit. Bristol is sure to have been posted with accurate up-to-date information from London. At last Malet could learn the full story of how the parliamentary session ended and hear Bristol's informed comment on the progress of events.[30]

The King's journey to the North had filled the Country leaders with deepest misgiving. They feared a military 'coup' and began to strengthen themselves against one. For the first time the two Houses published 'ordinances' that dispensed with the royal assent. And jointly they issued a series of orders directed to military officers appointed by the King and responsible to him. It was a small step from these orders to a formal assumption of responsibility for the armed forces of the Crown.[31]

Before the Houses adjourned for their summer recess on 9 September two events of great importance took place. The Commons broke with the Lords and on their own authority issued an order ending Laud's innovations, which was intended to bind all the subjects of the Crown; and some members of the Commons attacked the prayer book and provoked a spirited defence. During the recess in the cities and towns, and above all in London, the Puritan fanatics put into effect the Commons order on innovations. They tore up the rails round communion tables and swept them clear of crucifixes, tapers and candlesticks. They defaced paintings and broke up statues with axes and hammers. They destroyed stained-glass windows and left behind a shambles of rubble and broken glass. This wanton destruction and the attack on the prayer book aroused a widespread reaction. There was a growing nucleus of men who wanted a reconciliation between King and Parliament. It included many in the Commons who had been working with the Country for reform.[32]

Members of the two Houses returned to Westminster after their autumn recess to find an atmosphere of tension and fear. Pym was determined to wrest from the King control of the means of waging war. He tried to discredit him as a trustworthy head of the armed forces. He invented or exaggerated stories of Royalist 'plots' against Parliament. When news reached England that the Irish Roman Catholics had rebelled against the English, his supporters called it the Queen's Rebellion and suggested that she had lent them her secret support. On the night of 22 November, against intense opposition, he pushed through the Commons a Remonstrance of the State of the Kingdom which contained a long rambling recital of all the misdoings of the last fifteen years. Ostensibly, it was a petition asking the King to entrust his government only to those in whom the two Houses had confidence. But, if he did not grant this request, it threatened to cut off his funds and to fight the Irish rebellion without his agreement. In fact it was an instrument of propaganda designed to enlist support throughout England against the King. And it was this that its opponents, including nearly half the Commons, found most repugnant. To them it looked like an outright attack on the monarchical order.[33] Sir Edward Dering, one of the knights for Kent, objected to the form of it. 'When I first heard of a Remonstrance,' he said, '. . . I did not dream that we should remonstrate downeward, tell stories to the people, and talke of the the King as of a third person.'[34] The Remonstrance was passed three days before the King returned from Scotland to Whitehall. It marked a major split in the Country opposition to the Court and an important step in the disintegration of the Country alliance itself. The Country's strength and near-unanimity had stemmed from a broad-based aim to redress abuses. That aim was virtually achieved by the time that Malet was promoted to the bench in July 1641. Pym and his friends were determined to force from the King guarantees for their own safety and the permanence of their reforming work, which the King was not prepared to give. Those who were willing to take up arms in order to get their guarantees from the King eventually became Parliamentarians. Those moderates who were willing to defend the constitution from further change became Royalists. Most attempted to avoid either of these extremes for as long as possible and so the period between the passing of the Remonstrance and the outbreak of the Civil War was politically confused as individual members searched their consciences and made their several decisions.[35]

Pym attempted by every means in his power to weaken the King's support in the Lords, so that Lords and Commons could jointly supervise the selection of the King's ministers and his commanders for the armed forces. When the Lords blocked a second bill to deprive the bishops of their votes, the London Puritans organized a monster petition praying the Commons to get the bishops and popish lords removed from the Lords. The canvassers covered every ward in the city and used pressure and threats to drum up support. The document itself was twenty-four yards long and signed by 20,000 people. A Middlesex justice of the peace, called Long, heard that 10,000 men were going to march on the Commons to present it. He feared a breach of the peace and called a meeting of justices of the peace. They already had a writ from the Lord Keeper calling on them to suppress riots and unlawful assemblies. They now issued warrants for 300 men armed with halberds to guard the Commons and 200 duly appeared in New Palace Yard—where only 400 petitioners and fifty coaches actually arrived. The Commons imprisoned Justice Long in the Tower for interfering with the petition. Had it been contrary to the policies of the Country majority they would, no doubt, have thanked him for his efforts.[36]

Encouraged by the City members of Parliament, the citizens of London came down to Westminster in their hundreds, armed with swords and staves to intimidate members and peers. The mob poured through the doors of Westminster Hall and milled round the entrance to both Houses. By 28 December only two bishops dared appear in the Lords. When twelve of the bishops complained that they had been so menaced and assaulted that they dared not vote in the Lords, Pym got the Commons to vote that they be impeached on a charge of high treason.[37]

The climax came when Charles learned, as Pym intended he should, that Pym and his followers intended to impeach the Queen of high treason. Charles decided to strike first. Malet was sitting in the Lords on 3 January 1642 when Sir Edward Herbert, the Attorney General, read out the articles of impeachment against five members of the Commons and Lord Mandeville in the Lords on a charge of high treason. Malet and the Master of the Rolls were sent to the Commons to ask for a conference by a committee of both Houses. As they entered the Commons chamber they must have passed the King's serjeant-at-arms who was waiting outside for an answer after asking for the arrest of the five members.[38]

The King's bungled attempt to arrest the five members led to his own flight with his family to the comparative safety of Hampton Court and to renewed attempts by both sides upon places of strategic importance. The two Houses secured the port of Hull and dispersed a Royalist attempt to occupy Kingston-upon-Thames which lay on the road to Portsmouth and contained the Surrey county magazine. The City trained bands blockaded the Tower. The King's lack of strength forced him to send a conciliatory message to the two Houses on 20 January. Lords and Commons could not agree on the answer they should return.[39]

There were locally organized outbursts of popular feeling expressed in the form of petitions addressed to the King and the two Houses and presented by a substantial following. Accompanied by another 1,000 on foot, 3,000 men from Hampden's county of Buckinghamshire rode into Westminster. They tendered to the Commons another petition asking that popish lords and bishops should be ousted from the Lords. More significantly they declared that they were ready to live and die in defence of the privileges of Parliament. In their turn they received the thanks of a grateful House. They moved on to the Lords with a different petition asking that wicked counsellors be punished and the kingdom put into a 'posture of defence'.[40]

Pym's policies were breaking against the determination of the Lords where a small majority of disheartened peers was still holding out against him. They would not agree to parliamentary control of the militia and they refused to take away the votes of the bishops and popish lords. Pym decided to use the Buckinghamshire petition as a pattern and to support his demands with the full weight of organized support from other counties which were nearest to London. Essex, Hertfordshire and Middlesex all submitted to the Commons petitions which varied in detail yet were unanimous on two points. First, they demanded the removal of votes from the bishops and popish lords and asked that the kingdom be put in a 'warlike posture of defence'. Secondly, the signatories offered their lives and estates in defence of King and Parliament, an ominous pledge. By linking the King with Parliament, they avoided the charge of treason and secured the backing of many who believed that the King was being misled by evil counsel. The petition from Essex was subscribed by 20,000 signatories and attended to the Commons by 2,000 horsemen who numbered some of the principal knights and gentlemen of the county. The Hertfordshire petition was taken to Westminster by 4,000 supporters. In time similar petitions arrived from further afield.

In an hour-long speech in the Painted Chamber, Pym laid before the Lords a further petition from London and those from Essex, Hertfordshire and Middlesex. He represented the petitions as the cry of all England. He asked for the cooperation of the Lords and warned that if necessary the Commons would act alone.[42]

Under the weight of these petitions and others the constitutionalists in the Lords were losing heart. The King had given them no lead and no guarantees. They were fearful of his attempts to secure the ports of Hull and Portsmouth for the entry of foreign troops. One by one those who had been loyal to the King began to slip away to the country. Others could see no hope of peace save by acceding to the demands of the Commons. On 1 February the Lords agreed to petition the King to entrust the fortresses and militia to men in whom Parliament had confidence. On 4 February a further petition arrived from Surrey, listing many grievances, including complaints about bishops and popish lords. On 5 February, the Lords passed the Second Bishops' Exclusion Bill, which was intended to deprive the bishops of their votes in the Lords.[43]

Faced by defeat in the Lords and massive support for Pym's policies from the counties, the King gave way. On 14 February he gave his assent to the Bishops' Exclusion Bill. He hoped by concessions to stand more firmly on the issue of the militia. In the meantime, the Commons had embodied their proposals for the militia in an ordinance which provided, that the two Houses should exercise command over it through lord lieutenants to be appointed by them in every county. They intended that the ordinance should be passed by the two Houses and, if necessary, would dispense with the King's assent.[44]

All through February and March petitions flowed in to the two Houses from the towns and counties of England. In the main they supported the two Houses and asked for further reforms.[45] Often the petition for the Lords would first receive Commons approbation so that it could be delivered to its destination with added authority.[46] The emblem of the petitioners was the Protestation, a copy of which they often stuck in their hats like a favour or cockade.[47] By now it had become more than a shibboleth to distinguish between Protestant and Roman Catholic. The Commons had ordered it to be circulated throughout the country with a protest at the attempted arrest of the five members. Its promise to defend both King and Parliament was the nearest they dared go towards a threat of war against the King himself.[48] On 8 February hundreds of

Kentish Puritans presented a petition to both Houses listing a whole series of grievances. Like others before them they offered their lives and estates in the service of the King and Parliament and they asked that popish peers might be ousted from the House of Lords. Malet, of course, knew the political climate in Kent as he knew it in the other counties of his circuit from which petitions had come. He must have known that there were many men of influence in Kent who held views quite different from those expressed in the petition. At that time he can have had little idea what their reaction would be or how it would affect him personally.[49]

It was inevitable that the Puritan petitions should not go without some challenge. In fact the challenge came from the City of London where the Puritans had gained control of the Common Council. The Commons had ordered the Common Council to appoint a committee of safety to be responsible for City defence and to control the trained bands. Three of the new committee were parliamentary Puritans who were able to ensure that the Commons effectively controlled the trained bands. This caused resentment among a substantial minority of citizens with conservative views and it culminated in a petition which they presented to the Lords and Commons on 24 February. This pointed out that by Act of Parliament and royal charter the City had always enjoyed the privilege of ordering its own arms and asked that this should continue. It had over 330 signatures which included those of some of the most influential citizens. The Commons knew that they must take salutary action because the petition said, in effect, that the acts of the two Houses were already illegal. They decided to impeach the two principal organizers, Sir George Benyon, a prominent silk merchant, and Sir Thomas Gardiner, the recorder of the City.[50]

The Commons were also angered by the actions of Sir Edward Dering who finally broke with the Country alliance after voting against the Remonstrance. In January 1642 Dering crowned his offences by publishing a book of his own speeches justifying his position. He was foolish enough to identify the views of other members by their initials. The Commons voted his book to be burned, consigned him to the Tower for nine days and excluded him from sitting in their House. He joined the growing band of those who had been evicted from the Commons for opposing the policies of the majority.[51]

Judge Reeve and two serjeants were given leave to prepare themselves for circuit as early as 21 February[52] but Malet stayed on for another week at Westminster. With the Master of the Rolls he carried to the Commons the King's final answer to the Militia Ordinance, which the two Houses took as a direct refusal.[53] Chief Justice Bankes of the Common Pleas was given leave to go circuit on 25 February[54] and on 3 March Malet opened the assizes at Hertford. He was at Chelmsford on 7 March, Southwark on the 12th and East Grinstead on the 17th.[55]

Lacking the royal assent to the Militia Ordinance, the two Houses passed a joint resolution on 15 March that 'the ordinance agreed on by both Houses for the militia doth oblige the people and ought to be obeyed'.

On the same day Charles, on his way to raise forces at York, issued a declaration that 'his subjects cannot be obliged to obey any act, order or injunction to which His Majesty hath not given his consent' and forbidding them to obey the Militia Ordinance. The two Houses countered with a further joint declaration that the King's declaration was a breach of privilege.[56]

The Sovereign was not then, as now, bound by constitutional custom to give his assent to bills passed by his two Houses of Parliament. Elizabeth had used the veto as a normal procedure. She held no Parliament in which she did not at some time exercise this right. In doing so she caused no resentment or comment. Her two Houses were busy witholding their consent to the bills of the other.[57] There were a number of more recent occasions when the royal assent had been withheld. Sir Simonds D'Ewes, the diarist, said that it had been withheld more often than it was given.[58] Now the two Houses had dispensed with the royal assent; their Ordinance, if it was to have any meaning, would have to be imposed upon the subject by the unlawful use of force. The Ordinance would hasten the disintegration of the Country alliance by forcing men to choose between the Royalist and Parliamentarian alternatives.

Malet finished the assizes at East Grinstead either late on Friday 18 March or upon the following morning. No doubt most of this news had reached him by then. There only remained Maidstone and then his circuit would be over.[59]

4

The Great Business at Maidstone

'He never named in my hearing what the great business was,
wherefore he desired a good grand jury.'

SIR ROGER TWYSDEN
Testimony to the House of Commons, 1 April 1642.

In Malet's time there was a story told of old Judge Doddridge who sat
on the bench in King James's day. They called him the sleeping judge.
He had a habit of closing his eyes in order—so he said—to concentrate
on the argument in court. He knew that grand juries varied a great deal
from one county to another. In some they used to impanel the minor
gentry; in others there was a stiffening of leading magnates. He had strong
views about this and once reprimanded a sheriff because his jury lacked
rank and quality. The sheriff was a 'merry man' and remembered. When
the judge came again to that town a jury was returned, whose names
were read out in a sonorous voice by the crier. There were twenty-two
in all and they began 'Mamilian King of Tozland, Henry Prince of Godman-
chester, George Duke of Somersham . . .' right through to 'Richard, Deacon
of Catsworth'. The titles were all fictitious and there was not a plain
man among them. When all the names were called the jurors were duly
sworn by the marshal. All this time the judge sat with his eyes closed,
not seeming to notice. To this day, no one knows for certain whether
he heard and kept silent or whether he was fast asleep all the time.[2]

Malet had known Doddridge. As a student he had listened to his reading.
As a barrister he had seen him dine in Middle Temple Hall, where the
judges and serjeants added their lustre to the enjoyment of feast nights.
Doddridge had sat in the Court of King's Bench under six successive
chief justices, spanning two reigns, a total of fifteen years. He was a heavy
man. Awake he was a force to be reckoned with. In court, with his
head forward and his heavy jowls and numerous chins disappearing into
his ruff, he looked almost childlike. Malet knew that story and now it
may have come to his mind as the clerk and the crier performed their
ritual duet at the Maidstone assizes. Occasionally, the harsh voice of the

crier and the dull monologue of the clerk would be punctuated by the voices of individual justices, coroners, stewards, chief constables and bailiffs of hundreds as they answered their names, and by a long drawn out jostling and pushing as the various officers laid upon the table the inquisitions, indictments and recognizances for which they were responsible and retired towards the back of the crowded courtroom.[3]

At last the noise died away. The light from the lattice windows picked out the scarlet robes of the presiding figure so that they stood out among all the sober clothes of the people present. A judge was expected to look his most impressive at the opening of the assizes and Malet sat on a dais at one end of the room with a full-dress mantle of scarlet and miniver over his robe; it was hooked around his neck, open and folded back at the front to show the white lining, a vivid contrast to the scarlet cloth on the outside. He had a strong, thoughtful face with a well-trimmed beard and moustache. Round his neck he wore the ruff which had not gone out of fashion on the bench. On his head, over his serjeant's coif and black skullcap, he wore the limp black-cornered cap that was the proper dress for the opening of the assizes. On a lower plane, on either side of him and in front, packed tight as sardines, sat the justices of the county of Kent. Their presence on the bench gave to them an added prestige and to him the sanction of local support. There were the barristers and attorneys in black gowns and falling bands—and there were the great mass of officials and others who had been summoned by the sheriff, all dressed in their Sunday best to do honour to the judge and the occasion. Between the bench and the two wooden bars that separated the court from the public was a table where clerks were arranging in neat rows all the documents that the clerk had received. Amongst them was the sheriff's warrant for summoning the assizes and attached to it a schedule listing by hundreds the names of all those named for the grand jury. The clerk should then have called them. They stood there in the court waiting to serve. It was now that Mr. Justice Malet took the first step in a chain of events that was to lead him to the Tower and England to war with herself.[4]

At the last Maidstone assizes Malet had accepted the grand jury of minor gentry that the sheriff had presented; not one juror could even lay claim to the title of 'esquire'.[5] For many years this had been normal for grand juries in Kent.[6] During the assizes that March and in the preceding summer there had only been two grand jurors above the rank of 'gentleman' in the whole of the Home circuit.[7] Malet knew this and yet he now suggested a change. Perhaps he was thinking of Doddridge. Perhaps he was heeding the advice of William Lambarde who used to preside over quarter sessions in that self-same court.[8]

The judge interrupted the normal sequence of events and spoke. 'It is very necessary to have a good grand jury' he said. 'In other parts gentlemen of good account serve on the grand jury. I will not command you nor persuade you to this service. I only think to acquaint you with

it. If you do it, you do a good work to your country.' The judge was
not very explicit. Why was it 'very necessary to have a good grand jury'?
He must have foreseen some important and unusual duty that it would
have to discharge. He did not say what it was.[9]

There was a pause while Malet's words sank in. No one hastened to
do as he suggested.[10] Apart from the justices probably few people knew
what he had in mind. Not all the Kent 'gentlemen of good account'
were there and not all who were there could or would do what he wanted.
In Kent, as elsewhere, these gentlemen were to be sought among the
justices of the peace.[11] Some of the working justices were absent about
the King's business, serjeants-at law, minor officials in the navy and so
on. Four were ill. Only two members of Parliament were present on
the bench that morning. They were Sir Humphrey Tufton of The Mote,
Maidstone, who was member for Maidstone, and Richard Lee of Great
Delce near Rochester, who was member for Rochester. (Augustine Skinner,
who had succeeded Dering as knight of the shire, arrived later in the
proceedings.) Eight of the justices were absent from the bench, sitting
in the Commons.[12] Six of the justices who were present on the bench
were also in the commission of oyer and terminer. Among them were
Sir Roger Twysden the antiquary of Roydon Hall and Richard Spencer
of Orpington. They were not allowed to serve on the grand jury.[13] Finally
there were some who knew what the judge had in mind and who had
no intention of leaving the bench to do his bidding.[14]

If the judge's words were meant to be a cue to those who knew his
meaning, it was inevitable that those who understood should first respond.
Sir Edward Dering of Surrenden Dering knew exactly what the judge
meant and at last he said that he would serve and came off the bench.
Then some of the justices stood up and said they would not serve. Probably
Sir Michael Livesey the Puritan was among them. There must have been
some opposition to the judge's purpose at this stage, although later it
seems to have got overwhelmed in a popular tide of enthusiasm.[15]

After Dering, Sir George Strode of Squerries Court, Westerham, rose
and offered himself. He was a well-built man of about Malet's age. He
was certainly a Royalist later in the sense that he took up arms for the
King. At this stage he was opposed to the actions of the Parliamentarians.
He shared with Malet a patron in the Earl of Bristol. The next to volunteer
was a justice called Thomas Blount of Wricklemarsh near Charlton, a
man whose family had recently settled in Kent. He said later 'I conceived
that something was on foot; and I desired to see the play.' So a Parliamentary
informer was included among the candidates for the grand jury.[16]

These three were joined by old Sir Henry Palmer of Bekesbourne, Controller of the Navy, a staunch Royalist with a family tradition of service
to the Crown. Palmer was followed off the bench by Anthony Hamond,
another Royalist, who was to continue to work for the King over the
years that lay ahead. The other volunteers from the bench were Richard
Hardres of Upper Hardres, a county magnate and a moderate in the Country

interest, and two minor squires, Stephen Lennard and Richard Amherst. Eight justices, therefore, had stepped down from the bench. They were joined from the body of the court by Henry Oxinden and Thomas Broadnax, who were entitled to style themselves 'esquire', and by nine gentlemen who had served on a jury before. In all there were nineteen.[17] Some of those who volunteered for the grand jury must have been anxious to bring the judge's 'Great Business' to fruition, but part of the jury seems to have been 'packed' by Blount who learned of a plan to name a special jury on the preceding night. It was going to be an eventful assize.[18]

It is interesting that the first to volunteer as a juror and the man to be chosen foreman was Sir Edward Dering. He was a man in his early forties, who naturally welcomed the limelight and was apt to be precipitate in securing it. Perhaps he saw a chance to gain something of the power that he lost when he was expelled from the Commons. It did not occur to him that under his titular leadership the actions of moderate men opposed to the majority in the Commons were likely to seem subversive—if not downright seditious. He did not see that a jury with a less contentious foreman would be more likely to win acceptance for whatever purpose it hoped to achieve. Nor, apparently, did his fellow justices. One of them ingenuously suggested that the choice of Dering as foreman was evidence that there was no intention to do anything to which Parliament might object.[19]

The judge's marshal administered the oath first to Sir Edward Dering as foreman.

'You shall diligently enquire, and a true presentment make of all such matters and things as shall be given to you in charge ... you shall present no man for envy, hatred or malice, neither shall you leave any man unpresented for love, fear, favour or affection ... so help you God.'

Sir Edward, too, had taken a decisive step and one that was to lead to his impeachment 'by the Commons assembled in this present Parliament in the names of themselves and of all the Commons of England'. Eighteen men followed him, placed their hands on the Book, three at a time, and swore to observe the same oath. When the last three were sworn, the clerk of assize named them while the crier counted them ending with the exhortation

'Good men and true, stand together and hear your charge.'

The clerk's bailiff beat the floor sharply with his white staff so that the murmur of voices was stilled. The crier proclaimed

'My Lord the King's justice straightly charges and commands all persons to keep silence whilst the charge is in giving to the grand jury upon pain of imprisonment.'[20]

The shuffling ceased and Mr. Justice Malet began to speak. His task cannot have been easy. As a judge of assize it was his duty to convey to the justices and jurors of Kent the offical policy of the King and Council on matters of weight within the county. In a sense the charge was the most important part of the assizes, because it called for a report from the grand jury about aspects of the county's condition in which the Council was interested and because it defined the major tasks of the sheriff and justices for the ensuing half year. In normal times Malet would have received his charge and instructions at the hand of the Lord Keeper before leaving Westminster. It is very doubtful if he received them on this occasion. The King had fled to York earlier in the month taking his Court with him. Because the King had fled, because they wanted to hear of Malet's great business, his audience must have listened with very close attention. If they expected to hear anything startling and controversial from the judge, they were disappointed. Malet gave them nothing that could be used in any subsequent proceedings in Parliament. Most of the justices knew what the 'Great Business' was; the great mass of people in the body of the court probably had little idea. Some of them must still have been puzzling over it as the judge finished his charge, while the indictments were put into court and the prosecutors sworn to their bills. They must have been still turning it over in their minds as the court rose and the people issued out of the courtroom and down the narrow stairs to the street below. The clerk of the gaol arranged the recognizances in three neat files on the table. Sir Henry Palmer, one of the jurors, asked Twysden if there was to be any petitioning but Twysden honestly did not know; other people must have asked questions too. It was probably a major topic of conversation as they sat over their dinners in the inns and houses of Maidstone, this 'Great Business' of Mr. Justice Malet.[21]

Malet had ridden into Maidstone on the previous Saturday. The judges were forbidden to ride circuit on a Sunday. The great mass of local people arrived on the Monday and some of the principal gentlemen came to the judge's lodging in the evening to pay their respects before the opening of the assizes on the following day. It was more normal for the judge to receive the country gentlemen before robing on the day of the assizes, but Malet had no brother judge to share with him the burden of the work and he was probably anxious to make an early start in the morning.[22]

One of those who went to see the judge on the evening of Monday 21 March was Sir Roger Twysden of Roydon Hall. Twysden was a cousin of Sir Edward Dering and like him an antiquary. Both of them were born and bred in Kent, devoted to their native fields and their families. Twysden had defeated his kinsman, Dering, in a bitter contest for the elections to the Short Parliament. Following tradition in Kent he did not stand for re-election in the autumn of 1641. He was a moderate, at times almost a simple, man who was disturbed by the actions of Royalists and Parliamentarians alike. He foresaw that conflict lay ahead. Faced with two unpalatable alternatives he was keyed up either to fight or to fly. He had almost, but not quite, decided to evade the issue by going abroad. And yet, if a solution could be found he was prepared to fight in his own stubborn way—with the pen which came readier to him than the sword.[23]

On his way, Twysden fell in by chance with Sir George Strode, a comparative newcomer to Kent. Strode had been brought up in Malet's native West Country at Shepton Mallet. As a younger son he had decided to make his fortune in the City of London, where he entered trade and married the daughter of an alderman. Strode was as constant as Dering was changeable, as decisive as Twysden was slow to act, as fearless as both were timorous when it came to the push.[24]

When Twysden and Strode arrived at the judge's lodgings they found Sir John Sedley of St. Clere, Ightham, and a number of other justices, who eventually left the judge. Twysden and Strode stayed on to continue their conversation, but both of them left soon afterwards. Apparently there was no talk of any 'Great Business' then, for Twysden says that 'nothing . . . passed there but common discourse'. Strode was later quite emphatic that he did not talk to the judge before the assizes about the grand jury nor about any task that it was to undertake.[25]

After taking their leave, Twysden and Strode went to the Star Inn in the High Street. They found most of their fellow justices sitting at supper. It must have been quite a gathering as about forty-five justices attended the assizes on the following day. The talk was general and turned round the petition organized by Sir Michael Livesey and Sir Anthony Weldon and submitted to the two Houses one and a half months before. Livesey attended the assizes but no one knows whether he was present at supper that night. Almost certainly he was not, for there is no word of any argument. Weldon was not a justice and would not have been there. In the event a number of people complained that the earlier petition did not represent the general view of the county. At the time this was a fairly widespread complaint in other counties as well. Too many petitions initiated by the Puritans and supported by a strong but active minority purported to represent the whole county from which they originated. Probably someone suggested that only the justices of the peace as a body and the grand jury at the assizes could claim to represent the county as a whole. Someone did say that if they did not like the February petition they could now draw up one that did have general consent. This motion was generally agreed. Twysden asked what would be the subject of the new petition and someone told him that this would depend upon the grievances advanced by the grand jury. That was the first time that he heard about a new petition.[26]

It is interesting to see how quickly county opinion had seemingly changed.

One and a half months ago a brave cavalcade claiming to represent the people of Kent had marched up Fish Street Hill towards Westminster. They had thanked the Lords for passing the Second Bishops' Exclusion Bill and demanded the punishment of evil counsellors and the removal of popish lords from the House of Lords. They were, in fact, a minority of Puritan enthusiasts encouraged by Livesey and Weldon; their petitions to the two Houses, like those of many other counties at the time, were based on a model sent down from London. Now the majority of justices in Kent wanted to disclaim those earlier petitions and to frame another that more truly represented the general feeling in Kent. Perhaps they were irritated by the way in which Livesey and Weldon had been stirring up trouble in the county. The justices were certainly not predominantly Royalist in outlook. They seem to have been genuinely concerned that Parliament should have misunderstood the people of Kent. They were clearly worried that Parliament had gone, was going, too far with its reforms. They were trying to effect a reconciliation between King and Parliament and not to censure Parliament for what it had done.[27]

Blount said afterwards that there was talk 'at large' about naming a grand jury.[28] Richard Spencer of Orpington was present and he was later accused of persuading both Dering and Strode to serve on the grand jury.[29] Spencer could have put his suggestion at dinner or it may have matured slowly during the ensuing discussion in his lodging. He and Twysden were both in the commission of oyer and terminer and thus barred from serving on the grand jury.[30]

When supper was over the party broke up, but it was too early to go to bed. Dering, Strode and Twysden went with Spencer to his lodging. Here Twysden referred to the dinner-table talk. Soon afterwards they were joined by Blount. Various of them suggested items worth a place in the petition. Twysden spoke of the great licence of the House of Commons in ejecting members and declaring unknown privileges. This was an allusion to Dering's recent past and certain to gain his support. However, a motion on this issue was eventually laid aside because it was decided not to include anything which could give offence to either House.[31]

The meeting in Spencer's lodging is important for a number of reasons. The fact that Spencer was the host, that he invited the others, lends colour to the later accusation that he persuaded Dering and Strode to offer themselves for the grand jury and to solicit the rest of the grand jury to consent to the petition. At this meeting four men formed a definite intention to frame a petition and began to discuss its form and content. They already felt that it ought to have the widest possible support in the county. They now agreed to word it so that it would be acceptable to Parliament. Blount, the informer, must have said very little and listened a great deal. He could hardly have objected to the framing of a petition acceptable to Parliament, but he must have felt strongly opposed to a lot that Twysden was saying. Twysden knew that men had already been imprisoned for less. Indeed, he already had Dering's example before him. Yet neither he nor the others appear to have been suspicious of Blount.[32] And that is odd, because less than three months before Blount had actually taken the trouble to attend the Commons in person in order to inform against two men from his own county.[33]

It looks as if the judge asked for a good grand jury because someone told him of the intention to frame a petition; but who told him? Since the discussion at supper was apparently very vague it was almost certainly one of the five who gathered in Spencer's lodging that night. It does not appear to have been Twysden, for long afterwards when he was no longer under threat of imprisonment he wrote of his only meeting with the judge before the assizes 'nothing ... passed there but common discourse'.[34] It could scarcely have been Blount. It might have been Dering, who eventually took the lead, or Spencer, who was later accused of inciting him to do so. It could well have been Strode in spite of his later denial at the bar of the House of Commons, and yet denial of the truth is out of keeping with the character that emerges from the rest of his evidence. He was the most intransigent, the least apologetic of them all. It is tempting to think that there was a deep plot between Bristol, Malet and Strode to win moderate opinion in Kent by playing on the vanity of Dering and Twysden and persuading each in his own way to take a leading part. Strode was a stronger character and eventually a stauncher Royalist than Dering or Twysden or Spencer. The House of Commons later did its best to prove that a premeditated plot existed, but was unable to find sufficient evidence.

When the court reassembled after dinner on that first day of the assizes, Tuesday 22 March, the grand jury was absent. The judge, as before, was sitting in the old court house, as it was called, where by tradition Crown (criminal) cases were tried. It was built in Elizabeth's reign for quarter sessions and assizes. It was an attractive timber-framed building with high lattice windows and many gables, and it stood by itself in the middle of the High Street, resting upon square wooden pillars. It was too small for the two judges who normally rode the circuit. In 1608 the borough erected a second building for *nisi prius* (civil) cases a little distance to the east of the court house which then became known as the 'old' court house to distinguish it from the new or upper court house. This was a building similar at first glance to the old, but with additional ornamental features, particularly capitals and plinths at the top and bottom of the pillars. The system worked well when there were two judges of assize each sitting in his own court, but when there was only one it was simpler for him to move from one court to the other than to try all the cases in the same court. Each 'side' had its own associate responsible to the clerk of assize for the clerical work. The clerk of assize was John Eldred who had held the post since 1625. The two associates were Daniel Everard and John Lee. The parties, the witnesses and counsel were only concerned with one of the courts, either the crown court or *nisi prius*. The assize

judge was a victim of the administrative machine. When Malet wished
to hear cases upon *nisi prius* he must descend the narrow stairs facing
the cage for rogues and vagabonds and walk up the road to the upper
court house, less than a bowshot away.[35]

It may well have been in the upper court house that the grand jury
assembled that afternoon to frame their presentment of the state of the
county in reply to the heads of the judge's charge and to consider the
indictments that had been laid before them. These followed the familiar
pattern: stealing goods or money, breaking and entering, robbery with
violence, sheltering criminals; and there was one man accused of calling
the King a papist.[36] The jury seem to have hurried through this part
of their work for Serjeant Wilde later alleged that

> 'Their duty, was to have enquired diligently of the matters given them
> in charge; . . . yet they leave other matters which they were charged
> with as accidents and trifles, and insist upon this [the petition] which
> they had nothing to do with, as the main and principal business.'[37]

Once the general business was out of the way Dering and Strode moved
that a petition might be drawn and directed to Parliament. No one had
so far suggested the main items that it ought to contain. Blount said
later that he and others spoke against it, but Dering and Strode conjured
the jury to secrecy and instructed them not to talk to anyone about it
until it had been agreed and presented to the judge and the rest of the
bench. They explained that the juror's oath bound them to keep silence
about the petition.[38] For the moment the opposition was quelled.

The tactics of the moderate constitutionalists and the Parliamentarian
supporters make interesting comparison. Amongst the moderates there was
nothing premeditated, for everything was openly discussed. The plan was
only half a plan, for it saw the importance of putting justices of sufficient
stature and moderate views on the grand jury and yet failed to ensure
that enough of them got there.

Looking at the grand jury as a whole one is struck by the fact that
in spite of the judge's encouragement it was not predominantly composed
of men very powerful in the county. Dering, Strode, Hardres and possibly
Hamond were men of great influence in the county; the rest were parochial
gentry, differing from the grand jurors of the previous summer in that
one of them was an impoverished knight and six were entitled to style
themselves 'esquire' rather than 'gent.'.[39]

None of the knights and esquires among the jurors was so strongly
for the King as Palmer or as strongly against the Parliamentarians as Strode.
Hamond and Dering came nearest. But even Hamond was later to falter
for a while. And Dering had once been one of Pym's strongest supporters.
He was now seeking a middle way that would be acceptable to the two
conflicting parties. Hardres and the Oxindens were moderates; it took
them another six years to come out into the open against Parliament.

Lennard, Amherst and Broadnax were minor squires swimming with the Parliamentary stream.[40]

Before the assizes began, Strode, Dering, Twysden and Spencer do not seem to have been very successful in their canvassing. Perhaps it was part of their plan that they should have left a sufficiently favourable majority on the bench after the grand jury had been sworn. Possibly they had canvassed the wrong people and the judge's intervention caught them unprepared, in spite of the talk on the previous evening. They may have conceived themselves to be the leaders of a movement so generally accepted that there was no need to organize for its success—a common fault with the King's supporters at the time. In the court they managed to secure for the grand jury only two further allies from the bench, Palmer and Hamond, and the first of these, when he volunteered, did not even know whether there was going to be a petition or not. If Dering and Strode had been at all sensitive to the aspirations and determination of their fellow jurors, they would have dropped talk of petitions on the grand jury, and raised it in open court where they did later command an overwhelming majority. As it was, they totally underestimated the opposition among their fellow jurors.

By contrast Blount moved secretly and effectively. From the talk on the previous night he knew there was to be a petition, moderate if not Royalist in complexion, and he knew there had been talk of having the right grand jury. It seems almost certain that he encouraged most of the nine who were against a petition to volunteer for the jury. How else could the voting of the grand jury later in the week have been so unrepresentative of the views of the great mass of people present at the assizes, who, as we shall see, voted for the petition by an overwhelming majority? For the moment the minority appeared to have been overawed by Dering and Strode who were, after all, influential men in the county. No doubt, too, it was difficult to oppose a petition whose principal points had not yet been formally proposed. Perhaps Blount never really spoke out on that day. He had a strong reason for playing a waiting game. He had ensured that his small opposition occupied a key role out of all proportion to its numbers. He could wait until the plan was unfolded—and then act.

Towards evening the grand jury returned to the court. The clerk of assize called their names and asked if they were agreed upon any bills. Sir Edward Dering replied 'Yes' and handed over the true bills which the jury had found. Amongst them was one indictment which has come down to us in its entirety and it is interesting not only for its language but also as a reminder that articles of impeachment were not the only documents of the day to use exaggerated and condemnatory phrases wholly foreign to modern usage. The indictment runs to about 650 words but the gravamen of the charge was that Edward Fairbrother:

'said, published and in a loud voice pronounced these malicious and seditious words following in English namely: Kinge Charles that is now Kinge of England (meaning our said Lord Charles that is now King of England etc) is a Papist, falsely, maliciously and seditiously, advisedly and directly in the hearing of various subjects of the said Lord King, with that intention . . . to withdraw the cordial love, due fidelity and allegiance of the same lieges and subjects of the same Lord King from that Lord King . . .'

This and other true bills would later go for trial by petty jury.[41]

Dering then addressed the judge and the rest of the bench and told them that it was the wish of many to petition Parliament from the assizes as other counties had done. He suggested that three of the bench should join three of the grand jury in framing it. If they could not agree he would drop the matter. Mr. Justice Malet replied that this fell outside the scope of his commission and did not concern him as judge. He would, therefore, leave Dering to consider it with the justices of the peace. He then left the court and went immediately to try cases upon *nisi prius* in the upper court house.[42]

The justices had some notion of what was in the wind. They had been present at the dinner discussion on the preceding night. Although eight of their number had left the bench to serve on the jury, the majority accepted Dering's proposal readily and there was a general discussion about what was the best way to draft the petition. Eventually Twysden moved, and it was agreed, that the grand jury should nominate some of the justices and the justices some of the grand jury to draw it up. By its very novelty the motion must have helped to ensure that the architects of the petition had the initiative and were thus able to elect like-minded people to the drafting committee before any opposition could be mobilized.[43]

Those who were chosen went off to a private lodging in the town, Twysden and Sedley among them. Dering and Strode were almost certainly also on the drafting committee since they were later alleged to have proposed the petition and to have played a major part in persuading the others. With the possible exception of Strode, none of those four was a whole-hearted Royalist. Sedley was more for Parliament than King. But they all wanted a 'good understanding' to be 'speedily renewed between His Majesty and the Houses of Parliament'. They wanted reconciliation. Two of them, Dering and Twysden, had grown up in Kent where there were no very extensive traditional strongholds of private patronage. Since both were capable of a measure of organization and leadership they had been free to play at county politics in a relatively unfettered arena. With the people of Kent resenting outside interference these two were typical of Kent. They were both closely in touch with feeling amongst the gentry inside the county and at the same time curiously isolated both from the Puritan stirrings below the surface and from national feeling outside. In the year 1642 men everywhere in England thought of their county when they talked of their country. Nowhere was this more true than in Kent where leaders of county opinion could, on occasion, be totally wrong about the mood and temper of the Commons. So they continued with the work of planning, attempting to reconcile two forces that were becoming irreconcilable. Various clauses were presented. Some were approved, some corrected and some expunged. Sedley moved that a clause about papists should include provision for their children to be brought up in the reformed religion. In Twysden's view this was perhaps the hardest and least justifiable clause of all. The remaining clauses were agreed and, since it was now evening, one or two of the drafting committee were nominated to meet after supper to draw up their requests in the form of a petition.[44]

That night the petition was put down in writing. Twysden should have had a hand in drafting it, but he was ill and did not appear. Going back to his lodging through the Star Inn he met Blount who was clearly not satisfied with what they intended to do. Twysden's biographer suggests that his illness may have been brought on by his chance meeting with Blount. Whether that is true or not, the evidence suggests that he had recovered sufficiently by the next day to take a healthy interest in the petition and a major hand in redrafting some of the clauses. When Twysden came to write his journal he could not remember the point on which he and Blount differed. This suggests that the difference was over a point of detail rather than principle and that the incident had no great importance for him at the time. Probably its significance only occurred to him in retrospect.[45]

Staying at Maidstone for the assizes was a Doctor Piers, a doctor of law (a 'civilian') who had relatives in Kent. He heard the talk and gathered that the petition was to cover a wide variety of subjects. He saw an opportunity to jump on the band wagon. He drafted a clause designed to help his profession and it was probably on this night that he handed it to Spencer who promised to see that it was included in the petition. It certainly did eventually find its way into the petition and it was to add fuel to the flames, for 'civilians' who pleaded in the ecclesiastical courts were anathema to the majority in the Commons.[46]

On the following morning Twysden and Spencer, who had not attended the meeting of the previous night, asked to see a copy of the petition so that they could agree not only the heads but the detailed wording. The drafting committee then met in a private house in the town and considered the draft once more. There was some discussion and a number of alterations were proposed. The changes were mostly aimed at giving a more exact meaning or avoiding offence to Parliament. Twysden does not say in his journal that he was there, but some of the alterations are pedantic enough to be his. Apparently, all the objections at this meeting were finally transformed into agreed amendments. They resolved to put the petition publicly to the county on the morrow so that it could be laid before Parliament.[47]

We know that the petition was not presented in open court before Friday 25 March.[48] But Blount says in his evidence that Sir Edward Dering and Sir George Strode presented the heads of the petition on the day after the jury was sworn. This must have been a meeting at which the representatives of the grand jury on the drafting committee reported back to the grand jury as a whole; such a meeting must have taken place, but is nowhere explicitly reported. It was now that Dering and Strode encountered difficulty. Of the nineteen on the jury, nine protested against it. The evidence is not conclusive, but there are some grounds for believing that the jury was divided like this:

For the Petition	*Against the Petition*
Edward Dering, kt. and bt. (JP)	Thomas Blount, esq., (JP)
George Strode, kt., (JP)	Richard Hardres, esq., (JP)
Henry Palmer, kt., (JP)	Stephen Lennard, esq., (JP)
Anthony Hamond, esq., (JP)	Richard Amherst, esq., (JP)
Robert Sooles, gent.	Henry Oxinden, esq.
Charles Clarke, gent.	Thomas Broadnax, esq.
Henry Lee, gent.	Thomas Cattlett, gent.
John Harflete, gent.	Thomas Roper, gent.
Fortunatus Woodgate, gent.	Bonham Fance, gent.[49]
John Horsmonden	

The jurors of lower status, who were only 'gentlemen' or less, supported the petition by six votes to three. Their betters opposed it by six votes to four. No doubt exception was taken to individual clauses. No doubt, too, Blount reiterated a point that he had made on the preceding day; it would contradict the petition of Sir Michael Livesey that had already been delivered in the name of the county. The petition had failed in its aim that it should have general consent. It had a bare majority of one. Its supporters lacked two of the twelve that would have been needed to find a true bill on indictment. Its opponents numbered nine and they must have been adamant, their opposition steadfast and intense. It seems that the majority forced the nine to withdraw, although it is not completely clear whether the nine were asked to withdraw now or later when the petition was read in open court. Dering must have known then that the petition could never be presented to Parliament in the name of the grand jury and the justices of Kent. If it was delivered, it could not represent the view of a united county, only that of a large number of people in it. Although conciliatory in tone, because it opposed the majority in the Commons and was opposed by a minority within the county, it would fail to carry conviction. Blount saw this too; he went out with his supporters and used the interval to solicit their signatures against it.[50]

In due course, the whole jury returned to the courtroom and Sir Edward Dering as foreman delivered the petition to the bench in the name of the grand jury as a whole. He was living out a part that had ceased to have meaning. His opponents on the jury asked the judge to take note of the fact that they were not agreed with their foreman. There were mutual recriminations and threats. Strode said that his opponents deserved to have their names posted for failing to support the petition. They replied that the supporters of the petition ought to have their names posted.[51] In the heated exchange someone seems to have said that anyone who spoke against the petition or absented themselves from it ought to be punished.[52] Malet had to say that he could not accept the petition in the name of the grand jury.[53]

On the Friday the petition was presented in open court while the judge was again trying civil cases.[54] Sir Edward Dering, though he could not claim a united jury, could still hold the limelight and the approval of the great majority present by reading it in public. Spencer sponsored it from the bench. Twysden and Strode supported him.[55] Augustine Skinner, one of the two knights of the shire, was present and showed no distaste for it, although, like the judge himself, he did apparently refuse to set his hand to it. Even at this public meeting there were one or two suggested amendments and one at least was firmly approved on the grounds that the original wording might have given offence to Parliament. In a climate of opinion where this was possible it is not surprising that the petition was accepted with an overwhelming majority.[56] What is surprising is the disappearance of the opposition represented by the minority of nine on the grand jury. Either they had weighed up the situation and decided that they could not command an effective opposition in the courtroom or they were, as Jessup suggests, ordered to withdraw now and not before.[57]

By general consent the petition was handed to Augustine Skinner, as knight of the shire, on the spot. He seemed to approve it and promised to support it in Parliament. Sir Edward Dering moved on the bench that three copies should be made, one to the House of Lords, another to the Commons and a third to the King, but Twysden opposed the idea of sending a copy to the King, pointing out that this was unnecessary since the petition was addressed to the King through Parliament. Twysden says that there were 2,000 people present when the petition was read out, but the court house simply could not hold that number. It was probably agreed first in the courtroom and then read from the top of the stairs to the people gathered outside. The authors seem to have been at great pains to ensure that the petition had a wide approval. It was decided to allow time till the next quarter sessions in under four weeks' time so that if any of the justices found that any part of the petition was unpopular in their divisions, the offending part could be altered or struck out.[58] Spencer said they would have an order of the court to publish the petition.[59] Strode arranged for an attorney at law named Pope, who was living at Maidstone, to get copies made for distribution throughout the county to any who were prepared to pay for them.[60] They decided to ask the gentlemen in each division to collect signatures for it.[61] Dering reckoned that they would get 40,000 hands to the petition and proposed that they should all come up to deliver it.[62] Spencer said they should all meet at Blackheath on Friday 29 April and this was agreed.[63] The choice of Blackheath was unfortunate: it was a notorious place of assembly for rebels preparing to attack the City of London.[64]

The assizes ended that day with the crier's time-honoured valediction:

'All manner of persons that have here appeared before my Lord, the King's justice at these assizes and general goal delivery may now depart in God's peace and the King's and keep your day here upon a new summons and God save the King.'

The judge stepped down from the bench and preceded by the sheriff stepped out into the open air. The trumpets sounded and the sheriff's men were waiting below to escort him back to his lodgings.[65]

In the evening Strode came to the judge's lodgings late, told Malet about the petition and asked if he had read it. Malet said 'No.' Strode asked him if he wanted to read it. He replied 'Not during the assizes.' Then Strode told him that he would send him a copy and asked him to show it to 'the earl'. He meant the Earl of Bristol. Strode was later accused of intending that the earl should show it to the King and that its publication throughout the country should hinder the operation of the Militia Ordinance. That night he got a copy transcribed for the judge.[66]

On the morning of Saturday 26 March Strode wrapped a copy of the petition in a sheet of paper and sent it to the judge by Pope, the attorney.[67] Pope caught Malet just as he was taking horse for the journey back to London and gave it to him. Malet probably thrust it into one of the deep pockets of his serjeant's coat; at all events he did not read it until he got home. On the Sunday, back at home and with church and dinner behind him, he rode to the Earl of Bristol's house in Great Queen Street, with his copy of the petition. Bristol read it through and saw its significance. He called for his servant and got him to copy it out.[68] Because it is long, but important to the story, it is reproduced in full in Appendix II.

In the main the petition reflected the local interests of its originators and their desire to bring together the King and his two Houses of Parliament. It was couched in moderate and respectful terms. The majority of its seventeen clauses must have been unexceptionable to the Country opposition in both Houses. Apart from requests dealing with national and local economic problems, there were, for instance, thanks for the laws so far enacted by the Long Parliament, a request for a stricter enforcement of the laws against papists and another for a general synod of divines on the lines proposed in the Grand Remonstrance. But some of the clauses were contrary to the wishes of the majority in the Commons or of the Puritan core inside the opposition. There was a clause asking that the liturgy of the church might stay in its present form and another asking that bishops and episcopal government might remain. This latter would not find favour with those who had voted for the 'root and branch' bill. Two clauses may have been lacking in tact. One asked the two Houses to reply to the King's conciliatory message of 20 January; this carried the clear implication that they were at fault in failing to reply. Another clause asked that the judicial vacuum, created by the abolition of the High Commission Court, might be filled so that wills could be proved and crimes like incest could be punished.

But two clauses in particular really struck home. One asked for a law to regulate the militia, so that men would know whether to obey the King or Parliament and another asked that no order of either or both Houses, not grounded on the laws of the land, might be enforced on the subject until enacted by Parliament. Both these posed the problem of honest law-abiding citizens in the face of an unwarranted assumption of power by the two Houses. Both could be seen as an attack upon the Militia Ordinance, upon those who gave it the effect of law and upon those who sought to enforce it. It was these two clauses which gave the Kentish petition of March 1642 its constitutional importance.[69]

No doubt Bristol reminded Malet of what happened to Benyon, the chief promoter of the London petition of 24 February. They are almost certain to have discussed the sequel that was played out while Malet was on circuit. The newly elected Common Council had presented to both Houses a counterblast to Benyon's petition disavowing it completely. They were able to outvote the Lord Mayor and Aldermen on this issue and thus present their own petition as that of the 'Mayor, aldermen and the rest of Common Council of the City of London'. By then Benyon's petition had been published throughout the kingdom as a pamphlet. The Commons thanked their present petitioners, but the Lords went further. They ordered copies of Benyon's petition to be burnt by the common hangman and the new London petition attacking it to be printed and published forthwith.[70]

Meanwhile, the gentry of Kent dispersed to their homes. The active supporters of the petition had a lot to do before quarter sessions met on 19 April. Their organization at the assizes had been poor; their organization for signatures must be better. They were, after all, used to canvassing—the activity which preceded the elections for the Short and Long Parliaments had been well planned and executed. Then Dering and Twysden had been on opposite sides. Now they were united. In the previous autumn, too, Dering had set his supporters to get hands for his petition in favour of a reformed episcopacy and the existing liturgy. Many of the parish clergy had worked with them and the churches had been the centres at which they got the necessary hands. Now the clergy helped again and their churches were a focus for action.[71]

At Royden Hall, Twysden got copies made for distribution among his friends and then rode out to secure their support.[72] Sir George Strode not merely canvassed for the petition but spoke out strongly against Parliament's proceedings.[73] In Maidstone, Thomas Stanley, the mayor, was the driving force.[74] At Pluckley, Sir Edward Dering addressed the parishioners in church after evensong and solicited their support.[75] His neighbour,

George Chute, of Surrenden Chute, was also distributing copies. One of these came into the hands of Richard Lovelace, the poet, who eventually presented the petition to the Commons.[76] Some of the younger generation were active too. There were Sir John Mayney and young Sir Henry Palmer. Both were newly knighted by the King and anxious to demonstrate their loyalty. And there was Anthony Hamond, who had left the bench at the assizes in order to volunteer for the grand jury and support Dering's petition.[77]

All this activity took time to develop. The ingenuous Twysden was quietly and amicably discussing events with men who took a different view. On the day after the assizes ended, Sir Henry Vane, the elder, sent for him to dine at Fairlawn. Twysden does not tell us what they discussed. It is not unlikely that Vane's invitation was prompted by a desire to hear at first hand about the petition. It was almost inevitable that Twysden should mention it at dinner and that Vane should question him about it. Vane was a cousin of Twysden by marriage, but politically they had grown apart. Shorn of his offices under the Crown, Vane had thrown in his lot with the Country, a fact of which Twysden was aware. An old hand at duplicity, Vane must have played his cards well, for he does not seem to have given Twysden any hint that he was against the petition. On the following day Twysden rode over to William James of Ightham and found him to be the first man of intelligence and integrity who was against it. The two Houses had yet to mobilize their forces.[78]

5

Monday 28 March

'If any one moment can be selected as that in which the Civil
War became inevitable, it was that of the vote of March 28,
by which the Kentish petitioners were treated as criminals.'

S. R. GARDINER [1]

On Monday 28 March business in the Commons was well under way
before the Great Tom of Westminster had struck nine o'clock or the
Lords had begun their prayers.[2] Honourable members sat crowded on
either side of the chamber, five rows reaching upwards from the floor
of the House and round behind the Speaker's chair—a gallery of faces
framed between white collars or ruffs and broad-brimmed steeple hats.
Mr. Speaker Lenthall, in black gown braided with gold, sat in his chair
upon the floor of the House, but raised above it so that he had a commanding
view of every member he could see. (Some behind his back were out
of his control and could never catch his eye.) He too wore hat and sword
like the other members. Held above his chair by a board that ran down
its back were the emblazoned arms of Charles I, a reminder that although
he was elected by the Commons, he was 'enabled' by the Sovereign.
Behind him was the great east window of St. Stephen's Chapel. A false
roof completely hid the pointed arches of the chapel roof and the top
of the window itself which was now filled with plain diamond-paned glass.
Blinds across the upper part of the window masked the glare of the morning
sun. The lower casements were opened to prevent the atmosphere of the
crowded chamber from becoming too heavy. In front of the Speaker
the Clerk of the Commons House, Henry Elsynge, sat at a table with
his assistant, John Rushworth. Their table, none too big for its work,
was covered with a cloth and piled with journals and books. Across one
corner, so that it might encumber the table as little as possible, lay the
mace, the symbol of the Speaker's (and the King's) authority.[3] The House's
business that morning was at first merely a good deal of routine and
a long discussion about the office for foreign postmasters.[4]

Sir Simonds D'Ewes, the diarist, sitting at the bottom end of the tier of benches on the Speaker's left and opposite the south end of the Clerk's table, made scribbled jottings on large foolscap sheets, enough for his clerk to amplify later into two full pages of his journal.[5] Next to him sat another diarist and strong Parliamentarian, John Moore, the member for Liverpool, writing in a fine, almost indecipherable, hand in a small notebook.[6] Opposite them across the table sat Framlingham Gawdy, the member for Thetford in Norfolk, another taker of notes. He wrote in pencil and his spelling was wholly—and delightfully—his own.[7] Then D'Ewes, as he so often did, left the chamber for his midday meal (dinner, they called it) and a breath of fresh air.[8] He was not alone in this. The practice was widespread, and annoying to Mr. Speaker Lenthall. On one occasion the Speaker had been goaded into telling the members that 'they were unworthy to sit in this great and wise assembly that would so run forth to their dinners.'[9] The truth was that Lenthall also missed his dinner and it irked him to sit on while members came and went as they pleased.[10]

Before D'Ewes returned in mid afternoon the discussions about the Kentish petition were over for the day. They are covered in his diary by a short cryptic note 'Ve M for the next ensuing passages.'[11] We are sure of his meaning because in his entry for 1 April he wrote 'See Mr. Moore's journall for the rest.'[12] Unfortunately John Moore's narrative for this period has not survived and this is a double loss because Moore was appointed later in the day to sit on the joint committee of the two Houses for the Kentish petition.[13] For our knowledge of what went on in the Commons we are dependent upon the printed journals of the two Houses, upon the diary of Framlingham Gawdy and upon the original manuscript draft journal of the House of Lords. This last was kept by the Clerk of the House; it tells us more than the printed journal about the course and sequence of events.[14]

While D'Ewes withdrew for his dinner Pym and a number of his closest adherents remained in the chamber.[15] Pym himself sat on one of the lower tiers on the left of the Speaker and close to the bar of the House. Behind him was Henry Marten, the libertine republican, and probably Denzil Holles, the impetuous member for Dorchester. John Moore remained in his place on the same side of the House; on his tier, but closer to the Speaker, was the young Sir Henry Vane. There were Sir John Evelyn, Sir Henry Mildmay, the lawyer, John Glyn, the member for Westminster, and William Pierrepont, the member for Great Wenlock in Shropshire. Sir Walter Erle was present. There was Sir Arthur Hesilrige, whose place was up in the gallery.[16] A substantial number of Pym's adherents had chosen to forego their dinner on this particular day. It did not do to leave things to chance. These tactics by the opposition leaders had already secured the exclusion of the bishops. It was Lord Falkland who remarked that 'they who hated bishops hated them worse than the devil and they who loved them did not love them so well as their dinner.'[17] It looked now as if the same might become true of Malet and the Kentish petitioners. Pym and his supporters held the initiative. The petitioners themselves felt secure in the traditional freedom of Englishmen to petition. Those who were still prepared to defend that freedom in the Commons were not alive to the danger that threatened it. Pym was totally against a reconciliation. He saw clearly that he must crush any form of popular petitioning which cast doubt upon the legality of what the two Houses were doing. Before the moderate constitutionalists were alive to his purpose and before any new popular movement was fairly begun, he must break it—once and for all. He had chosen the time when the enemy was weak. He had massed his forces for the blow and now he must deploy them with all the skill at his command.

While D'Ewes and others were still out of the chamber, the House was told that a certain Francis Jones had laid an information about a Kentish petition. The information was read and then Jones was called to speak to it. Jones seems to have talked to some member of the Commons who wrote down what he said. His story was committed to paper in a way calculated to cause alarm in the House. The statement said that the petition was read in open court at the Maidstone assizes; this carried at least the suggestion that the judge was present when it was read. It mentioned the clause asking for the government of the bishops to remain. This was calculated to anger the majority in the Commons, who wanted bishops abolished altogether. It reported the clause asking 'that the liturgy and common prayer book might still remain', because it was known that the majority in the Commons wanted them changed. It gave the impression that the petition asked for those to be punished who spoke against it or did not support it. This may have been a serious threat in the heat of the moment at the assizes, but it certainly formed no part of the petition itself. The next quoted heading is equally misleading; 'That all the ministers and people might be brought into an uniformity to this.' In the petition 'this' was a national synod to settle religious differences; in the information, it appears to refer to the punishment of those who disagree—or to the petition itself. Well down the list were two clauses that bore on the Militia Ordinance. It is odd that these did not get more prominence either now or in the evidence brought out during the ensuing week, because when Dering, Strode and Spencer came to be impeached the first clause in each case charged them with conspiring to frustrate the Militia Ordinance. This was their real crime in the eyes of Pym and his supporters, but today it was played down, for until they had succeeded in working both Houses into a ferment of anger they could not be sure of gaining majority support to arrest its perfectly innocent authors. One other clause about 'the privilege of Parliament and the King's Majesty's regal power' was garbled, but for the most part the others were correctly represented—only shorn of the more tactful wording of the originals. The written statement ended by saying that Sir Edward Dering had pressed that a copy of the petition be sent to the King, 'which was denied, as I think.' Jones said that Sir Roger Twysden and Richard Spencer had been equally active in contriving and presenting the petition. He does not appear to have mentioned Sir

George Strode. There was further evidence that Sir Edward Dering said he could get 40,000 hands to the petition and that they would all come up to deliver it. In a sense this was true. Dering had said that he hoped to get 40,000 hands. He may have said that they would all come up to deliver the petition. He cannot have expected all 40,000 signatories to proceed to London in a body and yet this was just the sort of statement that the Commons would cite as evidence that he was seeking a breach of the peace—or worse.[18]

Without delaying to hear the next witness who was waiting to give evidence, the House ordered that the Lords should be asked for a conference and that 'Mr. Justice Mallet' should be present to be examined about the truth of the business. Sir John Evelyn was sent off with the message. The House then called Mr. David Browne, who, like Jones, submitted his statement in writing with his signature upon it and spoke to it orally, confirming what Jones had said. He gave a wealth of circumstantial detail about Dering's part in the affair and a garbled account of some of the clauses.[19]

When Browne had left the chamber, Pym, Pierrepont, Glyn and Marten were appointed members of a committee to withdraw and prepare questions to be put to Malet and to manage the coming conference with the Lords.[20] It was unusual for as many as four members to manage a conference and it is worth considering those who were assigned to the task. Collectively they represented the broad streams of opinion within the Country opposition. Pym, 'King Pym' they called him now,[21] had emerged as the clear and undisputed leader of the middle group which was the core of the Country alliance. Since he had been accused of high treason in January he was implacably opposed to the King. He knew how to touch chords of greatness and principle when he chose, but he had no trouble in forgetting the same principles when it suited his practical purpose. He was above all a realist and he had chosen to command, in person, the forces in the Commons ranged against those whom they regarded as 'the ill affected gentry of Kent'. After him, William Pierrepont was well chosen on four counts. He was one of the wisest men in the House and could be sure of a strong following of moderate members. He was close to the inner councils of the Country leaders. He was one of the best orators in the House and had spoken at the impeachment of Sir Robert Berkeley. And lastly, he was a Presbyterian elder and therefore unsympathetic to bishops. John Glyn, more probably an Independent than a Presbyterian, represented— like Pym—the middle group of members. He was an inveterate committee man, a lawyer and a strong advocate who had already managed or helped to manage the impeachments against Strafford and the bishops and the case against the Duke of Richmond in a conference with the Lords. Henry Marten was in politics an extreme radical and on religious issues an atheist. He had no use for Kings and certainly not for Charles, who had once insulted him. He was a man of acute intelligence and very great charm, whose talents do not seem to have been in any way impaired by his libertine tastes. He was an eloquent speaker, brilliant in debate.[22]

These were four of the best speakers the House could muster; their task was to persuade the Lords that it was now a crime to petition for a reconciliation between King and Parliament and to question the declared and unlawful policies of the majority in both Houses. It is not at all certain that they ever left the Commons chamber. In the *Journals* their report follows hard upon their appointment. It looks almost as if they had their questions already prepared and it was Glyn, the lawyer, who made the report. He asked that six questions be put to Malet.

1. Do you know of a petition publicly read at the assizes at Maidstone in Kent? To whom was it directed?
2. Who framed that petition? Had you any notice of it before it was publicly moved?
3. Was there anything expressed in it concerning the militia or the King's message of the 20th January?
4. Was there any motion made to send this to the King? If yea, who made that motion? And what speech was there of a former petition to the Parliament? And what the passages were?
5. Was there any speech of a number of persons to come with this petition? And when?
6. Who was the foreman of that grand inquest? And whether was that jury returned by the sheriff? Or, did you give directions for some of them to be of that jury?

The House heard the questions and authorized the committee to put any other questions that they wanted. They agreed to ask the Lords to join with them in sending for Sir Edward Dering, Sir Roger Twysden and Richard Spencer.[23]

Until this moment no evidence had been given against Strode. Dering was certainly a prime mover; all the witnesses were agreed on that. Francis Jones had identified Twysden and Spencer as being promoters of the petition. But if Strode had not been named in the hurriedly drafted informations and oral evidence, there were people there who knew he was implicated. Glyn and his fellow inquisitors knew more about the happenings at Maidstone than had so far appeared in the evidence. In the temper of those who remained in the House during dinner on that day it was unlikely that any architect of the petition would escape with impunity for lack of a small thing like first-hand evidence.

Sir John Evelyn returned and formally reported to the Speaker that the Lords 'would give a present meeting'. The time had come for the Commons to meet the Lords in the Painted Chamber and for the four appointed speakers to demonstrate to their supporters that they were worthy of their role.[24]

The Lords sat later than the Commons that morning and the *Journals of the House of Lords* suggest that Malet resumed his duties as assistant in his accustomed place on the inner side of the woolsacks.[25] After a month on circuit it must have come as a renewed shock to see the two empty benches where the bishops had sat, a splash of red serge on the right hand side of the chamber, and to hear prayers said and no bishop to say them.[26] Malet was probably the only judge on the woolsacks; his was the shortest circuit and there is no evidence that any of his brother judges had yet returned.[27] Lord Keeper Littleton still sat as Speaker on the upper sack. There had been times of late when sickness had kept him away. As spokesman of King to Parliament and Parliament to King he was subject to pressure from both and the strain was beginning to tell.[28] But the real interest centred on the serge-covered benches of the peers. They were sparsely filled, but not noticeably more sparsely than a month ago;[29] the records suggest that there were just under forty peers present.[30] Five of the peers who were most strongly against the Militia Ordinance a fortnight ago were no longer present in the Lords. They had lost heart and retired from the parliamentary scene. Eventually they joined the King. However, on 28 March there were about a dozen peers present in the Lords who supported the King, while there were about a score who had consistently supported the Country opposition.[31]

The Militia Ordinance was, as we have seen, an act of rebellion. It could only be imposed upon the subject by the unlawful use of force. The Kentish petition posed the first overt, if mildly worded, challenge to the Militia Ordinance. Now that the challenge had come, the question arose whether all the peers who voted for it were prepared to employ force upon innocent subjects in order to impose their will. Perhaps some of the more moderate, who had voted consistently with the Country peers to date and who were gradually becoming unsympathetic to their aims and methods, might change their views. If so, would they be enough to shift the balance and protect the long-standing right of the subject to petition Parliament? These and similar considerations must have been exercising Malet's mind that Monday morning.

Prayers over, the business of the day was begun. There came a debate about whether four officers of state should attend the King in York for the feast of St. George. While the discussion was in progress the gentleman usher informed the Lord Keeper that the knights, citizens and burgesses of the Commons House stood without. Following normal practice, the Lords continued with their business while Malet must have braced himself for the message that he knew was almost certain to come. At last the debate came to an end and it was resolved that the four peers should attend the House. The Lord Keeper was ordered to signify the resolution to the King and a committee was appointed to draw up reasons in writing.[32]

The peers sent for the messengers of the Lower House and sat waiting, their hats on their heads. Through the open doors a group of Parliament men advanced bareheaded to the lower end of the chamber. The Lord Keeper rose from his place and, supported by his purse bearer and the

Clerk of the Crown in Chancery, went down to the middle of the bar to await their coming with the silken purse bearing the Great Seal of England in his hand. He was followed closely by a number of peers. The group of Parliament men advanced to meet him at the bar. Heading them was Sir Walter Erle, who mounted the small dais prepared for him. Erle was an attentive committee man and a member of the middle group in the Country alliance. Like many of the most active, he was a strong supporter of various colonial projects, an aggressive opponent of episcopacy and one of the architects of the Grand Remonstrance. The Parliament men made their three bows to the Chair of Estate. Then Erle announced that the Commons had sent to their lordships a bill about Irish affairs which had passed the Commons and which they wanted their lordships to expedite. For Malet anticlimax must have been absolute. Erle humbly delivered to the Lord Keeper a copy of the bill. The Parliament men made their bows and withdrew. Then the business of the House continued once more.[33]

After an interval, the gentleman usher announced for the second time that morning that the knights, citizens and burgesses of the Commons were without. This time the group of Parliament men was headed by Sir John Evelyn. Once more the party from the Commons met the Lord Keeper and his supporters at the bar of the House. They brought the message for which Malet must have been waiting. 'The knights, citizens and burgesses of the Commons House desire a present conference touching some information which they have received from Kent, which concerns the breach of the privileges of Parliament and the disturbance of the peace of the kingdom; and the House of Commons do likewise desire that Mr. Justice Malet may be present at the said conference to answer such questions as they desire may be asked him.' The messenger and his supporters made three bows to the Chair of Estate and left the chamber. The peers returned to their places and the Lord Keeper reported the substance of the message he had received.[34]

The pattern of attack was beginning to unfold. Petitioning was still no crime. But if it could be alleged that the petition infringed the privileges of Parliament or the peace of the kingdom, then its supporters might be arrested and imprisoned. All the Commons needed was a statement from one or two accusers and the leaders could be sent for as delinquents, committed to the Tower, the Gatehouse, or the Fleet, and left kicking their heels while the Country leaders went to work in the county. In due course the prisoners would be released without trial on a punitive bail and with the best of reasons for curbing their enthusiasm in the future. It had happened before. Malet was all too familiar with cases of the kind.

The Lords could not refuse the request from the Commons and after consulting the House the Lord Keeper called the messengers to the bar again and sitting on the upper sack with his head covered he announced 'Their Lordships will give a present conference in the Painted Chamber as is desired and Mr. Justice Malet shall be present at it.' Sir John Evelyn's party bowed and withdrew.[35]

Now 'a present conference' only meant that the Commons were to assemble at once in the Painted Chamber, for they had to be ready and waiting for the Lords. While they did so the Lords continued with their business.[36]

Then at last, the Lord Keeper obtained consent to an adjournment in order to meet the Commons with a conference of the whole House.[37] The serjeant-at-arms and the purse bearer moved into the centre of the chamber, picked up the mace and Great Seal and attended the Lord Keeper as he left the House. They made their way through the intervening lobby (by which the Commons messengers had so lately entered) to the Painted Chamber where the Commons were already standing hats in hand. Behind the Lord Keeper came the peers. More bows, and the Lords took their seats in the centre of the chamber, their hats on their heads to emphasize their superiority. It was not a tradition of which the Commons approved, but at that particular time they needed the support of the Lords; more important matters hung in the balance.[38] Even the judges stood uncovered while their Lordships sat in conference. After a great deal of pressure the Lords had magnanimously agreed that infirm judges and members of the Commons might sit at conferences (as long as they were decently out of sight behind a pillar) but they were never to be covered.[39]

Malet had been in this chamber a hundred times in the last year—as assistant to select committees for bills, at conferences with the Commons, and on his way between his seat on the bench in Westminster Hall and his seat on the woolsack in the Lords. It was said that Edward the Confessor used it as his bedroom and died looking at the walls that were later painted to give it its present name. The gilded and faded tracery still adorned its roof.[40]

John Moore's description of this conference has not survived and so we have to call upon precedent and imagination to determine what happened. Facing the Lord Keeper would have been the four men appointed to manage the conference for the Commons: Pym, Pierrepont, Glyn and Marten.[41] Standing round them and the seated peers and even behind the Lord Keeper's chair (a favourite place for D'Ewes when he attended these meetings) were the Commons, outnumbering the depleted Lords many times over.[42] We can imagine Pym beginning in the time-honoured way: 'My Lords, the knights, citizens and burgesses of the House of Commons, now assembled in Parliament have commanded me to present to your Lordships an information. . . .'[43] On such occasions Pym was accustomed to open with a long preamble, wordy and clever, playing on fears and emotions and unproven accusations to hide any weakness in his case.[44] We know that a copy of Francis Jones's information was handed over at this meeting and it is probable that either Pierrepont or Marten read it out while the other followed with a speech adding the substance of what Jones had said in his oral evidence, implicating Dering, Twysden and Spencer. A copy of the petition itself does not appear to have been produced and naturally the written and oral accounts without the petition would be calculated to alarm. Glyn, the lawyer, had already reported to the Commons the questions prepared for Malet and it was probably he who now put them to their lordships. Since Malet was an assistant to the Lords, it was improper for the Commons to ask questions of him direct. It was equally improper at such a meeting for the Lords to enter into any discussion. The meeting ended with a request that the Lords would join the Commons in sending for Dering, Twysden, Strode and Spencer as delinquents and that the Lords would appoint a select committee to join a select committee of the Commons 'to examine this business to the bottom'. In this the Commons messengers exceeded their instructions, because the House itself had not included Strode in their order about a message to the Lords.[45]

The Lords withdrew and the Lord Keeper resumed his seat on the upper woolsack. Then he formally reported the result of the conference and had the information of Francis Jones read to the House. The House ordered Dering, Twysden and Spencer to be sent for as delinquents. There was enough evidence about these three to establish at least a *prima facie* case that they had been promoters of the petition. But the Commons had also asked for the arrest of Strode and so hurriedly had their evidence been put together that there was apparently none to incriminate him. There is no record of any evidence about Strode having been received by the Commons as a body—whatever was reported to individual members behind the scenes. In the Lords there was a difference of opinion between those who had private information about Strode and those who did not feel justified in sending for him because they had no formal evidence. In that assembly there was only one man who had been an eyewitness of the events in question, only one man who could give first hand evidence about the guilt or innocence of Strode—and that was Malet. They examined him upon oath and under questioning he had to admit that on the previous Friday night Strode had come to him at Maidstone, mentioned the petition and expressed a wish that the Earl of Bristol might see it. Malet said that Strode then asked him if he wanted to see it, and he said 'Not during the assizes.' Strode replied that he would send it to him the next morning, when the assizes were ended. Mr. Pope, an attorney, had brought it to him from Strode as he was taking horse on the Saturday and he had not read it until he came to his own house.[46]

Malet knew that he was facing a mainly hostile House. He knew that petitioning was no crime in statute or common law, but he was well aware that it could be made to appear so in the present temper of the two Houses. He clearly hoped to show that he had played no active part in framing the petition during the assizes. He was on oath in an age when oaths mattered. He had to admit having seen the petition after the assizes were over. He must have realized that in explaining how he got a copy he was implicating Strode as an active promoter and, therefore, a potential delinquent. He could not have understood that in mentioning the Earl of Bristol he was implicating him as well. Until that moment no one could have guessed that it might be made a crime even to see a temperately worded petition and not report it to Parliament.

After listening to Malet's evidence, the Lords sent for Strode as a delinquent and appointed twelve peers to sit on the joint committee with the Commons and report the result to the House. The names of these peers are jotted down in the original manuscript draft journal of the House in the order in which they offered themselves and were accepted for that service; the names were rearranged in order of precedence before they were printed in the *Journals*. They are given below as they appear in the draft.

2. L. Cham [Earl of Essex, Lord Chamberlain]
3. Pemb [Earl of Pembroke]
4. Ley [Earl of Leicester]
1. Admiral [Earl of Northumberland, Lord Admiral]
5. War [Earl of Warwick]
6. Holland [Earl of Holland]
7. Say [Viscount Saye and Sele]

4. Robartes [Lord Robartes]
2. Mand [Lord Montagu of Kimbolton, better known as Lord Mandeville]
3. Brooke [Lord Brooke of Beauchamp Court]
5. Capell [Lord Capell of Hadham]
1. St. John [Lord St. John of Bletso][47]

On that day roughly a quarter of the peers in the House were moderate constitutionalists, if not yet Royalists; eight of them later felt so strongly about the issue that they claimed their right to have their dissent to Bristol's imprisonment entered in the *Journals*. And yet out of the twelve peers nominated to the committee only one represented the moderate viewpoint and that was Capell, created baron in the week in which Malet had been appointed a justice of the King's Bench, and in that company something of an outsider, too unfamiliar with the ways of the House to be really effective. After Pym made his famous speech on grievances at the beginning of the Long Parliament, Capell had been the first man to stand up and present a petition in the name of the freeholders of his county. At that time he had sided with the Country alliance to get abuses removed; now he was opposed to what it was doing. Perhaps he was elected to the committee because of his past friendship or because the majority felt themselves strong enough to allow one moderate constitutionalist to attend their counsels.[48]

But Malet need expect no help from the rest. Collectively they were a powerful and united body, bound by strong ties of friendship and kinship, of commercial and political interest, and of subversive conspiracy. If there was one worried, weak man among them, he was there for a purpose; the Earl of Leicester was lord lieutenant of Kent, unwillingly charged with granting commissions under the Militia Ordinance. The other ten members were solidly against the King. The first to secure his election to the committee was the Earl of Essex, the emerging general of the Parliamentary forces. He was supported by his kinsmen, the Earls of Warwick and Holland, who were brothers. Lords Mandeville and Robartes were sons-in-law of the Earl of Warwick. Warwick, Holland, Saye and Sele, Brooke and Robartes were all Puritans accustomed to meet regularly with Pym and Oliver St. John in Warwick's house or Brooke's, ostensibly to transact the business of the Providence Island Company. Mandeville, who had become the leader of the Country opposition in the Lords, often entertained its strongest supporters from both Houses in his home. Pym had moved his lodgings from Westminster to Chelsea, so as to be near him. The Earl of Northumberland, proud and remote, was linked through one sister to the Earl of Leicester, whom she had married, and through another, the attractive and disloyal Countess of Carlisle, to both the Earl of Holland and Pym with whom she had very close friendships. The Earl of Pembroke was a friend of Lord Saye and Sele who had persuaded him to throw in his lot with the Country. Pembroke had been a member of the council of the Virginia Company. And lastly there was Lord St. John who had been summoned by writ to the Lords on a promise to support the King and who had actively supported the Country opposition ever since. With the sole exception of Capell, every man on the committee had for some months been a consistent supporter of the Country in the House and most of them had been active in its counsels behind the scenes.[49]

The Lords then sent a message to the Commons by Serjeant Ayloff and Serjeant Finch (apart from Malet they had no judges to send) to say that they had ordered the arrest of Dering, Twysden, Spencer and Strode and that they had appointed a committee of twelve Lords (of whom five were to be a quorum) to meet with a committee of the House of Commons and examine the business further. The sitting had lasted longer than was usual and they adjourned until 4.00 p.m.[50]

Meanwhile, in the Commons it had been formally resolved that Dering, Twysden, Spencer and Strode should be sent for as delinquents by the serjeant-at-arms. The news of Malet's evidence to the Lords seems to have passed to the opposition leaders in the Commons during the morning. They therefore ordered the attendance of Pope, the attorney, who gave Malet a copy of the petition, the clerk of the assize and the under-sheriff for Kent. These would help them get at the truth of the matter.[51]

There was some lack of 'correspondency' (as they would have described it) between the two Houses about the arrest of the four principal actors—Dering, Twysden, Spencer and Strode. Having asked the Lords to join with them in sending for these four, the Commons, without waiting for an answer, themselves ordered the arrest. They were clearly determined on this, whether the Lords joined with them or not. An order from the Commons and a warrant from the Lords were issued independently on the same day and served independently on the people concerned. We know that Twysden was arrested by order of the Commons on the following day, but it was not until the day after that he was served with the warrant from the Lords. Neither the warrant nor the order showed any cause for the arrest. Both Houses were thus outraging the principles of English justice that Coke had been at pains to demonstrate in his Institutes. Twysden was not slow to notice the fact.[52]

The Commons proceeded with other business until Serjeant Ayloff and Serjeant Finch came as messengers to give the reply of the Lords following the conference of both Houses on the Kentish petition. The Upper House, having appointed their committee of twelve peers, asked the Commons to appoint 'a proportionable committee'; that meant a committee of twenty-four. While the messengers waited outside the chamber for a reply, the Commons quickly nominated a committee of their own and sent the messengers back to the Lords to say they had done it.[53]

It is important to understand how members were appointed to select committees of the Commons at this time. It was an accepted convention that members who were against a proposed policy should not be named to a committee set up to formulate it. That meant, in effect, that those who were not opposed to the Kentish petition were automatically debarred from the committee set up to send for 'delinquents' and 'examine the business to the bottom'. Pym's closest supporters had the advantage, too, that they were organized, whereas those who opposed them were not. At the beginning of the Long Parliament it was ordered that 'everyone who names one for a committee to stand up and name the party'. Members could not name themselves and they could only name others if there was prior consultation and agreement, or at least an understanding. Pym and his friends had taken the initiative away from the privy councillors and occupied key places where they could catch the Speaker's eye and the attention of the Clerk whose duty it was to record the names of committee members. By careful planning and concerted action they could secure nominations of members who would support their policies.[54]

The Commons committee, like that from the Lords, was unrepresentative of the voting strength in the House. It included twenty-four members in all and everyone was an active member of the Country opposition. With the exception of Sir Edward Boys who represented Dover, there was not a single member representing a Kent constituency. The aim of the committee was to frame policy which had wide application not only to Kent but to the other counties as well; to make a salutary example of the authors rather than to persuade them to different views; and, above all, to prevent the distemper from spreading. Most significant was the inclusion on the committee of five members with views more radical than those of Pym's own middle group: Sir Arthur Hesilrige, Sir Henry Vane the younger, Sir Henry Mildmay, Sir Henry Heyman and Sir Peter Wentworth. At this time there were only seven men with such radical views among the most active committee men in the Commons; yet five of those seven managed to find places on this committee of twenty-four. On the other political wing were Sir Hugh Cholmley, an Anglican, and Sir John Holland, a moderate, both of whom would probably have favoured an accommodation with the King at that time. The great majority came from the middle group and included Pym himself. Seventeen out of twenty-four were Independent or Presbyterian Puritans; they would deal firmly with the Anglican pretensions of the Kent petitioners. The full committee, as it appears in the *Journals of the House of Commons*, consisted of:

Mr. Pym	[John Pym—Tavistock Borough]
Sir Arth Haselrig	[Sir Arthur Hesilrige—Leicestershire]
Sir Ro Coke	[Sir Robert Cooke—Tewkesbury Borough]
Mr. Whitacre	[Lawrence Whitaker—Okehampton Borough or William Whitaker—Shaftesbury Borough]
Sir Tho Dacres	[Sir Thomas Dacres—Hertfordshire]
Serjeant Wilde	[Serjeant John Wilde—Worcestershire]
Sir Sam Rolle	[Sir Samuel Rolle—Devon]
Mr. Reynolds	[Robert Reynolds—Hindon Borough]
Mr. Jo Moore	[John Moore—Liverpool Borough]
Sir Jo Corbett	[Sir John Corbett, Bt.—Shropshire]
Sir H. Mildmay	[Sir Henry Mildmay—Maldon Borough]
Sir Ro Harley	[Sir Robert Harley, KB—Herefordshire]
Mr. Trenchard	[John Trenchard—Wareham Borough]
Sir Edw Boyse	[Sir Edward Boys—Dover]
Sir Peter Heyman	[Sir Henry Heyman, Bt.—Hythe; Sir Peter died in the previous year]
Sir H. Vane Junior	[Sir Henry Vane, Junior—Kingston-upon-Hull Borough]
Sir Wm Massam	[Sir William Masham, Bt.—Essex]
Mr. Peard	[George Peard—Barnstaple Borough]
Sir Hugh Cholmeley	[Sir Hugh Cholmley, Bt.—Scarborough Borough]
Mr. Cage	[William Cage—Ipswich Borough]
Sir Peter Wentworth	[Sir Peter Wentworth KB—Tamworth Borough]
Sir Jo Holland	[Sir John Holland, Bt.—Castle Rising Borough]
Mr. Ro Goodwyn	[Robert Goodwin—East Grinstead Borough]
Mr. Rowse	[Francis Rous—Truro Borough][55]

By the time that Serjeant Ayloff and Serjeant Finch had returned, the Lords had adjourned. It was not until the clock had struck four, and prayers had been said, that they were able to report that the Commons had appointed their own committee to meet that from the Lords. After Malet's evidence in the morning session it was inevitable that Bristol should be asked what he knew of the Kentish petition. He produced a copy and it was read out to the House in full. Until this moment the Lords had been unaware of its contents in detail. They asked Bristol if he had taken a copy of the petition and he replied that Malet had shown it to him and that he had got his servant to make a copy of it. The House pronounced it a 'seditious and dangerous petition and of very ill consequence'. Because Bristol had read the petition and had not told the House of it, he was commanded to withdraw while they considered what to do. Malet was also commanded to withdraw because he had delivered a copy of the petition to Bristol. So Bristol and Malet left the chamber together and the House debated the issue.[56]

Eventually, Malet was called back to the Lords and questioned about his part in the affair. It is probable that he spoke from his place standing by the woolsack. If he had been invited to kneel as a delinquent at the bar of the House, that would not have passed unremarked in the *Journals*. He said that when Sir Edward Dering put forward the petition, he told him that this business was outside his commission. He had delivered a copy of the petition to the Earl of Bristol at three o'clock on Sunday afternoon. Sir Humphrey Tufton, the member for Maidstone Borough, Richard Lee, the member for Rochester, and Augustine Skinner, one of the knights of the shire, were all there at Maidstone when the petition was being considered. The name of Bristol's servant who wrote out the petition was Theophilus Brown; he was out of town but would be back that night. When Malet was done, some peer suggested that he had committed a great offence, contrary to his duty as a judge of assize and an assistant to their lordships' House, in not revealing the petition to the House until he was forced to do so. The motion was supported and opposed and Malet was ordered to withdraw while a debate took place. The discussion was prolonged by eight peers who supported Bristol and Malet against the twenty or so who were united in the popular interest. Then the question was put whether there were not some parts in the petition scandalous, dangerous and tending to sedition. And it was resolved that there were. It was now proposed that the Earl of Bristol for concealing the petition should, for the present, be committed to the Tower until the business could be further examined. Before the question was put, eight Lords claimed the right to enter their dissents to the question and their request was formally (and, no doubt, reluctantly) granted by the majority. They were:

The Earl of Bath	Lord Mowbray
The Earl of Monmouth	Lord Grey de Ruthyn
The Earl of Dover	Lord Howard of Charlton
The Earl of Portland	Lord Capell.[57]

So the Lord Keeper put the question from his seat on the upper woolsack. The outcome was certain but there must have been some dramatic tension as each peer rose uncovered in his place and said 'content' or 'not content' according to his conviction. It was the custom to begin with the most newly created baron on the bench at the back of the chamber and for the peers to vote in reverse order of precedence, ending with the great officers of state, sitting at the top of the earls' bench immediately on the left of the Lord Keeper. The Earl of Northumberland, as Lord High Admiral of England, was the last and most senior to give his vote, but by then he could not affect the outcome. The Earl of Bristol was to be committed to the Tower. Then it was put to the question that Justice Malet be committed to the Tower until the business could be further examined. This time none of the peers claimed their right to enter a protest in writing. The motion was carried.[58]

6

Retribution

'The object of all this is to frighten them and prevent the paper being presented and by an example of severe repression to prevent others in the future from entertaining any idea of opposing the principles of the present government.'

GIOVANNI GIUSTINIAN,
Venetian Ambassador in England, 11 April 1642.[1]

For the rest of that week—indeed, for the whole of April—the persistent inquisition into the happenings at Maidstone continued. In the Commons Pym, unusually, arranged for the whole House to hear the evidence of witnesses. The powerful joint committee of the two Houses could interrogate them later; meanwhile the whole affair must be given wide publicity and exceptional handling in order to emphasize its gravity.[2]

On Tuesday 29 March the Commons listened to Blount, the informer, while he told them the story of the petition. 'Some of the Heads were so high,' he said, 'that I wish I might not reveal them myself.'—but he did so at length and for the first time a complete copy of the petition was read to the House. When he withdrew, Augustine Skinner and Sir Edward Partridge, the baron for Sandwich, were both questioned about what they knew. Neither had volunteered to speak on the previous day and they clearly did not then consider it as seriously as Pym and his supporters. When they had done, Blount was called in once more. The Speaker thanked him on behalf of the House and asked him to wait so that a committee of both Houses could question him.[3]

Upon the evidence of these three, the House sent for a number of ministers as delinquents, for preaching in favour of the petition. They included Dr. Richard Shelden, Mr. Higgins, Mr. Copley and Mr. Crumpe. They sent for Dr. Piers, the doctor of civil law who happened to be staying in Maidstone and who proposed the clause about doctors of the civil law. And finally they sent for eight people who were the balance of the nine on the grand jury who opposed the petition. They were

Richard Amherst, Thomas Broadnax, Bonham Fance, Richard Hardres, Henry Oxinden, Stephen Lennard, Thomas Cattlett and Thomas Roper.[4]

Neither House sat on the Wednesday for it was the last Wednesday in the month and kept as a fast day by both Houses, the Lords in Westminster Abbey and the Commons in St. Margaret's, Westminster.[5]

On the Thursday the Lords sent to the Commons a copy of the Kentish petition which the Earl of Bristol had delivered.[6] One other event of importance to this story happened on that day. The Earl of Leicester, the lord lieutenant of Kent appointed by Parliament, had been slow to grant commissions to his deputies under the Militia Ordinance. In the meantime, the King had sent a warrant to the sheriff of Kent declaring that the Militia Ordinance was against the law. The Commons ordered their members of the joint committee for the Kentish petition to consider this and prepare an order that would extend to the whole kingdom 'for that and all businesses of the like nature'.[7]

On Friday 1 April the Commons serjeant was asked what had happened to the warrants he had been ordered to serve on Dering, Strode, Spencer and Twysden. He reported that three of them were at the door. Only Dering was absent and he had promised to come with his man on the following day. Spencer was the first to be called to the bar of the House and made to kneel as a delinquent while the petition was read over to him by the Clerk. The Speaker asked him what he knew of it and allowed him to stand while he gave his reply. Spencer made excuses. The petition read to him was not the same as the one he had agreed, which was only an embryo and had never been delivered to the House. As soon as he had found it distasteful to the House he had tried to stop it. The Speaker commanded him to withdraw and to wait upon the joint committee of both Houses. Meanwhile, he was returned to the custody of the serjeant.[8]

Spencer was followed in succession by Strode, by Twysden and by Dr. Piers. As each entered the Commons chamber he knelt at the bar as a delinquent and then stood up to give his reply. Strode was made of sterner stuff than the others. He admitted his part without excuse. He denied, however, that he handed a copy of the petition to the judge before the assizes. Since he was so frank about the rest, he was probably speaking the truth. Twysden, too, pleaded ignorance of any plot or design for a petition before the assizes began.

'It was table discourse the first time I heard of it. The judge said, it was very necessary to have a good grand jury. It seems he knew the matter better than I did; but he never named, in my hearing, what the great business was, wherefore he desired a good grand jury: And in Kent, there is ever as mean a grand jury returned, as in any county whatsoever.'[9]

Dr. Piers was then heard. He explained that he was there solely by chance and that his authorship was confined to the claim for civil lawyers which Spencer undertook to have inserted. Apart from this he took no part in the petition. Strode, Twysden and Piers were left in the serjeant's custody, but Piers was discharged on 2 April.[10] Both Houses were busy with an answer of the King to one of their messages; they agreed to put all other business aside, except that of the Kent and Irish committees, until they had considered it.[11]

Since its creation on the Monday, the joint committee for the Kentish petition had been meeting to examine witnesses. At first it concentrated on the four prisoners, Twysden, Dering, Strode and Spencer. The committee put thirty questions to each of them, and then, finding that their answers agreed and that no unlawful act was disclosed, demanded the answers to nine further questions on oath. While making clear to each prisoner that he need say nothing to incriminate himself, the committee clearly hoped that each would incriminate the others. Again, it failed in its aim.[12]

Meanwhile the committee had begun to assume new and unusual powers. It had already begun to examine witnesses upon oath.[13] It got the authority of the Houses to meet when and where they pleased,[14] to call what witnesses they thought fit and to send for papers and records.[15] It secured orders from Lords and Commons that it could make as many subcommittees as it wanted, that witnesses should wait upon it and not depart without authority[16] and that it should have power to bail witnesses and dismiss them when they saw reason.[17] In the Commons Sir Henry Vane the younger tried to get the committee given power to inquire into similar petitions in any county in England. Sir Simonds D'Ewes opposed this proposal on the ground that any general order would remove the ancient liberty of the subject to petition.[18] On 5 May Pym reported that a petition similar to the Kentish one was hatching in Somerset where two members of Parliament, Sir Ralph Hopton and Thomas Smith, said that they had a commission from the King to oppose the Militia Ordinance if it were put into execution there. The Commons sent for Hopton and Smith to serve in their House.[19]

Although the joint committee for the Kentish petition had secured the fullest powers to conduct its own affairs, the Commons continued to take the initiative. On 29 March they sent directly for a total of thirteen witnesses and 'delinquents'.[20] On 4 April they asked the Lords that the committee might spend a whole afternoon examining witnesses 'in regard the business is long and requires haste.'[21] On the following day the Commons ordered the committee to meet at 2.00 p.m. and especially the lawyers; they ordered four lawyers including Serjeant Wilde, a member for Worcestershire, and George Peard, who represented Barnstaple, to propose questions for Sir Edward Dering.[22] On 6, 9 and 14 April the House of Commons ordered its committee to meet in the afternoon. Of course it only had power to order its own members of the joint committee to sit and occasionally, as on 14 April, it sent a message to the Lords asking them to make a similar order. On 14 April the House ordered a further eleven witnesses to attend. These included one of the Seyliards who were later members of the Parliamentary county committee which was formed on the outbreak of the Civil War.[23]

George Peard, a one-time friend of Sir Edward Dering, made a series of attacks on the petition and its supporters, proclaiming that there were things in the petition not far from treason.[24] On Tuesday 5 April he reported that Sir John Mayney, Sir Henry Palmer the younger and Anthony Hamond were still labouring to get hands for the Kentish petition and he moved that they be summoned to the Commons. The House ordered them to attend and to bring with them the petitions for which they had been soliciting hands.[25] On the following day Peard delivered a written information against Sir George Strode which alleged that he had spoken 'verie dangerous words against the proceedings of Parliament'. According to this story, Strode had said that there was only one wise man in the House of Commons (meaning Sir Edward Dering) and they had put him out, that Parliament was about to impeach the Earl of Bristol, his son Lord Digby and Lord Cottington, because it would not allow one wise man to advise the King, and that he was ashamed that the bishops should have to appear before a company of boys. As soon as Augustine Skinner came into the House, Peard stood up once more and asked that Skinner might be heard as he had something important to say. Skinner then reported that the Kentish petition was still being strongly supported in Kent and that daily more hands were being obtained for it. He said it was reported in Kent that they would now come up to Parliament with it themselves 'and if they perisht, they perisht'. Sir John Colepeper, the Chancellor of the Exchequer, the other knight of the shire for Kent, must have been taxed with what he knew of the business for he said that he was indeed informed that the work of collecting signatures for the petition was still going ahead, 'which hee was very sorrie for and therefore wished that this Howse would make an order or a vote against it which he hoped would stopp the further proceedings of it.'[26] Colepeper was at that time one of the King's closest supporters and advisers. Like Simon Peter before him, he was not yet ready to speak up for his convictions—certainly not in that hostile assembly. Other speakers followed him and in the end the whole report was referred to the committee for the Kentish petition with new and enlarged power and authority.[27]

On 5 April the Lords, too, heard that Strode had spoken 'scandalous speeches' against both Houses of Parliament and the name of the informant was given as Sir Thomas Walsingham, the Commons member for Rochester. The Lords promptly authorized the Lords committee for the Kentish petition to examine Strode and any other witnesses they thought fit.[28] That business dragged on. During the next week the Lords ordered the attendance of sixteen witnesses against Strode. They included Sir Michael Livesey and Sir John Sedley.[29] Sedley had been a member of the informal committee which planned the Kentish petition on the day before the assizes opened at Maidstone. Now he was to give evidence against Strode and he must have done it to some purpose, for on 14 April he was approved by the Lords as deputy lieutenant for Kent.[30]

On Wednesday 6 April it was reported to the Commons that Dering had disappeared. The Commons sent a messenger to the Lords to tell them of his escape and to ask them to stop the ports and issue a proclamation to call him in. The request to stop the ports was an unusual one and it is probable that the Commons already knew that Dering had written a letter saying that he was leaving for Kent 'and wished himself beyond the salt water'. Details of this letter were not officially reported to the Lords by the Earl of Essex until much later in the day, but once Essex knew of them his first concern would have been to inform the leaders of the Country opposition in both Houses. The Lords at once ordered the Lord High Admiral to search and inquire at all ports. They ordered all mayors, justices of the peace, sheriffs, constables and other officers of the King to search, inquire and bring Dering back and they sent a message to the Commons to say what they had done.[31]

The next day in the Commons there was a report that the Kentish petition had been printed and this was referred to the committee for printing. The committee was ordered to hear evidence that afternoon and to report on the following morning. It was also instructed to submit on the following day the draft of an order to prohibit printing of this kind.[32] The committee completed its investigation quickly and John White of Middle Temple, the member for Southwark, was able to report that afternoon that Thomas Fawcett was the printer and that he would neither attend the committee when they sent for him, nor cease his work of printing. The House at once sent for Fawcett as a delinquent, and ordered the Master and wardens of the Stationers' Company to suppress Fawcett's press. They ordered the seizure of the Kentish petitions wherever they were found and their burning by the hands of the common hangman on the following Saturday in New Palace Yard, Westminster, at Smithfield and Cheapside, between the hours of ten and twelve. Fawcett was brought to the bar of the House, kneeling as a delinquent. When he was allowed to stand he confessed that the petition had been printed at his press, that he had no order to print it and that it had been brought to him by his servant, John Thomas.[33]

After he had spoken, Fawcett was ordered to withdraw while the Commons debated what to do with him. The House had actually voted that he be censured and the Speaker had stood to put the question whether he should be imprisoned, when Sir Gilbert Gerard, the member for Middlesex, rose and very reasonably pointed out that Fawcett had committed no offence against the House or any individual member; the House could not, therefore, give judgement. His support for the rule of law was partially successful. The House delivered no formal judgement. It simply laid the matter aside and continued to keep Fawcett in the serjeant's custody, until he became an embarrassment and was quietly released. Gerard's intervention is remarkable, for he was a close friend and supporter of Pym, a colleague in the Providence Island venture and a substantial contributor to Parliamentary funds. He was clearly concerned that the Commons were assuming powers to which they had no legal right.[34]

The measures to suppress the petition kindled a deep resentment that smouldered beneath the surface, not least in Kent;[35] while in London John Thomas continued to stoke the flames with further 'scandalous pamphlets' —by the end of April the House of Commons was once more sending for him as a delinquent.[36] Occasionally the Lords, too, took the initiative. On more than one occasion they ordered the committee for the Kentish petition to meet.[37] On Monday 11 April they ordered the clerk of assize for Kent to make written copies of any indictments and other records that the House wanted.[38] On Friday 15 April they heard that Captain Stanley, mayor of Maidstone, and Thomas Skelton, his serjeant, were still trying to get hands for the Kentish petition after it had been questioned in the Lords. They ordered the arrest of the two men and their appearance before the House to answer the complaint. On 22 April Stanley petitioned the House, complaining that he had attended for a whole week, and that he still had not learnt what he was accused of; he prayed to be discharged or bailed. His petition was referred to the committee for the Kentish petition. He was considered small fry, for when he was discharged on 3 May his bail was fixed at two hundred pounds.[39]

On 19 April the Lords asked for a conference with the Commons about a declaration to be set forth in these words:

> 'That whosoever shall go about to procure any counter petition against the militia, shall be accounted as a disturber of the peace of this kingdom; and that whosoever shall inform either House of Parliament of any such person or persons shall be accounted to have done good and acceptable service for the Parliament.'

The declaration was essentially simple, but it got bogged down in the slough of parliamentary procedure. On the following day eight peers were appointed to draw up the heads of a conference about it with the Commons. The Earl of Northumberland, as senior peer, was chairman and the committee was nicely chosen to support Pym's policies. It consisted of Lord Mandeville, who would provide the leadership and drive in committee that he was giving to the House as a whole, and Pembroke, Bedford, Salisbury, Holland, Paget and Howard of Escrick—all of whom might be counted on to lend their support. Salisbury and Paget were feeling some internal doubt about the worth of the men they were supporting, but this had not so far been apparent from their voting in the Lords over the last four months. There was not a single Royalist on the committee[40] though that is not altogether surprising. Four days previously the House had been called and it had became apparent that a number of moderate peers who were present at the end of March had drifted away to their country seats or to join the King. They included Lords Mowbray and Howard of Charlton, who had entered their dissent against

Bristol's imprisonment in the Tower, and Hertford, Huntingdon and Strange, who had avoided committing themselves deeply on either side, but who eventually sided with the King.[41] A tiny band of moderates remained in the Lords protesting against the more extreme measures of the Country lords, who were gradually forcing both them and a number of moderate Country supporters into the Royalist camp. These moderates were not represented on the committee for the declaration because the Lords also observed the Commons convention that people who opposed a policy could not be named to a committee to formulate it.[42]

On Thursday 21 April the Earl of Holland reported to the Lords the clause which the committee had drafted as the basis for a declaration to be made by both Houses. The committee believed that a simple declaration was not enough; it was necessary to show the need for its urgent adoption by alleging a deep-laid plot with ramifications throughout the country. The clauses were approved and messengers were dispatched to ask for a conference with the Commons in the Painted Chamber. This was readily accorded and it was the busy lawyer Peard who reported the conference to the Commons. His task was simplified because the Lord Keeper had given him the proposed clauses in writing. A number of members spoke in the debate and once more some of them reported that in Kent men were still getting hands for the proscribed petition. After some consideration, the Commons agreed in principle to the proposed declaration and asked that a committee of both Houses approve it in detail. It was referred by both Houses to the joint committee for the Kentish petition. It got shuffled backwards and forwards between the committee and the Commons. Finally, it was lost altogether.[43] The most effective way to prevent petitioning against the Militia Ordinance was not to issue threats but to make an example of those who had done it already.

Nevertheless, on 30 April the Commons did appoint another committee to prepare another declaration setting down the reasons for their actions towards the Kentish petition and petitioners. The committee contained seven of the members of the committee for the Kentish petition, Sir Robert Cooke, Sir John Holland, Sir Samuel Rolle, Robert Reynolds, William Cage and two of the strongest lawyers in the Parliamentarian interest, Serjeant Wilde and George Peard, who were the barristers principally engaged in preparing criminal charges against the petition's authors. Any Royalists who still remained in the Commons were once more excluded from the committee because they did not approve its purpose. However, the remaining seven members were very unrepresentative of the political groups within the Country alliance. Only one member, Edward Wingate, belonged to Pym's middle group. Three of the remainder, Henry Marten, William Strode and Henry Ludlow, were members of the extremist war group, while the remaining three were moderates, anxious for reconciliation: Harbottle Grimstone, John Potts and Sir Thomas Bowyer. Within a few weeks Bowyer was to defect to the King. It is difficult to discern a pattern in the selection of this committee, apart from a heavy weighting in favour of extremists.[44] Events were moving fast and it would be more salutary to impeach the authors of the Kentish petition than to explain why the two Houses had reacted so vigorously against it. The 'Paper War' was increasing in intensity. There were other declarations—about the Militia Ordinance itself, against the King's raising forces and a 'Declaration at large' that was finally published on 19 May. The two Houses were struggling to build up forces for the coming trial of strength and experienced members were needed for more important committees. This one never reported back to the Commons and it, too, faded away.[45]

Twysden had been lying with others in the serjeant's custody in confined quarters in a house in Covent Garden. During this time he was in touch with Peard who so far relented as to tell him that the House of Commons could distinguish between faults and saw very little against him. Presently, emboldened by this confidence, Twysden petitioned the House of Commons for his release on the grounds that he had answered their questions to the best of his ability and that his health was suffering. On Saturday 9 April the House of Commons ordered that Twysden and Spencer, who were still in the serjeant's custody, should be bailed upon the security of £10,000 to be found by them and £5,000 apiece to be found by their sureties, of whom each was to have two. At first Twysden was so staggered by the size of the sum fixed for bail that he almost refused to accept it. He was eventually persuaded to agree on the ground that it was only form, not good in law. Good in law or not, Parliament was in a position to exact these sums if he and Spencer defaulted. Strode remained in custody, following the new evidence produced against him by Peard.[46]

Although repeated interrogation had not revealed a case against Dering, Strode, Twysden and Spencer, Dering's flight provided an opportunity for the Commons to impeach and convict him in his absence and on Monday 18 April they ordered Serjeant Wilde and Sir Robert Cooke, both members of the committee for the Kentish petition, to prepare an impeachment and to bring it in on the following morning.[47] The next day, upon the motion of another member of their committee, Serjeant Wilde reported on the articles which he had drawn up with Sir Robert Cooke. The Clerk read them through twice. They were voted one by one and ordered to be engrossed.[48] Two days later the engrossed articles were read through again and ordered to be sent to the Lords at a conference. The lawyers, Serjeant Wilde and George Peard, were appointed managers. On the Friday of that week the Commons presented their impeachment to the Lords in the Painted Chamber.[49] It was a formidable conference. The articles of impeachment and the accompanying speech by Serjeant Wilde are spread over five columns of the *Journals of the House of Lords* (though the original document is lost). The title of the articles against Dering alleged 'high crimes and misdemeanours by him committed' and went on to specify them under four verbose and legal-sounding heads. The first alleged conspiracy to obstruct the Militia Ordinance. This article was based on the entirely false premise that the petition was unlawful, not the Militia Ordinance.[50]

The articles went on to list some of the 'dangerous and seditious' clauses in the petition, but in almost every case they misrepresented what the petition contained. They alleged, for instance, that there was a clause demanding that the House of Commons should say why they expelled Sir Edward Dering.[51] The petition contained no such clause; indeed Blount had already stated in evidence that this clause 'was upon debate omitted'. It is inconceivable that Wilde and Peard, the draughtsmen of Dering's impeachment, did not have a copy of the petition in front of them when they drew up the document. They were well aware that all the copies which could be found had been burned by the common hangman. They must have counted on this when they made their allegation.[52] The articles which reported the clause asking that people should not be bound by orders of either House deliberately missed the point. The petitioners did not object to orders, only those which were *ultra vires*. The articles alleged that the petition asked that people should not be bound by any ordinance of the Houses about the militia, unless the King agreed to it. In fact the petition had not asked this at all. It posed the difficulty of the subject faced with conflicting orders of the King and his two Houses and it asked for a law to resolve the conflict. The rest of the articles rambled on making lawful activities sound like felonies . . . offering himself for the grand jury when the sheriff had already returned one . . . persuading the grand jury that they were bound to secrecy by their oath . . . and so on. They included the acts of framing the petition, presenting it to the bench, publishing it and soliciting signatures for it. Throughout the document the wording was heavily interlarded with the adverbs 'unlawfully, wickedly and seditiously', although there was nothing either unlawful or seditious in what Dering had done. Finally the articles alleged that all these actions were great and high breaches of the privilege of Parliament, tending to sedition, and more in the same vein.[53]

When the articles had been read, Serjeant Wilde addressed to the Lord Keeper a long speech full of venom, demanding exemplary justice against the prisoners:

'A new brood of serpents which are continually hissing, maligning and practising against the pious and noble endeavours of both Houses . . .'

'This gentleman, the ringleader (a late member of the House of Commons, the great grand jury of the whole kingdom . . .) is contented now to descend so low as to become one of a common jury of the county; such is the meanness and pusillanimity of his thoughts . . .'

'Their duty was to have enquired diligently of the matters given them in charge; . . . and yet they . . . insist upon this . . . as the main and principal business.'

'He obtrudes upon them divers monstrous and seditious heads [clauses] and, by sinister suggestions, labours, and solicitations, which ought not to be used to a jury, and by a kind of violence offered to them, seeks to enforce them to a consent . . .'

'. . . instead of enquiring upon the statute of witchcraft and conjuration, he useth his conjurations and inchantments upon them . . .'

'. . . and sticks not to affirm, that he can have forty thousand persons to attend the petition, proclaims a meeting at Blackheath (a fatal and ominous place for actions of this nature); and all this under colour of a petition . . .'

'. . . a desperate design, to put not only Kent, but, for aught is known, all Christendom too into combustion carrying the sails full swoln with spight, arrogancy and sedition . . .'

'. . . might have spread the flame and contagion over all England, had not the great wisdom and justice of both Houses in due time prevented it.'

After this long oration the Lords returned to their own House where there were more urgent matters to discuss. It was not until the Tuesday of the following week that the Lord Keeper reported the conference and the House directed an order to the sheriff of Kent that Sir Edward Dering should appear before them on the following Monday or the House would proceed against him by default.[54]

The Commons had also to deal with the other principal actors. On Wednesday 20 April they sat three hours longer in the afternoon than they had intended in the morning. The Speaker had put the last question of the day. It was just after five in the evening and members were preparing to make their way home, when William Strode, the member for Bere Alston in Devon (and one of the five whom Charles had tried to arrest), rose with a petition in his hand from Sir George Strode. This asked that Sir George might, like Twysden, be bailed and that his petition might be referred to the joint committee for the Kentish petition. The timing was unfortunate. It was late and the House was unsympathetic. Perhaps William Strode was only concerned to discharge a distasteful duty for a kinsman who held different views. He was quickly opposed. George Peard of the joint committee leapt to his feet and alleged that the 'crimes and offences proved against Sir George Strode were much more foul than those proved against Sir Roger Twysden.' He asked the House to withhold bail. Peard was a lawyer and knew the meaning of the words. He knew that Sir George Strode had not yet been tried. When he said 'proved' he meant that his committee considered him too dangerous to go unpunished, whatever his rights under the law. Peard's action put William Strode in a quandary. If he rose to withdraw his support for his kinsman's petition, he would be infringing the rule of the House that no member might speak twice on the same subject without the consent of the House.

If he sat still he would appear to be condoning something of which neither he nor his colleagues approved. He rose and started to speak. He was at once interrupted by Sir Simonds D'Ewes who reminded the House of the rule and offered to do him the service of asking leave of the House to hear him. So William excused himself and said that he would never have handed in the petition if he had known Sir George's crimes to be so great. The petition was laid aside and Sir George Strode remained in custody.[55] On Tuesday 26 April the Commons ordered his impeachment to be brought in on the following Thursday.[56] On Saturday 30 April Peard reported progress not only on this, but on all the actions of the committee for the Kentish petition. He gave an account of the main events connected with the petition and felt it worth remarking that when Strode asked Malet to show a copy 'to the earle' he meant the Earl of Bristol. The implication was clear: there was, in Peard's view, a conspiracy.[57]

When Peard had done, he introduced the articles of impeachment against Strode[58] but it took time and a lot of discussion to get these articles and those against Spencer agreed by the House. The clerks, too, were heavily overworked.[59] Only on Tuesday 10 May were the engrossed articles finally read, agreed and ordered to be sent to the Lords on the morrow. They accorded a meeting almost at once. The conference concerned other matters, but at it the articles against Strode and Spencer were formally handed over to the Lord Keeper. Although the Commons had appointed five managers, Peard did what speaking there was. In one colourful sentence he alleged that Strode and Spencer were 'like Symeon and Levi, brothers in iniquity'. But no great polemic accompanied these impeachments as with that of Dering. The high-sounding phrases which accompanied the earlier impeachment had overlaid the thinness of the case for the prosecution. Peard now explained that the ancient custom was to forbear comments on first presenting the engrossed impeachment to the Lords. 'The House of Commons speaks the matter in the articles,' he explained. He went on to say that there was no point in making a speech, since the accused were absent and their Lordships were not yet sitting in judgement. 'But,' he said, 'when their Lordships shall assign a day, the House of Commons will be ready to make good the several impeachments against them.'[60]

The articles of impeachment against Strode and Spencer have survived to this day and are stored in the parchment collection of the House of Lords Record Office. They are engrossed on parchment roughly twelve inches wide. Spencer's is over four feet long, Strode's longer still. The writing of both is a fine round hand, the drafting almost monotonously emotive. Spencer's is marred by some blots and amendments. Strode's is in part meaningless because the scrivener omitted a line of text from a common draft. The Clerk's office was under great pressure and there was some urgency. The first head of the articles against both alleged at considerable length that they plotted to procure a petition which questioned the Militia Ordinance as invalid and against the law. It alleged that both were intending 'to stirre upp the people of this kingdome to disobeye the said ordinance and to raise sedition and tumulte in the countie of Kent and other counties of this realme against the Parliament.'

Spencer alone was accused of labouring with others on or about 16 March to be at the assizes in Maidstone in the following week to frame a petition to Parliament. It looks as if the idea of a petition might therefore have come from Spencer and this theory has some confirmation in the fact that it was in his rooms that Dering, Strode and Twysden gathered on the night before the assizes began.[61]

These two impeachments covered much the same ground as that against Dering, but there were differences. Strode's charged him with telling some of the grand jury that their names ought to be posted for refusing to present the petition, with giving a copy to Malet and saying 'that hee cared not for the Parliament.' Never before had a man been charged with this offence, although it is true that one man had been arrested in March for saying that Parliament was not worth a turd. Finally, the articles accused Strode of saying after Strafford's execution that his offence was not high treason. Spencer's articles accused him of saying that the petition would be accompanied by 40,000 people with intent to awe Parliament and of saying to Augustine Skinner, the knight of the shire, during the assizes, that no knight ought to lay claims upon the county without securing its agreement and that he had known knights hanged for failing in this respect. This remark, if true, was colourful stuff that probably sounded good at the time, but it was bound to ring hollow at the bar of the House of Lords.[62]

On Thursday 12 May Spencer and Strode were brought one after the other to the bar of the House of Lords, where, after they had knelt awhile, they were bidden to stand while their impeachments were read to them. Each in turn asked to be bailed and was bailed in the sum of £5,000 on condition that he kept the peace and had nothing further to do with the Kentish petition. The House ordered each to put in his answer to the impeachment within ten days. On the same day the Commons relaxed the conditions of Twysden's bail to allow him to go to his house in Kent.[64]

Strode and Spencer worked closely together to prepare their defence against impeachment. Each of them addressed a humble petition to the Lords in identical terms. They began by acknowledging with all thankfulness their lordships' great favour in bailing them quickly and allowing them time to prepare an answer to the articles of impeachment. They prayed that the same five lawyers might be assigned to each of them for their defence. They asked for a copy of their impeachment and for copies of all relevant petitions, orders and notes in their lordships' custody. The two petitions were written by different clerks. Spencer's is unsigned. Strode's is signed with a bold flourish, using a fine nib. Each is endorsed with the date, 13 May 1642, and the word 'Express'. The counsel they wanted included Chaloner Chute of the Middle Temple. Chute was already famous for his defence of impeached Royalists.[65]

After the Lords had granted them the counsel of their choice, it took Strode and Spencer eight days to put in their answers. These, like their petitions for counsel had many similarities, not only in form but in content. Both pleaded ignorance of the Militia Ordinance. Both claimed that two other petitions had been presented to Parliament by a few of the gentlemen and inhabitants of Kent in the name of the county and many thought it was in order for them to do likewise; but they had presented the ensuing petition to the body of the county and after some alterations and additions it was, as far as they knew, approved without dissent; that it was agreed that the petition should be brought to the Commons; all of which they thought it was lawful for them to do. Lastly, they firmly denied that they were guilty of the various crimes, misdemeanours and offences specified in the articles and ended by submitting themselves 'to the grave judgement of this most high and honourable court'.[66]

The plea that they did not know of the Militia Ordinance seems a weak defence. A resolution of both Houses on 15 March enforced the Ordinance upon the subject. The Maidstone assizes opened on 22 March. There was plenty of time for the news to reach both of them by then. Spencer alone was charged with conspiring to present a petition as early as 16 March ('on or about'), but even by then he almost certainly knew of the Ordinance. However, ignorance was a passable defence upon two grounds. First, the petition referred to the problem of regulating the militia, but nowhere did it use the word 'ordinance'. Secondly, while it was, even then, an established principle that 'ignorance of the Law is no excuse', the principle had not yet been extended in the courts to ordinances or resolutions of both Houses.[67]

The reference to a few people in connection with previous petitions was a telling one and the word 'few' occurred twice in each answer. The implication was clear and did not invite cross-examination. Earlier pro-Parliament petitions had not been well supported in Kent. This of Dering's was. No one had objected to it at the public meeting of the county. The work of gaining hands for it continued to prosper in spite of its proscription. It was Dering's petition which had majority support.[68]

Finally, the answers of Strode and Spencer enlarged on Spencer's original defence in his testimony to the Commons on 1 April. 'It was but an embryo' he said then. Now they said they had arranged for their petition to be brought to quarter sessions and, had it been brought, they planned to alter it. Again, the meaning is clear. If it was a crime to present the petition as it stood, then they could not be held responsible, because their arrest prevented their proclaimed intention to amend it.[69]

The impeachments against Strode and Spencer were dropped, although the Commons were still asking the Lords to proceed against 'the delinquents concerning the Kentish petition' as late as 14 June.[70] No formal charge was made against Twysden; he had the friendship of Peard. Twysden summed up the result as it affected Strode, Spencer and himself:

'Of my charge a stoppe was made, which after was layd aside as forgotten; and those two having by good advise put in their answer, there was no farther prosecution of them, onely wee were commanded to call in all ye copies of this petition had beene by us distributed which was done accordingly.'[71]

By then men were openly talking of civil war. The issue would soon be settled not in the House of Lords, but on the field of battle.

7

Reaction

'By arresting the originators of the movement, the Parliamentarian leaders simply handed over the organisation of opposition
in Kent to hotheads.'

ALAN EVERITT.[1]

The restless determination of the two Houses to suppress Dering's petition
and to punish the authors was, of course, fathered by fear, but it was
a very special fear. Neither Lords nor Commons were threatened by any
criminal conspiracy to promote a seditious petition. The action of the
Kent petitioners was not criminal and the petition was not seditious. The
Parliamentarians feared it not because it was unlawful, but because it was
lawful—and might spread. Giovanni Giustinian, the Venetian ambassador
in London, wrote on 11 April that Parliament was

'alarmed lest such a step, based as it is upon the laws, might be imitated
by several counties and make a wide breach in the hearts of the people.'

He continued in cypher:

'if it does spread, it may serve as a very effective instrument for restoring
the King to his former powers, and give back to England with tranquility,
the ornaments of its ancient greatness.'

Parliament was in no mood now to restore the King to his former powers
if they could in any way prevent it. They had good reason for mistrusting
him.[2]

Above all, the majority in Parliament feared the denial of their right
to raise, train and control armed forces independently of the King. There
was still more that might be against their principles, and which had little
practical short-term significance. But the eleventh and twelfth heads really
struck home.

'... that you please to frame an especial law for the regulating the

76

militia of this kingdom so that the subjects may know how at once to obey both His Majesty and the Houses of Parliament ... that no order, in either or both Houses, not grounded on the laws of the land, may be enforced on the subject, until it be fully enacted by Parliament.'[3]

By adopting the Militia Ordinance, the two Houses had overthrown the constitution and assumed sovereign authority in the face of the King's refusal to give his assent. The petitioners were accused of asking that the royal assent be obtained before the Ordinance was put into effect. They had not been so specific. Yet when the King withheld his assent, as with the Militia Ordinance, a bill did not become law, was not enforceable. That had been the constitutional position until now. Because the two Houses intended to alter the position, the petition was a serious threat to their immediate capability. Like others before them, they could only defend their assumption of sovereignty by the unlawful use of force against those who opposed them on constitutional grounds.[4] So it was that the first and most serious charge against Dering, Strode and Spencer alleged conspiracy to obstruct the Militia Ordinance. The preamble in the articles against Dering ran:

'That whereas an ordinance was lately made ... for the settling of the militia ...'[5]

Strode's and Spencer's both ran:

'That whereas the Lords and Commons ... have by an ordinance of parliament settled the militia ...'[6]

For this reason, too, when Blount's counter-petition was eventually delivered to the Lords it was laconically endorsed by the Clerk '1. Militia ...' The counter-petition did not even mention the militia, but everyone knew that it had struck a blow for the Militia Ordinance, just as Dering's petition had threatened it by posing the problem of moderate, law-abiding, citizens.[7]

The immediate aim of the majority in the Commons had been to suppress the petition in the county of its origin and to prevent its ever being delivered to Parliament. They secured the arrest of the Earl of Bristol and Judge Malet for failing to disclose its existence. They arrested the four principal authors and a number of smaller fry for promoting it and they arrested anyone reported as trying to get hands for it. They gave out that the promoters of the petition were to be severely punished. They declared that parts of the petition were scandalous, dangerous and tending to sedition. They ordered that copies should be seized and burnt by the hand of the common hangman. They imprisoned the man responsible for their printing. And they attempted to publish a declaration that anyone who procured a counter-petition against the militia should be accounted a disturber of the peace of the kingdom. Lacking an adequate case against the people they had arrested as delinquents, they had put them on bail at a figure which effectively stopped their further support for the petition. Giustinian at least was clear about the purpose.

'The object of all this is to frighten them and prevent the paper being presented and by an example of severe repression to prevent others in the future from entertaining any idea of opposing the principles of the present government.'[8]

Twysden tried to explain the action of the Houses against the petition and its authors. He asked

'. . . why the two Howses were so transcendently incenced at this petition? Why they laboured so earnestly the finding out a plot which was never imagined? Why they tooke so unheard of wayes in their proceedings? . . . Why they shewde so strange partialyty as to incourage petitioning in some, yet make this crime so heynous, as it is certayn a lawyer of the Howse [George Peard of the Inner Temple] went so far as to say there were in it things not far from treason?'

He concluded that it was not really strange. Having decided to govern the country by votes, orders and ordinances without the King's assent, they must now be prepared to enforce obedience to their will.[9]

Certain it was that since the attempt on the five members the Country members of Parliament had consistently organized, encouraged, sponsored and commended petitions favourable to their cause. They even looked for the help of the judges where they could get it. On 9 April the House of Commons sent Pym and Glyn to thank Judge Reeve, not only for allowing a debate at the Nottingham assizes on a petition asking the King to return to his Parliament, but also because he gave the petition his support and offered to be the first to subscribe to it. The passage affords an interesting contrast to Parliament's reception of the Kentish petition and its treatment of Malet. Petitions were in order, providing only they suited Pym's purpose and that of his fellows.[10]

Petitions hostile to the views of the majority in the Commons had hitherto been presented largely with impunity, if not with the earnest rapture and wide publicity that greeted those in the Country or Parliamentarian interest. In the main the King had so far discouraged the circulating petition as a means of influencing policy. Royalist petitions had not been organized on the same scale as those supporting the policies of the opposition or its Puritan core. Occasionally moderate constitutionalists had been harried and imprisoned as delinquents for counter-petitions against the Country policies. Before the Kentish petition the Commons had twice taken a very tough line indeed. The twelve bishops were impeached because they petitioned that they had been intimidated by the mob. That was a unique opportunity to imprison them until their votes had been taken away by the peers who were left in the Lords. Benyon was impeached for petitioning that the City's militia might remain under the control of the Lord Mayor and aldermen. At all costs the Commons, having gained effective control of the only disciplined military force within reach, must keep it. In both cases limited punitive reprisals were sufficient. The bishops' petition was never in danger of infecting the people at large. The London petitioners were intimidated by the imprisonment and questioning of a few. They were too close to the Commons which effectively controlled the City's own militia. But the Kent petitioners were different. Their awe of Parliament was diminished by distance and a belief that the two Houses could not, or would not, contain all of them by force. The more Parliament harried the authors, the more the petition continued to gain ground. That was why the remorseless questioning and investigation went on day after day, week after week, until it was overtaken by the shadow of greater events.

But the actions of the two Houses, like most repressive measures imposed by a majority on a determined minority, succeeded only in provoking a strong reaction—in this case inside Parliament, in the country at large and in Kent in particular.

Giustinian wrote in his dispatch of 11 April:

'. . . many parliamentarians of moderate views, filled with a sincere zeal for the public good, have strenuously opposed this deliberation [the attempt to repress the Kentish petition] in lengthy offices [speeches], arguing that they ought not to put obstacles in the way of so just a demand when they have hearkened to other counties making petitions which merited censure rather than acceptation.'

and then in cypher:

'But the overbearing influence of the contrary party has refused to admit these arguments, valid as they are, and they are proceeding with great ardour to prevent this effort making further progress.'

Other counties, including Somerset, contemplated making a similar petition and this apparently stirred Parliament into an even greater severity against the authors of Dering's petition. Giustinian explains this in code in another dispatch:

'as if they hoped at least to defer if not to extinguish completely the first sparks of this fire which threatens to break out in so many quarters.'[11]

But the reaction was strongest in Kent. In *The Community of Kent and the Great Rebellion* Alan Everitt tells vividly how 'by arresting the originators of the movement, the Parliamentarian leaders simply handed over the organisation of opposition in Kent to hotheads.' He describes the new promoters of the Kentish petition as sharing some broad characteristics. They were young, they were closely linked by ties of marriage and of blood, they were spoiling for a fight and they had little to lose if the battle should go against them.[12]

Action against Dering's petition had not been confined to the two Houses or to committee. Pym saw the importance of mounting a counter-petition in the county itself in order to discredit Dering and his supporters and to prevent people of other counties from combining for similar ends.[13] The right moment was clearly at the next quarter sessions when Dering's petition should have been finalized, while he and his fellow promoters were on bail as delinquents, his petition proscribed and his supporters under threat of imprisonment if they continued to help.

Quarter sessions opened at Maidstone on Tuesday 19 April and a good many magistrates appeared on the bench who had not been accustomed to attend.[14] Blount was there [15] and so was Richard Lee, the member for Rochester. There may have been other Kent members of the Commons sitting on the bench, which was predominantly Parliamentarian in sympathy: the core of moderate opinion had been broken and many of the active remaining supporters of Dering's petition were young men of impoverished families who were not in the commission of the peace and were not, therefore, entitled to sit on the bench. Dering's petition was not presented for support and further consideration as he had hoped. The magistrates and gentry discussed the counter-petition. They publicly disclaimed the old one and protested against it. In court only one man voted against the motion. While this was happening a number of Royalists were holding a meeting in favour of Dering's petition in a nearby tavern. Eventually, Richard Lovelace, the poet, and some companions strode into the courtroom and furiously shouted 'No! No! No!' Then, to emphasize their contempt for the court, they clapped their hats on their heads. They said that they had heard about a new petition to be presented to Parliament, that they had a copy with them and there were many falsehoods in it. Lovelace lifted it over his head and tore it in pieces. He then delivered a condemnatory speech and gave a copy to the clerk of the peace. The magistrates apparently took no action against him and a 'Mr. Browne' reported to the Commons on the Friday that Dering's petition had been publicly disclaimed at quarter sessions; he said not a word of any opposition.[16]

Now the Parliamentarian supporters in Kent, under Blount's leadership and with the active encouragement of the two Houses, were making great efforts to collect hands for this counter-petition. They knew that Dering hoped to secure 40,000 signatures for his own petition in the five weeks between Friday 25 March and Friday 29 April. Blount's aim was to secure a comparable and substantial number of hands, if possible, between about 21 April when the counter-petition was framed at quarter sessions and 29 April when Dering's petition was to be presented to Parliament. With Dering fled and his supporters bailed upon substantial sums that would ensure their compliance with the Parliamentary will, with the petition proscribed and every possible copy burned, Blount must have felt that he had at least a sporting chance. By 18 April Giustinian was still not certain whether the remaining supporters of Dering's petition intended to continue or desist from their efforts. And Blount had the full weight of the two Houses behind him.[17]

Hostility to Parliament's handling of the business had been growing in Kent. Some rumblings of the reaction had already reached Westminster, mostly through Peard.[18] On the morning of 28 April a confused report of the preparations reached the Commons. There would be seven or eight thousand people at Blackheath on the following day. It was enough for the Commons to work on. They dispatched the young Sir Henry Vane to ask for a conference with the Lords, and they appointed Pym and Holles as managers.

Pym's handling of the conference was calculated to alarm. He began by reporting that a large number of people planned to meet the following day at Blackheath to support the rejected petition, but he added, typically, that there were reports given out that they intended to shed blood. If he could frighten his audience, he knew it would help to unite them in a common hatred against the petition's supporters and he was not above inventing talk of blood-shedding where there was none before. Finally, he asked that Major-General Skippon and the committee of the militia of London might be instructed to prevent any tumultuous and disorderly assembly to the disturbance of the peace or any one coming into the city of London with arms and weapons. This last request was an ingenious one, for every gentleman of the day carried his sword on a journey and on public occasions. In this sense any large gathering of gentlemen could be made out to be a tumultuous assembly bent on disturbing the peace—or worse. The Lords agreed to the Commons's request.[19]

At five o'clock on the morning of 29 April two men arrived on Blackheath to prepare for the main body of the petitioners who were to follow them. They were bidden to make arrangements for food and clothing. The main body was due four hours later. We do not know how many people eventually assembled on Blackheath. We do know that Richard Lovelace assumed their leadership and that a number variously estimated as between 280 and 500 men marched the six and a half miles to London. They came down Long Southwark two abreast with Richard Lovelace and Sir William Boteler at their head; past the courthouse where Malet had held the assizes less than a month ago, on towards London Bridge. At last they came in sight of the great stone gateway on the bridge itself, the gateway that was London's first defence against insurgents from the south. In front of the gateway and across the staples at bridgefoot a chain was drawn and a company of soldiers, from the Yellow Regiment of the Trained Bands, stood waiting. The commanding officer of the regiment, Sir John Wollaston, alderman and member of the militia committee of the City of London, was there to supervise the operation in person. Captain Bunce, the company commander, demanded of Lovelace and

Boteler what their intention was. They told him that they had come to deliver a petition to Parliament and read it out to him. He asked them why they came armed and they told him that they only carried the arms of gentlemen. Bunce allowed a small party of the petitioners to cross London Bridge, but not until he had taken possession of their swords and arrested one of the foremost as he turned his horse southwards away from the bridge; the man had a bundle of the proscribed petitions about him. The House of Commons rose before the party could reach them and so the petitioners were frustrated until the following day.[20]

On 30 April, upon the motion of William Strode, Sir John Wollaston, who had been responsible for the operations at London Bridge on the previous day, was admitted to the Commons. He made his report at the bar of the House and supported by some of his colleagues he reported that he had arrested one of the Kentish petitioners because he was carrying a bundle of the printed petitions which the House had ordered to be burnt. After Wollaston had withdrawn, he and his party were called in again by the Speaker who thanked them on behalf of the House. The committee for printing was instructed to find out who had printed this great bundle of petitions and to whom it had been delivered.[21]

A little later the serjeant informed the Speaker that some gentlemen of Kent were at the door and wanted to present a petition to the House. Lovelace and Boteler and about fifty supporters, who had managed to elude Captain Bunce at London Bridge, were called in and they lined up at the bar of the House—without their swords. They presented their petition and then withdrew. Lovelace delivered the petition and it was read by the Clerk. The House recognized it as the one which they had ordered to be burnt by the common hangman. Richard Lee then read out a statement he had written on the events that had taken place at Maidstone at quarter sessions and delivered it to the Clerk. He included in his report the part played by Lovelace in breaking up the meeting.[22]

Lovelace was then called in and he was asked by the Speaker from whom he received the petition and who authorized him to present it. He replied that he had been given a copy by George Chute, a near neighbour of Dering, on the day after the assizes and that he had been commanded to deliver it by the gentlemen assembled at Blackheath. Questioned, he admitted that he knew a similar petition had been burnt by the common hangman and that some gentlemen had been questioned about it. He knew nothing of the bundle of printed petitions that had been seized on the previous day. The *Commons Journals* record that he agreed that there was another petition at quarter sessions which he had torn.[23]

When Boteler's turn came, he had to admit that he had come from York on Wednesday 13 April, that he had also been to Hull on the way back, that he had heard of a petition that was never delivered, but never heard of any Parliamentary censure, that he had heard a paper was burnt, that he knew nothing about an order of either House to do with the petition, and so on. The House committed Lovelace to the Gatehouse and Boteler to the Fleet, and ordered their supporters to wait while it attended to other business. The Commons had to meet the Lords for an important conference and they discussed whether or not they should put off dealing with the other petitioners until Monday. At last the Speaker called them in and told them that the House intended to let them off with a warning because they were 'young gentlemen, misled by the solicitations of some not affected to the peace of the kingdom'.[24]

Later in the day the Commons secured the agreement of the Lords to what they had done and to the committee for the Kentish petition sitting specially to interrogate Lovelace, Boteler and any other witnesses that might be produced.[25] On Wednesday 4 May they ordered four of their lawyers to be added to the committee and to prepare charges against Lovelace and Boteler.[26]

If their treatment was intended to mollify the rank-and-file supporters of the petition, it failed in its aim. The rest of the Kentish Cavaliers left Westminster and returned to Kent very angry men. Giustinian reported:

'They have put it about that they will come back very soon in greater strength and numbers for the purpose of compelling parliament to return again to the straight path of the laws, to preserve for the Protestant Church its ancient pastors [the bishops] and to assure the King, their lawful sovereign, the tranquil possession of the prerogatives enjoyed by his predecessors.'[27]

All this prompted renewed Parliamentary pressure for a Kentish counter-petition 'whereby they may discredit the first and so dissipate all idea among the people of other counties of combining for the same purposes.'[28] Blount's task had not been easy. While his counter-petition had been supported by the majority of remaining justices at quarter sessions, there was clearly a great deal of strong opposition at Maidstone. His meeting there had been broken up in disorder. He was unable to secure a substantial number of signatures by 29 April when Lovelace presented Dering's petition. Some fourteen days after his own petition had been framed, the records suggest that he had only managed to secure some 6,000 signatures from the Canterbury area. His supporters in other parts of the county had only been able to secure a few hundred more. It was then judged better that he should quickly present those that he had than that his supporters should complete their lists or even collect what they had. The counter-petition must go to Parliament with a minimum of delay.[29]

On 5 May, accompanied 'by many knights and gentlemen of the county of Kent', Blount brought the petition to the two Houses. His petition recalled Livesey's of the previous February, thanked Parliament for all that they had done, disclaimed the one framed at the previous assizes and denied that it was 'the act of the body of the county, as it seems to speak, forasmuch as it was disavowed by many of the then grand jury, and justices on the bench, and since by all us your petitioners, whose names are underwritten.' Finally, the petition asked Parliament to accept their vindication of themselves and the county, and ended with a wordy exhortation to Parliament to lift their hearts above discouragements and an equally wordy declaration of their resolution to maintain the King's person and dignity and the power and privileges of Parliament.[30]

In the Commons Augustine Skinner now had an opportunity to redeem his reputation, which must have suffered through his passive acceptance of the events which took place at the assizes. He moved that the supporters of the counter-petition be admitted to the House. Thomas Blount and his party were allowed to enter and take up their position at the bar of the House. Blount delivered a short speech in which he asked that the militia might be quickly settled and the ports put into trustworthy hands. He handed in his petition, addressed to Lords and Commons, in the name of the county of Kent. He and his supporters then withdrew. The petition was read by the Clerk and two or three members spoke in support of it. The Speaker called Blount in again and thanked him. He used the words 'and as for the militia you know what has been done'. Blount was so flattered by this attention that he forgot the rules, if ever he knew them, and asked the House to direct him to carry the same petition to the Lords. The Speaker had to tell him that he had not leave from the House to hear him speak a second time or to reply.[31]

In the Lords the petitioners were asked to withdraw while the House considered the matter. They were then called in again and the Lord Keeper thanked them on behalf of the House.[32] The petition lay on the Clerk's table among a host of other documents that would later find their way into the records of the House. For the moment the back of the petition was endorsed as an aide-mémoire against the time when the minutes should be written. The endorsement read:

'1.   Militia
2.   14 days
3.   6,000 hands and upwards and all Canterbury
4.   Many hundreds more have subscribed'

There is no mention of the militia in Blount's petition and it is, therefore, interesting that the word 'militia' should have appeared on the back of the petition in the Lords and that the Speaker should have referred to the militia in the Commons ('As for the militia, you know what has been done'). Both Houses saw Dering's petition principally as a threat to the Militia Ordinance. That is why they moved so energetically against it.[33]

The proceedings against Lovelace and Boteler, like those against Dering, Strode and Spencer, gradually petered out. On 12 May Boteler petitioned the Commons for bail and they refused it. Instead they ordered Peard to bring in the charges against Boteler and Lovelace on the following Monday. When Monday came, no charges were brought. On 19 May the Commons resolved that the charge against Boteler should be brought on the following Tuesday, but nothing happened and so he remained in the Fleet prison. On 17 June Boteler again petitioned for bail. His case was supported by Edmund Waller, the member for St. Ives in Cornwall, but his petition was only granted after a lengthy debate. He had to pay £10,000 and his two sureties £5,000 each. On the same day the Commons ordered that his impeachment be brought in on the following Monday morning. But it never was. On 8 July the Commons ordered his bail to bring him in on the following day; the reason is obscure. At a later date Boteler caused considerable offence to the Lords by attending a conference of both Houses, for on 11 July Peard was reporting that the Lords 'tooke much offence that Syr William Boteler shoulde come to the conference and there as ytt were outface both Houses'.[34]

Meanwhile, Lovelace in the Gatehouse at Westminster was inspired to compose the poem 'To Althea, from Prison', one of the finest and most poignant lyrics. He also prayed for his discharge on bail on 17 June, so that he could serve against the rebels in Ireland.[35] The document was delivered to the Clerk by Edward Bayntun, the member for Devizes, a moderate man who was not afraid on occasion to face Pym himself and tell him he was wrong. He must have been a good friend of Lovelace for with some difficulty he arranged for bail.[36]

8

Paper Warfare

'These paper skirmishes left neither side better inclined to the other; but by sharpening each other drew the matter to an issue.'

EDWARD HYDE, EARL OF CLARENDON.[1]

From 28 March until 2 May 1642 Malet remained in the Tower.[2] We have no record of his stay. We do know that it was not a healthy experience for a man of sixty. Sir John Eliot and Sir Walter Raleigh had lain there in a damp cold cell where the foul river water seeped up inside the walls. Both fell a prey to consumption. Without the warmth of a fire in winter Eliot died there at forty. Raleigh survived his thirteen years of imprisonment by sheer force of will. Probably Malet was not kept in close confinement for he was old and his offence relatively minor. Perhaps they let him exercise on the top of the inner wall, where once Raleigh used to walk.[3]

Several of Malet's acquaintances had already been in the Tower for short periods in the recent past. One was Sir Edward Dering, the principal cause of Malet's present confinement. He had been imprisoned there from 2 to 11 February.[4] Others were Sir Ralph Hopton, a neighbour and fellow justice in Somerset, who spent eleven days there in March, for defending the King in a Commons debate,[5] and Sir Thomas Gardiner who had supported Benyon's petition and was briefly in the Tower for refusing to defend Sir Edward Herbert because he was given too little time to prepare his case.[6] There was also Justice Long, imprisoned for impeding the London petition.[7]

Malet had no lack of fellow prisoners. For most of his stay there was the Earl of Bristol, his friend and patron. The records suggest that each of them had a keeper of his own, a man responsible to the lieutenant governor but paid by the prisoners so that they could enjoy a measure of freedom.[8] They would have been able to procure clothes, clean linen and money for food. Probably, too, they would have been allowed their own servants.[9] Archbishop Laud had been imprisoned there without trial since March of the previous year.[10] Ten other bishops had been held there since they complained that the mob by violence and threats had prevented them from sitting and voting in the Lords; in fact they were bailed very soon after Malet.[11] In the meantime, there was almost an embarrassment of talent for services on Sundays. In such surroundings Malet must have found it strange to hear a sermon from William Peirce, the Bishop of Bath and Wells, who had been a fellow justice in Somerset until the Bishops' Exclusion Act had removed him from the commission of the peace.[12] Besides these, there was Arthur Magennes who had become garrulous over a drink in Chester, where he boasted a sympathy with the Irish rebels and an intention to visit Lord Maguire, one of the most notorious.[13] For the last week of Malet's stay there was Colonel Beeling, who was said to have solicited 20,000 men from France for Ireland upon a promise to deliver the kingdom.[14] These two had no funds to maintain themselves in prison, but their crimes appeared to be minor and the lieutenant governor had himself contributed to their food and lodging.[15] In contrast to these improvident prisoners there was Sir George Benyon, the promoter of the London petition which had so angered the two Houses. Since 26 February he had been held almost continuously in the Tower. On 8 April, following impeachment by the Commons, he was sentenced by the Lords to two years in gaol. He was a wealthy man and we can be sure that he had all the luxuries that money could buy.[16] Finally, there was Daniel O'Neill, one of the King's officers who was implicated in two army plots. He had got himself transferred to the Tower on the grounds of illness and secured a measure of freedom inside it. He was busy plotting to escape and managed to leave disguised as a woman three days after Malet was released on bail.[17]

The Earl of Bristol was a leading figure in the Lords and it was natural that he should petition the Lords for his release before Malet attempted to do so. They would then see which way the wind was blowing. As early as 7 April Bristol prayed the House for his freedom because his questioning had failed to show that he had any hand in promoting Dering's petition. On the next day he submitted another petition asking to go out of the Tower either on parole or with a keeper for his health's sake so that he could attend to his affairs. At sixty-two he was two years older than Malet. He must have been very miserable lodged in the Tower during the wet April weather. He pointed out rather pathetically that the request he was now making had been granted when he was in the Tower on the most serious charge of treason. He might have added that he was fourteen years younger on the last occasion. His petition was allowed on condition that he returned to the Tower at night. Malet made a similar petition three days later and was granted a similar dispensation.[18]

The case against the Earl of Bristol was the most slender of all. He had never been directly concerned with the petition; his only offence was that he concealed its existence from Parliament for a period of less than twenty-four hours. He complained that under the law he would have done nothing wrong if he had concealed so serious a crime as treason for so short a time. He found it odd that he should have been imprisoned for concealing a petition to Parliament which had been publicly proclaimed in Kent, while Justice Long was committed for hindering one that had been canvassed in London.[19]

On Friday 15 April the Lords ordered the examination of Bristol and Malet on the following Monday. When Monday came, they said it was to be before the Lords committee for the Kentish petition that afternoon. They seem to have been anxious to maintain their own privilege against the Commons. By the following day they must have capitulated to pressure, for while the earl was to be examined by the Lords committee that afternoon, they ordered the judge to be examined by the committees of both Houses. The earl's examinations showed that he had had no hand in promoting Dering's petition. Even Lord Saye and Sele had to admit that Bristol was guilty of no more than receiving the petition, of having it copied and concealing it. Bristol petitioned the Lords for his own release. He pointed out that nothing had emerged in his examination except what he had already admitted in the first instance. On the same afternoon they ordered his unconditional release from the Tower that evening. Malet was still to be kept under restraint. On 23 April he petitioned the Lords for bail, but the House decided to postpone a decision for four or five days and it was not until 2 May that he was finally released on bail.[20]

During the dinner recess on 2 May Malet was brought from the Tower to the Lords and as soon as prayers were over he was freed upon a modest recognizance of one thousand pounds, 'unto our Sovereign Lord the King'. It was a condition of his bail that he should attend the Lords when required, but this was meaningless because that was part of his duty as an assistant. One of the clerks wrote laboriously in the manuscript journal of the House:

Thomas Mallet, Miles, unus justiciarius de
Banco Regis, recognovit se debere Domino Regi
in mille libris, levari ex terris, bonis et
catallis suis, ad usum Domini Regis, &c.[21]

Easter Term had already begun. Malet was needed to support the Lord Chief Justice in the King's Bench and eventually to act as assistant to the Lords once more. Bramston, the Lord Chief Justice, still had articles of impeachment pending against him. Heath sat in the King's Bench and continued on occasion to act as assistant to the Lords. Berkeley was still under arrest. Lack of judges was straining the service of the Lords and even important messages were carried to the Commons by masters in chancery.[22]

Ever since Malet had first set out on circuit for the Lent assizes the flow of circulating petitions had continued. While Parliament was sitting, and particularly this Parliament, petitions had in the past usually been addressed to the two Houses. This had become almost a custom of the constitution. There were always exceptions. Peers, bishops and army officers quite properly regarded themselves as having a special relationship with the Crown. But when the King moved first to Hampton Court and then to York it was a sign that he was no longer willing to accept the advice of his two Houses. And so the practice grew of addressing the King direct, either to enlist or offer support against the two Houses to to persuade him to accept the advice of the Houses and return to Whitehall.[23]

The two Houses set out to enlist popular support. While dealing harshly with the authors of Dering's petition, they sought to show that their policies for Church reform were moderate and reasonable. On 8 April they issued a joint declaration that they wished only to remove what was evil and offensive from the government and liturgy of the Church.[24]

Despite the efforts of the two Houses Charles was gaining a great deal of support throughout the country, whenever he chose to take Hyde's advice and adopt a conciliatory tone. And then on 8 April, apparently without consulting Hyde, he announced that he proposed to go to Ireland in person to suppress the rebellion. He intended to raise an army of 2,000 men and to arm them from the magazine at Hull. He would himself draft a militia bill that would meet the needs of the two Houses. Not unnaturally this declaration revived all the old suspicions that he intended to equip himself with an army and march on London. The reaction of the two Houses was immediate. They rejected the King's proposal and refused to allow him an army for Ireland.[25]

Meanwhile the King had received from the two Houses a request that the arsenal at Hull be moved to the Tower. At the time the Queen was abroad trying to raise forces from Holland and Denmark. Hull was a vital entry port and in the face of Sir John Hotham's refusal to cede it, the Queen urged her husband to take it by force. On 14 April Charles sent an answer to the request of the Houses. This time, advised by Hyde, he stood upon the letter of the law, refused them and pronounced the appointment of Hotham to be illegal, which it was.[26]

The Houses issued an endorsement of Hotham's conduct commanding the garrison at Hull and a direct order that the magazine should be moved from Hull to the Tower. The King sent the young Duke of York with a small following into Hull and followed him with a large force in person. The affair was botched and Sir John Hotham again refused him entry. Charles sent a message to the two Houses asking for Hotham to be punished. Meanwhile he refused to assent to his own militia bill, because it had been substantially altered by the Lords. As soon as the Houses heard this, they issued a declaration requiring all persons in authority to put their original Militia Ordinance into execution.[27]

From this time onwards each side made urgent preparations for war. The Houses issued another peremptory order for the removal of the Hull magazine and held a review of 8,000 men of the London Trained Bands in Finsbury Fields. The King failed to win help from abroad and realized he must depend upon backing from his followers at home. He called together the gentry of Yorkshire, explained that the Houses were opposing him with force and asked them for a guard to protect his person. Failing to get sufficient support he ordered the Yorkshire gentry to come in arms to protect him, he called out a regiment of the Yorkshire Trained Bands and he ordered Major-General Skippon, the commander of the London Trained Bands, to join him. Skippon was appointed by the two Houses and, of course, he refused. On 20 May the Houses passed the historic resolution that the King, seduced by wicked counsel, intended to wage war on his Parliament, that his action was a breach of trust and that all who helped him were traitors.[28]

In May Sir John Bankes, the Chief Justice of Common Pleas, left Westminster and followed the King to York.[29] In the middle of the month the Lord Keeper received from the King a command to issue proclamations and writs that next Trinity term be adjourned from Westminster to York. This brought the strain upon an already sick man almost to breaking point. If he disobeyed he would be removed from office; if he obeyed Parliamentary retribution was like to follow him more quickly than horses could take him to York. Perhaps because he feared to take the more resolute course, perhaps because the burden was too great to bear alone, he called Malet and the other judges together and told them of the command. The story got to the Parliamentarians and the issue was raised in the House of Lords on 17 May. They resolved that the King's action was illegal and 'contrary to the express writ that calls assistants to this House'. The Commons passed a similar resolution.[30]

This must have shown Littleton the weakness of his own position. The only way to escape being crushed was to come down firmly on one side or the other. But which? Finally, persuaded by Hyde he escaped to York taking the Great Seal with him. The Great Seal was the 'emblem of sovereignty', the only instrument by which on solemn occasions the will of the Sovereign could be expressed. To counterfeit it was high treason. To lose it was to suffer a major moral defeat. With its possession the King had won a great victory.[31] A number of peers and members of the Commons deserted the two Houses and followed the Great Seal to York. One of the first was Edward Hyde, whose drafting of the King's declarations had done so much to win moderate men to the royal cause. By the end of May the King had thirty-two peers with him at York, and only a handful were actively supporting him in the Lords. The Earl of Bristol was one of the last to go; he stayed till the middle of June to make two speeches urging a reconciliation between the King and the two Houses.[32]

All this time the declarations and answers between the King and the two Houses continued unabated. Lords and Commons said flatly in a declaration dated 19 May that they could not settle a revenue upon the King until he chose suitable officers and counsellors. They alleged a plot by the malignant party to promote 'mutinous petitions' in London, Kent and other places.[33] Almost at the end of a very long reply to this declaration, the King replied to the charge. He asked:

'Hath a multitude of mean, unknown, inconsiderable, contemptible persons about the Citie and suburbs of London, had liberty to petition against the government of the Church, against the Book of Common Prayer. . . . and been thanked for it: And shall it be called mutiny in the gravest and best citizens of London, in the gentry and communalty of Kent, to frame petitions on these grounds; and to desire to be governed by the known laws of the land, not by orders and votes of either or both Houses? Can this be thought the wisdom and justice of both Houses of Parliament?'[34]

The paper war between the King and the two Houses came to a head on 1 June when both Houses agreed a document known as the Nineteen Propositions and dispatched it to the King. It set out the minimum conditions which the two Houses felt they could accept in the circumstances. The Houses no longer asked for the right to recommend councillors and officers to the King. They asked simply for the right to approve officers of state, privy councillors, the two chief justices and the chief baron. They asked for the control of the militia and the reform of the Church and they demanded that the King should, in future, take advice and act through his duly appointed officers and not through private men and unsworn counsellors. This last was perhaps the most important of all. If 'evil counsel' were proffered to the King in future, Pym and his supporters were determined to know who had given it.[35]

Falkland and Colepeper drafted the King's answer to these propositions. This was a landmark in constitutional history for it completely abandoned the King's claim to 'divine right' and appealed to the idea of a mixed, limited, monarchy that consisted of King, Lords and Commons. The answer was so persuasive that Pym was in danger of losing support for the principle that the two Houses should approve privy councillors. As on previous occasions he silenced argument by reporting an immediate danger to the safety of the state—in this case the Royalist preparations in Gloucestershire.[36]

Trinity Sunday was on 5 June and in the following week the new law term began in an unusual and uncomfortable quiet. The judges and serjeants lacked a Lord Keeper for their customary procession to Westminster Hall. At the King's command Sir Robert Heath of the King's Bench had slipped away quietly to York in the short vacation between the Easter and Trinity terms. There was a strong rumour that Sir Robert Foster of the Common Pleas had gone with him.[37] Those who remained were conscious that, after the bishops and recusant peers, the judges had become some of the most unpopular people in the land.

On Tuesday 7 June the Lords were officially informed that Judges Heath and Foster had gone to York without leave of the House and they ordered their arrest as delinquents. Later in the week it turned out that they had been misinformed about Foster and on the Friday they received from Heath a carefully worded letter making his excuses and expressing the hope that the King would release him within a few days. Few people can have believed that he would return or that was what he hoped. The House promptly came to the opinion that the judges were not tied by their oaths and began to look for signs of defection among the remainder.[38]

On 7 June, too, the Lords took official notice of Malet for the first time since he was bailed over a month before. Before he escaped to York, Heath had been engaged in the examination of Colonel Beeling who was a prisoner with Malet in the Tower. The examination was still uncompleted and it had become clear that Beeling was seriously implicated. Rumours of further judicial defections were rife and the Lords now ordered not one judge but two to complete the work. They sent Chief Justice Bramston and Malet, who were the two remaining judges of King's Bench. But the Lords had no great confidence in either Bramston or Malet and so they ordered two serjeants to accompany the judges.[39]

In mid June three prisoners were brought over from Ireland under a strong escort. The two most notorious were Connor Lord Maguire and Hugh Macmahon, who had planned to lead a party of Irish Catholics against Dublin Castle at the outbreak of the Irish Rebellion. The third prisoner was Colonel Sir John Reade, a man of hitherto unimpeachable character who had allowed himself to be used as an intermediary between the rebels and the Earl of Ormonde commanding the forces against them. All three were brought before a committee of both Houses in the Court of Wards and from there committed to the Tower.[40] Lord Chief Justice Bramston and Malet were ordered to examine the prisoners and prepare a case against them. Malet finally handed over to this committee sixteen parcels of papers.[41] Maguire and Macmahon at least were plainly guilty and would suffer the traditional death of traitors.[42]

Long after term had begun Westminster Hall still wore a vacation look—almost as if the plague had frightened people away. In Malet's Court of King's Bench even the boys were now able to peep over the bar where a five-fold row of lawyers normally stood waiting for their cases to be heard. At other times the surly tipstaves could not have been persuaded to give bench room to the public for blandishment or bribes; but now they looked over the door as if it were a pillory, become suddenly courteous in their efforts to persuade people inside—for a consideration, of course. The barristers, instead of studying their briefs (for there were precious few briefs), were buying up all the latest pamphlets and standing in corners to read them aloud. Unkind people said they did it to keep their tongues in use lest their flow of talk should dry up with unwilling silence. In fact the business of the court itself had dried up and what was true of King's Bench was also true of Chancery, Common Pleas, the Courts of Exchequer, Wards and Requests. The courtiers had left London with the King. Litigation was almost at a standstill for men had other things to think about. Heaven and Hell, the two inns adjacent to Westminster Hall, were empty. The coaches had thinned out in New Palace Yard and about the Inns of Court. The cooks stood idly leaning against the door posts outside the King Street taverns, where once, when the courts were risen, clerks, solicitors and their clients had come to devour puddings and mince pies by the dozen. Trade of all kinds was slack. Many traders had been made bankrupt and men were railing bitterly against the times.[43]

During May and June there was a steady flow of petitions from Parliamentarians in the counties of England praying the King to forego his intended journey to Ireland and to return to his Parliament. At first they were framed in courteous terms, but they irked him and he replied sharply, referring to the answers that he had given the two Houses in the past. The men of Hertford petitioned him for an accommodation; the King said trenchantly that God had preserved him from the bloody hands of rebels and that his efforts to avert a civil war had kept him so long from raising an army that he was almost swallowed up by a desperate rebellion. The expressions 'civil war' and 'rebellion' were being used increasingly on both sides. Language was becoming less and less temperate. When the two Houses complained to the King about his reception of a petition from some of the gentry of Yorkshire, Charles replied that he had reason to believe that the petition was

'framed and contrived (as many of such nature have been) in London, not in Yorkshire.'

He went on to accuse the two Houses of having a double standard for petitions, refusing those which they disliked, preventing their publication and punishing their authors, while taking the greatest pains to publish and print the petitions which accorded with their wishes.[44]

In the meantime each side had taken a number of important steps upon the road to war. On 9 June the two Houses passed an ordinance calling on everyone to supply money, plate and horses for the service of the country. Great pressure was put on the members of both Houses to set an example. Even the assistants to the Lords were called on to contribute, but this was partly in order to see which of them were likely to be loyal to the two Houses. The King now made a determined effort to win a party for himself. He published a declaration promising to maintain the liberties and just privileges of Parliament and undertaking not to wage war except in his own defence. He got over forty peers at York to declare that it was not his intent to wage war on Parliament. On the very next day he issued his first commission of array for Leicestershire, directing the trained bands to muster under his own officers. Typically, Charles chose the wrong county in which to make a start and Henry Hastings failed to execute the commission in the county or to capture the magazine there. The Earl of Newcastle captured Newcastle for the King and the King dismissed the Earl of Northumberland from the post of Lord High Admiral. (He had long ago deprived Essex and Holland of their positions at Court.) Warwick managed to neutralize the position of Newcastle as a Royalist port by gaining the fleet for Parliament before Charles could appoint a successor to Northumberland. In London Lord Mayor Gurney had the courage to publish the King's commission of array and was promptly impeached. Lords and Commons appointed a Committee of Safety which was in effect a war cabinet and then they resolved to raise an army of 10,000 men. On 12 July they decided that Essex was to be captain general of the Parliamentary forces. Offers of help were pouring in to the King and the two Houses. Many of the peers with the King advanced him considerable fortunes to raise an army or raised troops or regiments themselves. Similar preparations were taking place on the Parliamentary side. And all over England the great majority of people who wanted peace began to wonder how far they would be pushed by the extremists on to one side or the other.[45]

9

The Last Circuit

'I was att Maydstone assises where yor brother Mallet caryed
himself stowtly and bravely.'

SIR JOHN SACKVILLE
to Sir Robert Foster, Judge of Assize for the
Western Circuit, 9 August 1642.[1]

Term lasted almost till June had run out. The summer assizes were due
to begin two weeks later. There was no Lord Keeper to bring the judges
together in Star Chamber, to confirm their choice of circuits or to give
them the main points which they should make in their charge. As term
drew to its close the Commons sent two of their number to question
Malet and Foster for allegedly altering the places of assize. They considered
whether Malet was a fit person to go circuit 'being complained of . . .
the last circuit he went.' And they again voiced a rumour that the judges
had been ordered to adjourn the next term to York. The judges were
questioned and denied any knowledge of the order. The Lords commanded
them to inform the House if any such order should come.[2]

The King did not overlook the lack of a Lord Keeper to direct the
judges. Possibly prompted by Lord Littleton himself, he sent directions
to his judges of assize from York on 4 July. Malet's copy was addressed
'To our trusty and welbeloved the judge or judges of assize for our counties
of Kent, Surrey, Sussex, Hertford and Essex.' Malet would have received
his copy some time between 6 and 9 July depending on the zeal and
fortune of the messenger. It was close-written on two pages and, except
on one point, conciliatory and non-contentious, as far as that was possible
in a document which sought to win the people to the King. It explained
that the points of the charge could not be given to the judges in Star
Chamber. It exhorted the suppression of popery. It proclaimed a resolution
'to maintain the lawes of this our kingdome; and by and according to
them to govern our subjects' and to maintain the just privileges of Parliament. Then came the sting:

'. . . but that we may not, nor will admit of any such unwarranted power, in either, or both Houses of Parliament, which in some things hath been lately usurped, not onely without, but against our royall consent and command. And we require and command you, as there shall be just occasion offered, in a legall way that you take care to preserve our just right in these cases.'

There were two more paragraphs ordering suppression of insurrections, riots and unlawful assemblies and enjoining the enforcement of peace in spite of the difficult times. Finally, it encouraged people to put their grievances to the judges or to the King himself; and it promised a sympathetic hearing. It commanded the judges to give a copy of the King's directions to the foreman of the grand jury or others wanting a copy and it empowered the judges to appoint counsel for the King in pleas of the Crown.[3]

The directions were well designed to help regain the initiative for the King and to win over the support of moderate people in the counties. The vehicle was well chosen. However unpopular the judges might be in London and with the Parliamentarians, they still had a great deal of prestige in the counties, where for eleven long years of personal rule they had been the main administrative link between the King in Council and his justices of the peace in the country.

Already the judges still allowed to go circuit were preparing for the coming assizes. The Lords acknowledged the double strain of work in the courts and as assistant to their House by granting to some—Mr. Justice Reeve, Baron Henden—leave of absence when the circuit was ended. On 8 July Foster was given leave to prepare himself for the Western circuit. On the following Monday two of the ship-money judges were allowed to go to their own houses until the Michaelmas term. Finally Malet was given leave to prepare himself for circuit. His was the shortest circuit and he was the last judge to go.[4]

On Thursday 14 July Malet opened his commission in the timber-framed town house at Hertford.[5] That same morning in the House of Commons Sir William Lytton, one of the knights for Hertfordshire, awoke to the danger. The assizes were a great occasion for swaying opinion, for moulding attitudes and for reaching local decisions on matters of national policy. On this occasion they were likely to be a cockpit of argument about the commission of array and the Militia Ordinance, about the King and his two Houses. In a situation where sentiment had not yet crystallized, the part played by Malet could well be decisive. If the Hertfordshire members continued to sit at Westminster, they could lose the battle for men's hearts and minds in the county where they lived. Lytton therefore moved and the Commons ordered that the 'Knights of Hertfordshire', Lord Cranborne, Mr. Robert Cecil, Captain Wingate and John Harrison should go down to the assizes there, ostensibly to further the proposals for bringing in money, plate and horse, and to put them to the county. In fact none of them was strictly a knight of Hertfordshire. Lord Cranborne sat for Hertford Borough and Captain Wingate for St.

Albans Borough. The other two lived in the county and represented constituencies outside it. Cranborne and Cecil were both sons of the Earl of Salisbury. The sympathies of all four at the time were entirely with the Parliamentarians. They would see that the Parliamentarian case was not lost by default.[6]

In the House of Commons, William Strode, one of the 'five members', began to turn over in his mind what the Parliamentarians would actually achieve by the order which Lytton had moved. Certainly, the four Hertfordshire members could help by bringing informal pressure on justices both in and out of court. But what could they do if Malet attacked the two Houses from the bench, perhaps even in his charge to the grand jury? If they interrupted, they were liable—and properly liable—to imprisonment for contempt. And yet it might become essential to stop him from developing his theme. Pondering the problem, Strode hit upon a solution that seemed to him right, because in his view the Commons had by now become a sovereign body transcending the Parliament of which it had once been a part and the judicature which was in the Parliamentarian view a corrupt and subservient body. Impetuously, he interrupted a report from committee to propose that the four members sent down to Hertford might have the authority of the House to interrupt the judge and to defend the honour of 'Parliament', if Malet should say anything derogatory to their proceedings. By 'Parliament' Strode meant, of course, the two Houses.[7]

Strode's motion provoked a debate. Members might have reservations about Malet himself, but the great majority respected the law. To them it was a crime to interrupt a judge in the execution of his office. D'Ewes suggested that the members might, if necessary, ask for liberty to speak when the judge had done. Sir Harbottle Grimston, the member for Harwich, thought about the implications for his own county and asked that a similar order be made for the Essex assizes at Chelmsford. D'Ewes saw the point and at once proposed that a general order should be made for the whole kingdom and that a committee be named to draft it; this was agreed. In due course the committee sensibly recommended that there was no need for an order; the task could safely be left to those members who were on the bench at the assizes. This is interesting, because Strode, the extremist, chaired the committee and D'Ewes, the moderate, failed to turn up.[8]

At Hertford the presence of four members of the Commons did not precipitate the sort of scenes that were later enacted in Kent. In his instructions to the judges the King had not mentioned his commission of array. The two Houses had not yet decided to use the judges as their mouthpiece to pronounce it illegal.[9]

Malet could not count on overt Royalist support in Hertford. The Earl of Salisbury, the Capital Steward of the Borough and owner of Hertford Castle since 1628, had at last come down on the Parliamentarian side and a lot of people followed his lead. The Parliamentarians were already strong in Hertford itself. For some time they had been training the militia. 'Young Mr. Keeling', the steward of the Borough of Hertford, finding himself chairman at the last quarter sessions had charged the grand jury to present the names of those who exercised in arms. The foreman of the grand jury happened to be their commander and flatly refused to return a 'true bill'. He reported the affair to the Commons and Keeling eventually ended up a prisoner in Windsor Castle.[10]

While the Parliamentarians in Hertford had been drilling in public and while the Earl of Salisbury had been making up his mind (and remaking it) there were powerful men working in secret for the King. Lord Capel was gradually accumulating a small arsenal at his seat at Hadham Hall. He himself was already with the King at York. Sir Thomas Fanshawe, a member that the Commons did not send down to the assizes, had smiths concealed at work in Ware Park. Large bodies of horse were being collected. But, so far, there was no physical conflict.[11]

Giving his charge at Chelmsford, Malet read out his instructions from the King. The quiet, measured, persuasive, reasonable phrases were calculated to make their mark with every man in the closely packed court. We can reasonably assume that Malet sensed, as every good lawyer senses, the effect of his words on his audience. It is part of a judge's task to interpret difficult passages to ordinary people. He may have stopped when he came to the part about 'unwarranted power, in either or both Houses of Parliament, which in some things hath been lately usurped' and explained in simple terms that this meant acts like the Militia Ordinance passed without the King's consent.[12] He may have gone further and cited his own arrest and imprisonment as another illegal act. Contemporary pamphlets accused him of saying these things and more.[13]

Malet's words, whatever they were, succeeded in convincing Robert Smyth, the sheriff, who a month before had been seeking the Commons's advice about whether he should publish the King's proclamation forbidding the trained bands to muster and exercise. They convinced the majority of the justices present, but they were only partially successful with the grand jury. Malet had a strong ally in Sir Thomas Bendish of Steeple Bumpstead, perhaps the most influential of the justices of the peace. That very same day Bendish drafted *A Remonstrance and Declaration*, got the sheriff, twenty-four of his fellow justices and six of the grand jury to sign it, and dispatched it to the King at York. The *Remonstrance* accepted the King's intentions expressed in his declarations and in the letter which Malet had read out. It ended by saying:

'Wee . . . doe assure and faithfully promise, that for the safety of your Majesties most royall person and posterity, defence of your rights and just prerogatives we will be ready according to our faith, allegiance, and late protestation to assist your Majesty with our persons, lives and fortunes whensoever you shall be pleased to command us.'[14]

Malet and Bendish between them had done a good job. There was no public discussion of the petition in court, as there had been at Maidstone in the previous March. The grand jury as a whole were not asked to approve it. That would have been impossible for only six out of twenty-three grand jurors were prepared to put their signatures to it. (Some fifteen out of about forty justices present had also withheld their signatures.) Instead Bendish seems to have privately solicited the signatures of all he knew would support it. In this way he avoided provoking an opposition and a counter-petition. The very moderation of the document must have made it difficult for many loyal justices not to put their names to it. Its wording suggests that it was agreed by the justices and grand jurors as a body. We know that could not have happened. The ruse was sufficient to fool one nineteenth-century historian and it probably fooled many Englishmen at the time. Because it represented a substantial achievement by the King in his efforts to win moderate opinion, it would for that reason alone have justified the wildest rumours designed to discredit the judge's handling of his charge. Perhaps the two Houses failed to punish the authors when they saw that there was absolutely nothing culpable in the declaration. There was no word of disapproval for Parliament; only a whole-hearted promise to assist the King with their 'persons, lives and fortunes'.[15]

Meanwhile much was happening that was soon to affect Malet personally and directly. Reports about the King's attempts to put into effect his commissions of array were beginning to arrive. Commissions had already gone out under the Great Seal of England to Leicestershire and Worcestershire. There were rumours of Royalist preparations in many other counties besides.[16] The Earl of Leicester, the lord lieutenant of Kent, had not yet granted commissions to his deputy lieutenants and this was essential if the commission of array was to be successfully resisted there. As early as 6 July the Commons pressed the Lords to get him to appoint deputies quickly. They wanted the deputy lieutenants who were members of the House to go down to Kent and put the Militia Ordinance 'in execution'. And they wanted the militia in Kent to muster on 20 July, three days before the coming assizes. The Lords agreed but ordered the muster to take place after the assizes at Maidstone would be finished.[17] The Earl of Leicester was a half-hearted Parliamentarian, deliberately vacillating. He knew that many of his deputies were equally unenthusiastic.[18] On 16 July the Earl of Warwick reported correctly that the commission of array was about to be put into execution in Kent and that Sir Henry Palmer had boarded one of his ships with a command from the King. Once more the Lords ordered the lord lieutenant to grant his commissions to his deputies. He still did nothing.[19] On Tuesday 19 July the Commons ordered Serjeant Wilde to draft an order to the judges instructing them to publish in open court in their charges to the grand jury in each county the declarations and votes of both Houses that commissions of array were illegal. On the following day Lords and Commons approved his draft and the Commons instructed their serjeant to send 'messengers of purpose' with the order of both Houses to the judges of assize.[20]

On Friday morning of the same week the business of the Commons was interrupted by Henry Marten from the Committee for the Safety of the Kingdom on a matter of urgent importance. Something was plotted at the next Kent assizes. There are two versions. Sir Simonds D'Ewes says 'that they had understood of certaine practices hatching at the next assizes in Kent.'[21] Framlingham Gawdy says that Marten reported 'some yll affected yn the countye of Kent entend to dyvldge somethyng of thys house that ys scandalous at the assyses.'[22] The knights of the shire, Sir Henry Heyman and the rest of what the Commons described as 'the Kentish members' were ordered to see that the circuit judge published the order of both Houses about the commission of array. The House made no less than four other orders on the same subject before the day was out. The 'gentlemen of Kent' were to withdraw and prepare their instructions. The order was to apply 'to all Kentish members'. Mr. Skinner was to have the orders in readiness. And finally the 'gentlemen of Kent' were named and ordered to

'go down to the said assizes; and use all diligence to prevent such inconvenience, or any other attempt that shall be offered, to the prejudice of the Parliament; and, by all lawful ways and means, to preserve the said county not only in peace among themselves, but in a right understanding of the proceedings of Parliament.'[23]

Malet opened the assizes at Maidstone on the following morning, Saturday 23 July. The members of the Commons sent down from Westminster had clear instructions from the House that as soon as they arrived they were to go to the judge of assize and acquaint him with the contents of the order and the instructions they had received. In the name of the House they were to require him to help them to carry out the commands of the House. They were to deliver to him the order of the Lords and Commons about commissions of array dated 20 July. They were to use 'all careful ways and means to hinder any proceedings that shall be attempted in the furthering the same commission'. These were their instructions.[24] There were seventeen of them; they arrived late and the court was already in session.[25]

The justices of the peace probably had their midday dinner in the Star Inn as their custom was.[26] Amongst them was Sir Roger Twysden, released from restraint by the Commons and now resolved to live quietly and avoid meddling in public affairs. Seeing such a large committee from the House of Commons he asked one of their number for the reason. His friend told him they were there about the peace of the county. This astonished Twysden, for the county was at peace and unlikely not to be—unless as he suggests 'some of ye Parliament's faction made it otherwise.' When the meal was over the committee chairman, probably Sir Henry Heyman, read out the Commons order of 22 July beginning with the alleged reason for it:

> 'Whereas the House hath been credibly informed, that some ill-affected persons within the county of Kent are now endeavouring to disperse rumours to the scandall of Parliament, and to censure the proceedings against the promoters of the late dangerous petition; and they have plotted for this purpose to meet at the assizes, the further to extend their malicious designs; . . . .'

He asked the justices to help the committee carry out their order, and then requested

> 'That, to this end, this committee may be seated at the bench, suitable to the authority and trust they represent, to be ready to perform the commands of the House as occasion shall require.'[27]

Heyman (if Heyman it was) carefully suppressed the portions which bade the committee first attend the judge, acquaint him with their various orders and instructions and seek his cooperation. It is clear from the subsequent behaviour of the justices that the committee's instructions were not altogether well received, even though they finished on a more conciliatory note than the Commons had intended.[28]

Twysden tells us that the committee first made their appearance on the bench on Saturday afternoon.[29] In fact only justices of the peace in the commission for Kent might sit on the bench and only nine out of the seventeen men sent down by the Commons had that right. Eight were attempting to assume a privilege that did not properly belong to them.[30] This must have irritated the justices already on the bench so much that they even grudged room to the members who were fellow justices. In his subsequent report to the Commons Sir Henry Heyman said that 'scarce any of the justices would vouchsafe them roome to sitt or stand conveniently.'[31] When Heyman rose and moved that a printed order of the House be publicly read, Judge Malet refused to agree, saying that his authority was derived from the Great Seal and that he could not admit anything which did not stem from that authority.[32]

Sunday 24 July was the seventh after Trinity and Malet went to pray in the parish church of All Saints, once the collegiate church of the archbishops of Canterbury. He sat inside the chancel in one of the massive oak stalls where the officiating chaplains of the college once used to worship. Robert Barrell, the minister, preached the sermon.[33] He was a colourful character, who had been nominated to All Saints by Dr. Abbot, the Puritan Archbishop of Canterbury. Long before Laud succeeded Abbot, Barrell had driven many of the Puritans from his congregation by adopting high church practices, erecting crosses once more and turning the communion table into an altar. Twice he was the subject of hostile petitions to the Commons, once for erecting communion rails, standing at hymns and turning to the East, and once for not preaching often enough and for being 'a common tavern hunter'. He was above all a King's man. He was reported as saying that he 'wished God would put it into the heart of the King to set the City of London on fire and burn up the Puritans.'[34]

It is not at all certain what Barrell said in his sermon. He was later summoned by the Commons as a delinquent 'for scandalous words uttered in a sermon preached by him on Sunday last at Maidstone, against the Scots; and other seditious expressions contained in that sermon.'[35] If he did speak against the Scots it was probably to say something unkind of a nation that managed to dispense with bishops. It is more probable that he commended to the grand jury Malet's charge which would have included the King's instructions. The pamphlets of the time charged him with

Supporting Judge Malet in showing that the commission of array was legal.

Preaching a seditious sermon before Judge Malet.

Speaking against Parliament.

Incensing the county against the proceedings of Parliament.

Urging his congregation to lend supplies to His Majesty.

Whatever he said, he was a brave man, for a number of members of the House of Commons must have been listening to his sermon.[36]

On the following Monday morning the committee sent two of their members, Sir Edward Hales (of Woodchurch and Tunstall and member for Queenborough) and Sir Humphrey Tufton (of The Mote in Maidstone and of Bobbing Court, member for Maidstone) to seek access to the judge. The court had just risen and Malet wanted the committee's message to be put to him. before all the justices of the peace. To that end he invited them to meet him in his lodgings after dinner. They accepted his offer and arrived at the hour he had named. Sir Henry Vane the younger (who had lands in Kent and was member for Hull) was now their spokesman. He told Malet that he had a message from the House of Commons. Malet replied suavely enough that he had come to Maidstone to do justice according to the law and he would accept anything compatible with that from the Commons. He asked if what they had to say could be said publicly. Vane replied that it could be public afterwards, but they wanted to tell him first. Malet asked if it concerned the King. Vane replied 'Not more than all things pertaining to the government of the Kingdom.' The verbal sparring went on. Malet wanted the committee to give their message in the presence of the justices. Vane was determined that Malet should hear him without them. Eventually Malet gave way and he and Vane retired to a private room.[37]

Malet and Vane were about half an hour talking alone. We do not know exactly how the conversation went. Vane himself reported to the

Commons that he asked Malet for his fullest cooperation in publishing the orders and instructions that the committee had brought. From the tenor of Malet's considered reply given later it would appear very unlikely that Vane told him precisely what orders and instructions the Commons wanted to be published at the assizes. It is still less likely, because it fell right outside his own instructions, that Vane asked him to read the Militia Ordinance; yet three news pamphlets later reported that Malet refused to read it. Probably Vane wanted to read out the order about the commission of array himself and hoped by concealing its nature and purpose to persuade the judge to give his permission. Twysden says that, when they eventually finished their private meeting, a statement of their discussion was read to the others and it emerged that Malet had refused Vane's request. By Vane's own account, Malet only refused to accede at once to Vane's request and asked for time to consider it. In the meantime someone on the committee published their orders and instructions to the justices of the peace.[38]

After some though Malet returned an answer by Sir Edward Hales and Sir Humphrey Tufton that he was prepared to help the Commons committee as far as was consistent with his commission and the law of the land. The committee then asked him to provide room for them when they came to sit on the bench. He considered this for a little time and replied that if they had sat on the bench without demanding it, he might have let it go. Now that they had demanded place on the bench, he felt it was so important that he could not answer without careful thought. The committee pressed their claim both with the judge and with the justices of the peace who were present. The judge explained that places on the bench were only for those who were authorized to sit there during the assizes and they were the judge of assize and the justices of the peace of the county. Failing to get an answer satisfactory to themselves, the committee decided not to sit on the bench that day. Instead they went away and prepared a declaration which they proposed to read to the county in court on the following day. The declaration would show how they had been hindered from putting into effect the instructions which they had from the House of Commons and that their intention was only to achieve peace in the county and a good understanding between it and Parliament.[39]

That afternoon the justices fell into an unhappy discussion about what answer they ought to return. A reply was drafted, but a number of justices had a hand in it and when it was finished it was laid on the table, still unapproved, still generally unacceptable because it was the work of many different hands and nobody cared to amend it. Twysden took it up, seeking only to shorten it to his own satisfaction, for he thought it too long. When he had done, he read it out and it was approved with one or two slight alterations. The justices then delivered it to the committee.[40] It ran thus:

'The answer of the justices of the peace the sayd 25 July 1642

'That the first demand being grownded (as wee conceive) upon misinformation, and in it, a great aspersion layd on this county, wee not knowing any such endeavors as are expressed, it beeing as wee hope, likely to continue in a secure peace; His Majesty's justices of the peace, having their auctoryty committed unto them under the Great Seal of England, dare not, in the execution of it, join with any not so authorized.

'That beeing demanded, this committee may sit upon the Bench for the performing the commands of the Howse of Commons, (unknowne to us) wee doe not know what place may bee sutable to the authoryty and trust they represent; nor that we have power to place any on the bench, not sent thither by the like auctoryty we sit there.'[41]

It was a gauntlet hurled at the authority of the Houses and one which the committee quickly picked up.

The next day the justices received the following reply in the forenoon by the hand of Sir Norton Knatchbull:

'Die Martis, July the 26 1642

'Whereas this committee have received an answer yesterday in the name of his Majesty's justices of peace of the county of Kent, with which they are alltogether unsatisfyed, and which tends very much to the disservice of the Howse of Commons; They, therefore, according to the instructions they have received from that howse, (whereof a copy is hereunto annexed) doe require the sayd justices, in the name of that howse, to be assistant to this committee in the execution and performance of the orders and commands of that Howse, as they will answer the contrary to the sayd Howse. And for this purpos this committee doth declare that they doe resolve to make their repayr to the bench, from tyme to tyme, (as they shall see cause), during these assizes, there to put in execution the orders and commands of that Howse as occasion shall require.'

'The instructions of the Howse of Commons to the Committee'

'And for your better performing of the orders, instructions, and commands you heerewith received from this Howse, the sherifs, justices of peace, mayors and all other his Majesty's officers are hereby requyred to bee assistant to you in execution and performance of the sayd orders and instructions.'

Not till now had the Parliamentary committee played their trump card, the order of the House of Commons requiring sheriffs, justices and mayors to assist them. Why did they wait?[42]

In the afternoon, as they had promised, the committee came once more into court. Some of them got comfortable places, but others had to stand with considerable inconvenience and crowding. When they arrived, Malet was trying criminal cases. The gaol calendar was heavy and there were a number of indictments carrying the death penalty. The committee had to wait three hours before they had an opportunity to put a motion or to speak to him. Henry Vane the younger was a proud, impetuous man and he must by now have been fuming. He acted as spokesman and moved the judge in the name of the committee that they might deliver some commands they had received from the House of Commons for the county and asked that the grand jury might be sent for to hear what he had to say.[43] Surprisingly, in the circumstances, he spoke 'exelently well, temperately and soberly' and explained that what he had to say was for the good of the King, the peace of the county and the maintenance of the laws and religion.[44]

Malet replied that he was willing to obey the House of Commons in anything consistent with his charge and the preservation of the law, and must have asked what were the commands that Vane wanted to deliver. Vane apparently refused to indicate their nature in court, for Twysden tells us that Malet said that he could not accede to Vane's request unless he first knew what he intended to say. He said that he would permit nothing to be said or done there, except what he was authorized to do by the King's commission and would rather lose his life. The argument went on for some time and a number of people shouted when Malet spoke and the others when Vane spoke. Finally Malet told Vane that if this continued he would be forced to adjourn the court. Vane told the Commons that because he could not be heard they withdrew rather than hinder the business of the court. Twysden says that Vane was commanded to retire by the committee and went home to Fairlawn. When they left some followed them crying for the 'Parliament', but they were not considerable in quantity or quality and the bulk of the people there paid little attention to them.[45]

After the court was adjourned a few young Royalists, angered by the behaviour of the Parliamentary committee, drafted a reply to the House of Commons and a petition to the King. They included Sir John Mayney of Linton Place near Maidstone (who had been active in soliciting hands for Dering's petition), Sir John Tufton (eldest son of Sir Humphrey Tufton, one of the committee members), Sir Edward Filmer (eldest son of Sir Robert Filmer who was one of Twysden's guarantors in his bond to Parliament) and Sir William Clerke (later killed in the Royalist cause at Cropredy Bridge in 1644). None of them was a justice of the peace.[46] The reply to the House of Commons was addressed to Augustine Skinner, knight of the shire (with Sir John Colepeper, Chancellor of the Exchequer). It reminded him that a committee of the House of Commons had been sent down to the assizes because the House had information that there was to be a disturbance of the peace in Kent. In the name of the commons of Kent it asked him to certify as their servant that the county was at peace and that the information was groundless. It asked for the name of the informer so that their honour might be vindicated and he might be punished. It ended by asking the Commons to afford the King full satisfaction on four counts:

'1. In presently leaving the town of Hull in the same state it was before Sir John Hothams entrance into it; And delivering His Majestie his own magazine.
2. In laying aside the militia, untill a good law may be framed, wherein care may be taken as well for the liberty of the subjects, as the defence of the kingdom.
3. That the Parliament be adjourned to an indifferent place, where His Sacred Majestie, all the lords and members of your House of Commons may meet and treat with honour, freedom and safetie.
4. That His Majesties navie may be immediately restored to him.'

There followed a long statement of their reasons. The whole was couched in such belligerent language that it was certain to bring down punishment upon those who were responsible for it.[47]

Their petition to the King included a copy of their instructions to Skinner and thanked him for the letter which the judge of assize had read in his charge to the grand jury. It referred to the danger of civil war and said that this was no time for grievances. It asked that, if the two Houses should agree to their requests, the King would be prepared to dispense with his extraordinary guards and meet his two Houses in some place where they would be free of rioting mobs.[48] Failing to find Skinner in court, the young Royalists set up so great a shout that they flushed Sir Roger Twysden from his nearby lodging to see what was going on. The clerk refused to accept the instructions and they tried to offer them to Twysden. He, too, refused because there were Sir John Baker, Richard Spencer and others who were senior to him on the bench. At last a young man, possibly the under-sheriff's clerk, was persuaded to read out the instructions. There were some members of the Commons committee sitting on the bench who listened in disapproving silence. Mr. George Chute and a fellow justice sent the instructions to Skinner, but he refused to accept them. Twysden heard that they were thrown at him.[49]

On Thursday 28 July Sir John Mayney, his brother-in-law Paul Richaut, Sir Thomas Bosvile and Sir William Clerke carried to the King at York this petition, a copy of their instructions for Augustine Skinner and their reasons. All were delivered into the King's hands at the court of York on 1 August.[50] This was fairly slow going for an important document, but a deputation does not travel as quickly as one man in a hurry. The Essex remonstrance had already reached the King. He was, therefore, well aware of what Malet was doing. He was aware, too, that the two Houses were unlikely to allow him to do it much longer. On 31 July he dispatched a letter to Malet telling him of a plan to deliver him safe from the two Houses and to use his services in Somerset.[51]

On 4 August Lord Falkland signed the King's answer to this last Kentish petition. In it the King sympathized with the petitioners' fear of a civil war and affirmed his intention to do everything possible to avoid one. He said that he wanted no other amends than the return of the town of Hull, his goods and his navy, the disavowal of the power to make laws without him and agreement about a safe place where he could meet Parliament with his Council to settle differences. He went on to list the injuries that the two Houses had done to him. He pointed out that they had been at pains to encourage and publish petitions against the laws and government of the country while they censured and imprisoned petitioners who were loyal subjects although they had committed no offence. He suggested that now their lawful rights were being taken away from his subjects by arbitrary power, they should provide for their own security by helping him to defend his person, the Protestant religion, the law of the land and the liberty of the subject. On his part he undertook to venture his life and crown with them in the struggle. The King assured his petitioners that he would do his utmost to protect their right to petition. He declared that they were not obliged to obey any pursuivants, serjeants or messengers who should try to prevent their doing their duty. And so that the whole county of Kent should know, he declared his pleasure that his answer, together with the Kentish petition and instructions to Augustine Skinner, should be read in all churches and chapels in Kent. They were printed in London and sold by Robert Barker, the King's printer.[52] The King was inviting the people of Kent to join with him in the fight to uphold the law and the constitution.

Malet had moved on and by Friday 29 July he was sitting in East Grinstead for the Sussex assizes. Here nothing remarkable occurred. There were so many indictments that politics receded into the background. Occasionally the cases touched on the problems of the times. A body of the King's subjects had been training 'peacefully' with muskets and pikes when a musket was accidentally discharged and a man was killed. There were popish recusants who refused to receive communion kneeling, people indicted for not coming to church; but for the most part the cases were routine and with routine punishments for the guilty. It was a short-lived lull in the gathering storm.[53]

On Tuesday 2 August the House of Commons was asked to provide time to discuss the Kent assizes of the previous week. The attack began with a reading of the county's instructions to Skinner for the House of Commons. This was calculated to provoke the anger of the Parliamentarians by its tone and demands: . . . 'delivering His Majesty his own magazine' (at Hull) . . . 'laying aside the militia' . . . 'That the Parliament be adjourned to an indifferent place' . . . 'that His Majesty's navy may be immediately restored to him.'[54]

Then Sir Henry Heyman reported the events of Saturday 23 July, explaining why it was that the committee of Kent members had been unable to see the judge before the assizes began and the difficulty they had experienced in finding room in court that day. Sir Henry Vane the younger followed him and reported at some length on the events of the following week. He alleged that when the committee asked for places on the bench, they could get nothing from the judge but 'dilatory and unsatisfactory answers'. Sir Simonds D'Ewes's very full report of Vane's speech in the Commons ends abruptly with the withdrawal of the committee from the courtroom 'rather than they would hinder the business of the assizes'.[55] It is very unlikely that Vane did not go on to tell of subsequent events and of the interchange of messages between the committee and the justices. One contemporary pamphlet reports Vane as saying that Malet 'did as much as in him lay incense the people of the county against the proceedings of the Parliament' and that he 'procured' some of the justices of the peace to draw up the instructions for Augustine Skinner. Another substantially confirms this. Both pamphlets say that the judge was to be arrested and there was talk of sending a troop of horse for him.[56] It is quite possible that the discussion was on these lines but it would have been a breach of privilege if the Commons had ordered the arrest of an assistant of their Lordships' House. Henry Elsynge, the Clerk of the Commons, was aware of this; the *Commons Journals* record two orders, that 'it be referred to the committee for the defence of the kingdom, to consider the fittest way to send speedily for Judge Mallett' and that the whole business of 'the last assizes in Kent' should be referred to the same committee.[57]

On the same day Malet opened his commission at Kingston-upon-Thames[58] and while he was there a messenger arrived with a letter for him from the King at York.

'To our trusty and right welbeloved Sir Thomas Malet, our judge of assize for our county of Surrey.

CHARLES R.

'Trusty and welbeloved wee greet you well. We [h]ave here a faire and wee believe a just report of your fidelity and courage in your circuite for our service. As wee shall never desire anything from our judges but what is just, and which by the knowne lawes of the land may and ought to bee done and there-in wee are confident yee will performe that trust which becommeth persons of your quality, soe bee you assured wee shall always bee carefull to protect you in doing our service in that just way as becommeth us to doe as a good master to a servant, soe usefull and soe neare to us and our crowne, and of whome wee have soe much esteeme. We understand your circuite is neare at an end, and the place being soe neare to the House of Parliament, wee doe foresee, that, answerable to some other parts of their accions, they may endeavour to send for you, and drawe you before them againe, and soe put some disgrace upon you: and dishonour upon us and our service for soe wee doe and shall esteeme it. But wee, having occasion to [use?] you in the countrey where you dwell, for the peace of the place, ch[arge] you upon the allegiance you owe to us, that you repaire to your owne home, with all convenient speed, where wee have use of your speciall service, and to that place wee shall addresse our dispatchs to you, and you must not faile to bee there ready to receave them and execute them with your best endeavour. And least any violence shalbee attempted to hinder you in your returne, wee have by a letter sent at this time also commanded our high sherrife of Surrey to attend upon you and carry you safe out of that county, and wee have also written the like letteres to others the sherrifes of the counties by which you are to passe, that they assist you if there shalbee occasion. Given at our court at Yorke the last of July 1642.'[59]

The two Houses would see that Malet was never again allowed to sit on the judicial bench—at least while they ruled. Meanwhile, the King wanted him in Somerset where he had authorized the Marquess of Hertford to execute his commission of array; he needed Malet's standing and support. The question—and one that must have occurred to Malet—was whether the King in York had power to protect his judges in the south. It is one thing to give orders to sheriffs and another to have them obeyed. Charles was forever an optimist, counting on loyalty he had done little to foster or reward. Like the people of whom the psalmist sang, he imagined such things as he was not able to perform.

In Westminster a warrant had been issued and a messenger dispatched to Kingston to serve it on Malet at the assizes. There is no record of who issued the warrant or precisely what it was for.[60] There is no trace of it in the *Journals* of either House or in the order book for the period. It was certainly not ordered by the Lords whose assistant Malet was.[61] The warrant could conceivably have been issued by the Commons, whose Clerk, mindful of privilege, might have been compelled to avoid reference to it in the *Journals*, but this is unlikely because on 1 August they asked the 'committee for the defence of the kingdom' to consider what was the fittest way of sending for Malet.[62] It is most probable that the warrant was made out not by this committee but by the Committee for the Safety of the Kingdom. Like other joint committees of both Houses it drew members from Lords and Commons in the proportion of one to two, so that the Lords were outnumbered by the Commons; and the Commons were determined to have Malet arrested. The noble members of this committee, like the Commons members, were staunch Parliamentarians to a man. Every one of the five peers had been on the joint committee for the Kentish petition appointed in March; Northumberland had been manager for the Lords. The ten Commons members of the Committee were all Parliamentarians; there was not a Royalist amongst them. Pym had been manager of the conference on the Kentish petition and Marten, Glyn and Pierrepoint had helped him prepare the questions that were put to Malet at that encounter in the Painted Chamber on Monday 28 March. It was Marten who, acting as spokesman for the Committee for the Safety of the Kingdom, had warned the Commons of a plot to be hatched at Maidstone this summer assizes.[63] The members of the Commons on the Committee probably counted on the strong Parliamentarian element from the Lords to cope with any question of privilege if it should arise in the Upper House. They could, too, rely on the support of Lord Mandeville, who, in the absence of the Lord Keeper, was now acting as Speaker in the Lords.[64] Finally, it is not completely certain that the warrant authorized Malet's arrest. There was talk later of 'a warrant from the Parliament for apprehending him', for this was in everyone's mind. If arrest without the formal order of the House of Lords would have been a breach of privilege, it was probably proper for a joint parliamentary committee to issue a warrant for the attendance of a judge. The formal statement in public in the assize court at Kingston only informed the judge 'that there was a warrant from the Parliament to appear before them'. The words would have been carefully chosen to avoid any hostility from the onlookers. It is possible that they were close to the truth.[65]

Kingston itself was tactically important. There was no bridge between Kingston and London. It lay on the main road to Portsmouth. It contained gunpowder works and cannon foundries and the county magazine of arms and ammunition for the militia. It had already been the subject of an attempted Royalist coup. The town itself appears to have been Royalist in sympathy and it seems likely that most of the justices assembled for the assizes were also Royalist supporters, if not very active. Any public show of force for the arrest of one of the King's judges was likely to provoke a hostile response. As an assistant to the Lords and a judge of the King's Bench, Malet must eventually return to Westminster; the problem was to persuade him to return now and voluntarily and thus to avoid the occasion for conflict with the justices of Surrey and the people of Kingston. The Commons had already seen in Kent the effect of verbal battles between Commons representatives and county justices; they cannot have been anxious to provoke overt opposition in Surrey as well.[66]

Timing was important. Kingston was the last assize town of this summer's circuit and it was best to serve the warrant when the assizes were concluded. The precedent of Judge Berkeley, actually arrested while sitting on the bench, was not a happy one. There was, too, the paramount need to uphold 'the King's peace' under whatever aegis. Peers and Commons were for the most part men of property and substance. They had a strong interest in preserving order and judges were growing scarce. Because the ship-money judges were forbidden to go circuit, there were only six judges available for assizes including Bankes and Heath who had escaped to York. It would help if Malet could complete his own circuit.[67]

The messenger with the warrant needed support and advice on the spot. The obvious choice was George Price, the sheriff, but he was not a man on whom the two Houses could count; he had some difficulty later in deciding where his allegiance lay.[68] The lord lieutenant charged with raising the militia was the Earl of Nottingham, a man without strong conviction who was to die very soon. The acting head of the county forces was Sir Richard Onslow, a member of Parliament and a deputy lieutenant. He was a strong Parliamentarian with no love for the King. In the preceding year Onslow made a speech comparing Charles I to a hedgehog who had wrapped himself in his own bristles. For this he had already been put out of the commission of the peace for Surrey. He was a connection by marriage to Denzil Holles, one of the members of the Committee for the Safety of the Kingdom. Now he accompanied the messenger with the warrant, in order to ensure Malet's safe return to London.[69] It is not clear whether the messenger was told to act under his orders or whether Onslow assumed responsibility for his actions. It was natural that he should take charge and that the messenger should accept his instructions. Onslow was a county magnate, he had local knowledge and he was clearly determined to help the man serve his warrant, while the messenger was simply a messenger.

On Thursday 4 August Onslow took his place upon the bench beside the judge and watched the proceedings in court. The routine of assizes was familiar to him, because he had been a justice of the peace. He no longer had any right to sit on the bench—as he himself said, he had been 'put out of the commission of the peace'—but no one challenged him. He gradually saw that the judge was aware of his intention, for he was spinning out time, perhaps realizing that he was unlikely to be arrested until after the assizes. Onslow sat on waiting for the court to rise, but at about ten o'clock the judge proposed to adjourn until 16 August and then to sit at Dorking and not Kingston. Onslow rose and told him that there was a warrant from Parliament to appear before them and that this proposed adjournment might be inconvenient. Malet replied that he had a service to perform for the King and that he was commanded upon his allegiance, or else he would willingly obey the Parliament. Without further ado Malet instructed the crier to proclaim an adjournment until 16 August at Dorking and the people left the courtroom 'in God's peace, and the King's'. The messenger served Malet with the warrant and the judge asked for time to go to his lodging and decide whether he would obey it or no. Onslow followed him to receive his reply and Malet showed him the letter of command from the King, that he should go home and that all sheriffs should protect his passage homewards. The sheriff had a letter direct from the King commanding him to protect the judge on his journey and Onslow told him

'that I conceived his duty to obey the commands of the Parliament and not the directions of a private letter to contradict that power and so required his assistance.'

The sheriff was afraid to obey Onslow's instructions without the authority of the Commons. Onslow, anticipating local resistance, was worried about his ability to take the judge to Westminster by force with the twenty-five horse at his command. He sat down and wrote a letter to his 'Honourable friend and kinsman Denzil Holles, Esq or in his absence John Hampden, Esq', leaving it to the consideration of the House whether they should find a greater strength of horse in view of the expected resistance. He wrote the letter clearly on a sheet of foolscap paper. The matter was urgent, there was no time for a fair copy. He folded it twice and then twice again. The address is blotted and smudged as though it was washed by the rain. Onslow was determined to hold the judge in town while he waited for an answer. He kept him confined to his lodgings with the passive agreement of the sheriff.[70]

10

Assize at Arms

'If in early Stuart theory they were meant to be 'lions under
the throne', when the day of reckoning came the Judges turned
out to be a somewhat mangy collection.'

G. E. AYLMER.[1]

Vengeance was coming, but at first it did not touch Malet himself.

On 30 July Robert Barrell, the Minister of All Saints, Maidstone, who
had preached on the Sunday of the Kent assizes, was ordered by the
Commons to be consigned to the custody of the serjeant. The charge
in the *Journals of the House of Commons* was general and vague; the news
pamphlets of the time elaborated it in a way calculated to ensure that
his continued incarceration would be acceptable to the public. Amongst
other charges one pamphlet accused him of 'endeavouring to prove the
legality of the commission of array and commending Judge Malet's speech
to that purpose'.[2] Twysden tells us that Malet 'spake not one word as
approving [the commission of array]'; he only refused to countenance
the reading of orders showing its illegality.[3] In the constitutional law
of the time the commission of array could have been lawful; the Militia
Ordinance was definitely not law. In the eyes of the Parliamentarians
it had become sedition to disagree with the majority in the Commons
and unlawful to encourage people to petition against their proceedings.
Since the courts could not recognize this interpretation, men must be
denounced and imprisoned and left without charge or trial. Barrell applied
for bail and on 19 August this was granted.[4]

On 2 August the Commons ordered Twysden, Strode and Spencer to
be brought before them. Twysden was committed to the custody of their
serjeant-at-arms without even being examined. He was lodged as a prisoner
near Charing Cross for nineteen days without being charged or questioned.
During this time he applied to the House of Commons for leave to go
into the country, but this was refused. When they found that there was
nothing for which he could be formally charged or condemned, the House
sent a messenger to tell him he might lodge at Isleworth with his brother-in-
law, Sir Hugh Cholmley. He refused to go and asked only to be charged

with a recognizable offence. They told him that 'in these times the House could not look at the nice observance of law.' He replied that this was all very well for people on the field of battle but should not apply to those who were not engaged. Meanwhile Strode and Spencer appear to have remained at large.[5]

On Friday 5 August the Lords heard that Chief Justice Bramston of the King's Bench had been commanded by the King to attend him at York.[6] If civil war should come, the Lord Chief Justice of England as Chief Coroner had authority to pronounce judgement of attainder on any rebel slain in battle, so as to work corruption of blood and forfeiture of lands and goods.'[7] Having been bailed in the sum of £10,000 for his part in the ship-money business and having an estate at Skreens near Roxwell, Essex, uncomfortably close to London, he could not afford to obey the King's command. He had been reinforced in this view by discussions with the Earl of Portland, the Earl of Lincoln and others faithful to the King's interests. The fact that Bramston reported the King's command to the Lords meant quite simply that he had no intention of going to York and wanted a formal order to stay and attend upon their House according to his writ of assistance. He got it.[8]

The other ship-money judges were in no great hurry to declare for the King. If they did, they would of course forfeit their bail. For the present, Chief Baron Davenport, now enjoying a holiday, managed to remain virtually neutral. Baron Weston, also at home, disappeared from sight and Baron Trevor, who was to emerge as a judicial vicar of Bray, remained at Westminster. Sir Francis Crawley of the Common Pleas was another judge who took time to make up his mind; though he did eventually join the King. For want of evidence in so serious a charge as high treason Sir Robert Berkeley had still not been tried. In November he was allowed to sit once more in King's Bench. In the view of the two Houses he had since his impeachment 'carried himself with modesty and humility'. That meant that there was no fight left in him.[9]

All over England the sheriffs' trumpeters at the assizes were heralding the clash between the forces of King and Parliament. Both sides appealed to the authority of the judges and called for the support of the sheriffs. Grand juries continued to represent their own views as the unanimous voice of counties that were, in fact, bitterly divided. In many places sheriffs and grand juries found themselves openly opposed either to the commissioners of array or to local members of Parliament. In one, at least, the sheriff's guard protected the commissioners. In others the citizens took to arms and repelled them. Almost incredibly there was no bloodshed, in spite of the great concourse of opposing factions and all the drilling and armed preparation. There seemed to be a conscious effort to avoid violence until the troops of both sides were ready for war. The judges continued to dispense justice, trimmed a little to the wind of the particular town where they happened to be sitting. Nowhere was this more true than on the Western circuit where Sir Robert Foster of the Common

Pleas bowed to every wind that blew.[10]

At Bath, Foster had an order from the King to forward the commission of array and another from the two Houses to declare it illegal. The first was backed by the physical presence of the commissioners led by the Marquess of Hertford. The second was supported by the sheriff and grand jury. The judge in his charge declined to notice both orders. But when the constables of some twenty-one hundreds pressed him to declare his opinion he pronounced the commission of array illegal and ordered the votes of both Houses pronouncing it illegal to be read in court. In Royalist Cornwall Foster could afford to be braver. In his charge to the grand jury he 'made a little noise' to the declarations and votes of both Houses, but when he came to the King's declarations 'he had vigour, voice and rhetoric to act that home.' Although Foster later joined the King at Oxford, he 'sayled betwixt wind and water very politiquely', so that in 1643 Parliament actually asked the King to continue him in office.[11]

In the counties of the Oxford circuit they were mainly for the King. There was little public opposition to Royalist sheriffs and Royalist grand juries and so Baron Henden had a comparatively easy time. He must have been seventy or so, and he managed to stay in office until he died eighteen months later.[12]

Chief Justice Bankes of the Common Pleas had already joined the King. On the Norfolk circuit he was the senior judge in commission with Serjeant Whitfield. In his charge to grand juries he read the King's charge to the judges, but he dared not pronounce the Militia Ordinance illegal although the King had written to him personally commanding him on his allegiance to do it. As Bankes put it himself 'it is not safe for me to deliver anie opinion in things that are voted in the Housses.' In spite of his allegiance to the King he managed to keep on such good terms with influential members of both Houses that in 1643 they asked the King that he, too, might continue in office.[13]

Sir Robert Heath, the judge for the Northern circuit, had also deserted Westminster. At York he read the King's charge to the judges and received in return a petition from the grand jury listing the steps needed to put the county on a war footing for the King's protection. He had certainly chosen his side, but he had also taken great care to write a humble submission to the Lords explaining his conflict of loyalties, acknowledging his duty to their lordships' House and expressing the hope that the King would release him within a few days. He was insuring himself against the two Houses winning the war.[14]

Sir Edmond Reeve of Common Pleas was the most strongly Parliamentarian of all the judges of assize that summer. He took the Midland circuit and at Leicester he had to face the King in person. Charles asked him to try Dr. Bastwick, a senior officer in the militia, for treason. Reeve admitted that the evidence was overwhelming but pleaded with the King to have him tried by all the judges, pointing out that a resolution of the whole bench of judges would be of more value to the King than the opinion of one judge sitting alone. Reeve said that if he tried the case alone he would only destroy himself without advancing the King's cause. The point was at least arguable, but by praying the King almost at once to release the man he acknowledged to be a traitor, he betrayed the real truth: his excuse was hollow and he was himself under Parliamentary pressure. Like Bankes (but on the other side) he was trying to satisfy both the opposing parties. The King refused him and took Bastwick to York.[15] Only Malet was firm and uncompromising in the face of an unconstitutional illegality which he could no longer tolerate in good conscience.

By careful trimming, the common law judges had postponed the moment of open conflict upon their circuits. But blood had already been spilt in one place at least. On 15 June in Manchester, in the County Palatine of Lancaster, Lord Strange backed by a band of armed troopers broke up a meeting of townsmen who were putting the Militia Ordinance into effect. They were beaten off and they retired leaving one of their number dead. For the moment that was an isolated outbreak of violence. Each side was busy mustering its forces, winning what it could without bloodshed. Lord Goring secured Portsmouth for the King. The Marquess of Hertford put himself at the head of a Royalist army in the West. In Warwickshire the Earl of Northampton stopped some Parliamentary guns on their way to Warwick Castle. Hampden arrested the Earl of Berkshire before he could execute the commission of array in Berkshire. Oliver Cromwell seized the college plate at Cambridge before it could be sent to the King.[16]

The war was to be fought by two minorities bitterly opposed. Each side was joined by many for their own protection, because they feared the consequences to their lives and estates if they remained aloof. The condition of many must have been summed up by Henry Oxinden of Deane in Wingham, Kent.

'Mee thinks my condition beetwixt the commission of aray and ordinance of Parliament is like his that is between Scylla and Charybdis, and nothing butt omnipotencie can bring mee clearely and reputably off . . .'[17]

In the spring there were few real Royalists and they of doubtful value to the King. As war approached so the King got increasing supplies of horse, foot and money from members of the peerage. When his standard was raised he was to secure a further access of strength from thousands of Englishmen who distrusted their King, his court and his policies—and yet held kingship dearer than life: Sir Edmund Verney, his standard bearer, who wished that he would submit to the two Houses, yet in honour could not forsake him, felt his position so keenly that he rode into the Battle of Edgehill without 'armes or buff cote' so that he could salve his conscience in death;[18] Lord Falkland, his principal secretary of state, accepted his service with deep misgiving and fulfilled his hope of dying in battle by riding into the advancing Parliamentary line at Newbury.

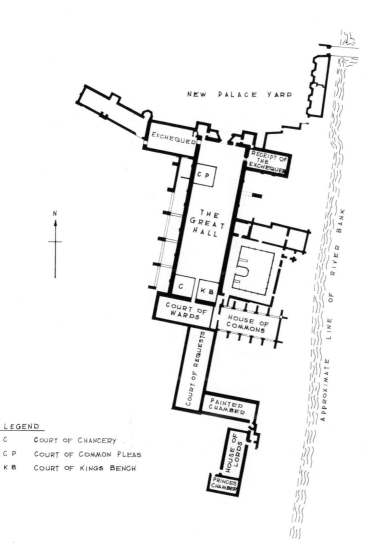

LEGEND

C   COURT OF CHANCERY

C P   COURT OF COMMON PLEAS

K B   COURT OF KINGS BENCH

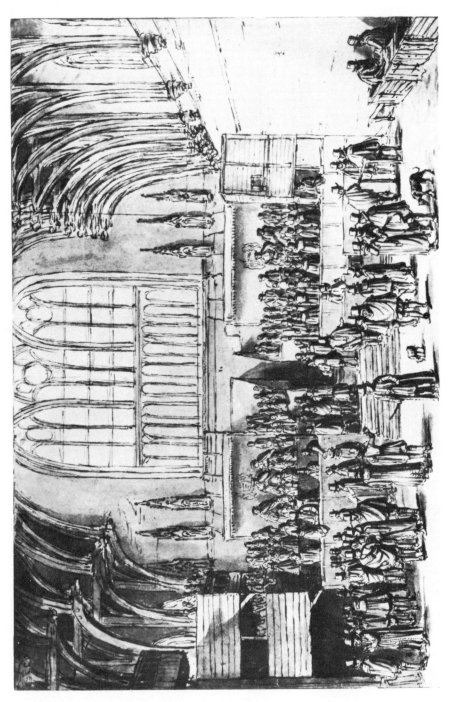

Westminster Hall, west end [actually south], with the Courts of Chancery and King's Bench in session

Market Cross   Upper Court House   Lower Court House
                                (*Nisi Prius* Court)   (Crown Court)

The Site of the Maidstone Assizes 1641–42

Gilt badge depicting head of Charles I. (See p. 198 n. 24)

Come Freind, ARRAY your selfe, and never looke,
To prosper in your Di=ō=cease your Booke
Meddle with it lesse: for you must Arme
If you intend to keepe your selfe from harme:
Vse now your power only against those
That are the Kingdomes friends (but yet our foes)

J: D: mallet

Mr. Justice Malet, aged about sixty

Mr. Justice Malet, aged about seventy-nine

The Commons Chamber during the Long Parliament

Lady Malet, c. 1661

DIEV. VOV: LANT, IE SVIS CONEN

Hatchments of Baldwin and Sir Thomas Malet in All Saints Church, Poyntington

They would rather die than choose the alternatives offered by King Pym and King Charles.[19]

We do not have to believe that Malet was a Royalist judge because he opposed the will of the two Houses. He was steeped in a strong family tradition of service to the constitution and to the Crown. He could trace his descent in an unbroken line from the first Great Chamberlain of England. He was proud of his great-grandfather who had been solicitor to Henry VIII. But his family are prouder to this day that a Malet was one of the guarantors of Magna Carta. When King and constitution were opposed it was the constitution which they tended to support. Malet himself was once an outstanding critic of Stuart abuses. He was now as strongly opposed to the unwarranted assumption of power by the Parliamentarians. In a sense he, too, rejected a choice between two evils. But his was a constructive, purposeful choice. He chose the path of duty as he understood it. And he was willing to suffer for what he believed.

Sir Richard Onslow's letter from Kingston-upon-Thames was read to the Commons on Friday 5 August. They resolved to arrest Malet, notwithstanding the adjournment of the assizes to Dorking; this confirms the view that there was originally no intention to arrest him until the assizes were over. They left the Committee for the Safety of the Kingdom to consider what force would be needed to bring Malet to Westminster and required the sheriff of Surrey and his officers to help in bringing him up.[20] This posed a problem for George Price, the sheriff, whose orders from the King were in direct conflict with those from the House.[21] And then Sir Philip Stapleton, a member of the Committee for the Safety of the Kingdom, was dispatched to the Lords to tell them of the Commons's resolutions. Stapleton reached the Lords before the morning's business was half done and they lost no time in agreeing with the Commons.[22] They sent James Maxwell, the gentleman usher of the black rod, with a serjeant-at-arms and a troop of horse to Kingston. Maxwell and Onslow between them had little difficulty in persuading the sheriff of Surrey where his duty lay. The King at York was too far away to protect him.[23] They fetched Malet from his lodging and took him south of the river to London Bridge and Westminster. You could use the horse ferry bridge if you were a small party, but this was out of the question for such a cavalcade.[24] The escort was the biggest that Malet would ever have while he was judge of assize. There were the twenty-five troopers of Sir Richard Onslow, there was the troop that the Lords had sent to reinforce them and there was the sheriff and his men.[25]

For Malet the latter part of the journey to Westminster must have been full of memories as they rode down St. Margaret's Hill (now Borough High Street), past St. George's Church, the White Lyon prison, which served as gaol for Surrey county, and past King's Bench prison towards London Bridge. At the bottom of St. Margaret's Hill Malet's party bore right down Long Southwark past the familiar landmarks. In the angle at the fork roads was the unfenced churchyard where the great Southwark market was held. Above the market place they could see the roof and dormer windows of the court house where Malet had held the assizes five months before. Ahead lay London Bridge and the staples at bridgefoot where Captain Bunce had halted the Kentish petitioners and disarmed Lovelace and Boteler three months before. Here the sheriff and his escort should have taken their leave.[26]

Malet was brought to the Lords early on the Saturday morning and formally committed to the Tower.[27] James Maxwell, the gentleman usher, entered up in his accounts 'for Justice Malet £3'. It was one of the smaller items in a month of heavy expenditure on messengers from the Lords to distant parts of the kingdom.[28]

Malet's story was reported in contemporary letters and pamphlets. It was told in both Houses and is certain to have been spread quickly by word of mouth. It is sure to have been widely known. Malet's stand against the members of Parliament at Maidstone made a strong impression upon Sir John Sackville, who was present.[29] Malet's arrest at Kingston-upon-Thames, his journey as a prisoner to Westminster and his imprisonment in the Tower were remembered long afterwards as an example of 'the most extravagant severity that had ever been heard of' by Edward Hyde, later to become Earl of Clarendon. Clarendon described Malet's arrest and imprisonment as being 'to the unspeakable dishonour of the public justice of the Kingdom'.[30] Clarendon was a biased observer, yet many who had not taken sides must have been shocked that such treatment should be meted out to a judge doing his duty according to his conscience. Malet's courage and fate must surely have helped to influence many moderate people to take up arms for the King against Parliament or at least to condemn in private the arbitrary use of force by the two Houses. Soon more would be forced to choose between public support for Parliament and loss of their property. For many, who were still undecided, that would be the final spur, forcing them into the Royalist camp.

11

Epilogue: War and Peace

'Judge Mallet (I dare say) will do them justice.'
THOMAS SMITH
to Joseph Williamson, 17 September 1660[1].

When Malet had been in the Tower for a fortnight he petitioned the Lords for his release. It was the day after the royal standard was raised at Nottingham; civil war was at last an official fact. Malet explained that he had in the West Country a hundred miles from London six young children whom he had not seen for five months as well as an uncle of eighty and another kinsman of about the same age, both of whom were sick and weak and needed his advice. He apologized for his offence and asked for his release. If they would not let him go, he sought permission for Jane, his wife, to remain with him during his imprisonment because, he said, 'it would be unto her a farr greater discomfort and griefe to be removed from him.' But the Lords were busy with other, more important, matters. It was not until 3 September that they considered his petition and then they did not release him. They agreed to his wife visiting him in the Tower, but not to her living there.[2]

Lords and Commons had to make special arrangements to bind over until the next Surrey assizes all those who were due to appear at the assizes which Malet had adjourned to Dorking.[3] The Commons ordered Colonel Sir Edwin Sandys to arrest Sir Edward Dering and Sir George Strode.[4] Sandys with a force of 500 Parliamentary cavalry overran Kent, rounded up many of the Royalists and impounded their arms.[5] Apparently oblivious that civil war had already begun, Sir John Sedley organized yet more petitions to the Lords and Commons and these he presented to them on 30 August.[6] On the same day the Commons sent their serjeant-at-arms to arrest the authors of the Kentish petition framed at the summer assizes. They ordered Sandys to support him in making the arrests. By 16 September Sandys had completed the initial work of subjugating the county and Kent remained under Parliamentary control until 1648.[7]

The two Houses gave the King an unexpected advantage by seeming to say in a declaration of 6 September that all who did not support them were delinquents and their property forfeit. That declaration gave Charles an army with which to advance on London. He pushed on from Edgehill, was thrown back from the outskirts of the City at Turnham Green and retired to winter quarters at Oxford.[8]

On 25 November Malet again petitioned the Lords for his release. He said that he was sorry to have offended their lordships. He explained that he had 'a wife and many children in great distresse and want since his restraint' and that his own health was deteriorating. Their lordships did nothing.[9]

While the Royalists rallied and attacked once more in the districts where they had strongest support, Malet spent four winter months more in the Tower before summoning courage to petition once more. He was old. His health was failing and he must have known that if he stayed long enough in his cold damp cell he would die like Eliot before him. On 17 March 1643 he petitioned again, representing his urgent need to leave the Tower with his keeper so that he could 'provide for the reliefe of his distressed family'. This time the Lords heard and granted his petition at once, with the proviso that he returned each night to the Tower.[10]

In April negotiations between the King and his two Houses, which began immediately after Edgehill, broke upon the King's intransigence. On 29 April Malet was sufficiently emboldened by their lordships' favour to ask that he might lodge at Serjeants' Inn in Chancery Lane, with freedom to leave it for his private affairs, for his health and to go to church. The Lords acceded to his petition but ordered him to come to the bar and engage his reputation that he would not stir from London or Westminster without their leave. On Monday 1 May he appeared at the bar of the House and formally gave his promise.[11] However the Commons got to hear of it and on Saturday 6 May a general concern was expressed in the House that he should have been released, bearing in mind the fact that he 'had done generall disservices to the two Houses of Parliament and had been sent for and committed by order of both Howses'. Finally they despatched Denzil Holles (who had now forsaken the field of battle) with a message to the Lords to remind them that Malet was sent to the Tower by authority of the Committee for the Safety of the Kingdom appointed by Lords and Commons and asking that he be returned to prison to await the order of both Houses.[12]

The message was only partly true. It may have been the Committee for the Safety of the Kingdom which had Malet arrested at Kingston-upon-Thames and brought to the Lords. It may have been that Committee which recommended that he be imprisoned. But it was the Lords who sent him to the Tower. No one knew this better than Holles, who had been a party to the earlier proceedings, but he believed that Malet at sixty was still a dangerous man capable of stirring up trouble for the two Houses in the West Country. Holles was prepared to use any argument which he thought the Lords would accept. And there were no Royalists left in the Lords.[13]

When Holles reached the House of Lords he found that the peers had risen. The Commons were seriously concerned that Malet might attempt to escape to the West Country before the two Houses met again. Upon their own authority they arrested Malet and kept him in custody until the Monday when they sent Holles once more to the Lords. He asked for and got Malet's remand to the Tower. A year ago the Lords would have taken the gravest exception to Holles's argument and the action of his fellow members. Now their constitutional position was precarious and they acceded.[14]

The year 1643 was one of Royalist victories. At Chalgrove Field Rupert forced Essex to abandon the blockade of Oxford. In Yorkshire Newcastle routed the Fairfaxes. In the West the Royalists defeated the Parliamentary forces at Stratton, Lansdown Hill and Roundway Down, captured Bristol and besieged a defiant Gloucester.[15] It was twelve months since Malet was imprisoned in the Tower when on 11 August 1643 he again petitioned the Lords that he might be confined to his chamber at Serjeants' Inn and be free to take the air for his health. The Lords were sympathetic, but this time they were careful to ask the view of the Lower House. The Commons undertook to send back a reply by messengers of their own. But they never did.[16]

Following the King's victories in the West, Somerset came once more under Royalist control. The King in Oxford seized the opportunity to issue a new commission of the peace for Somerset on 31 October 1643, confirming his own supporters in the county magistracy. Malet was included in the new commission. It may have heartened him that he was still in the mind and favour of his Sovereign, but it had no material effect, for he was still in prison. When he was released he never sat at quarter sessions.[17]

Not till the Parliamentary armies had won the battle of Marston Moor did the House of Commons turn their attention to Malet once more. And then on 22 July 1644 they proposed to the Lords that he be exchanged for three Parliamentary prisoners of war held by the King's forces at Oxford. The Lords agreed, but the proposal hung fire.[18] On 18 September Lady Malet petitioned the Lords reminding them that her husband had now been two years in prison, old and sick, while his children were in the country dependent upon the charity of friends. She asked permission to visit her children and to raise money from friends for her husband's wants. The Lords agreed to this request and authorized the issue of a pass for her, two maids, a man and a horse and a coach with another four horses and a coachman to go to Poyntington.[19]

Before Lady Malet could make arrangements for her journey, the Commons again asked the Lords if Malet could be exchanged, this time for Sir John Temple, Master of the Rolls in Ireland, a prisoner at Dublin Castle. They proposed that Malet should go in person to the King at Oxford to negotiate the exchange. The Lords took some time to consider the request and had to be prompted again three days later when the

Commons asked particularly that good security be taken of Malet before he be given his liberty. On 19 October the Lords agreed to the exchange provided that Malet put up substantial bail in case Sir John Temple was not released. But Malet, already nearly destitute, was unable to find anyone to go bail for him. Reluctantly the Lords agreed to accept his word that he would return to custody if Temple could not be released. When he attended the House they had second thoughts and fixed bail at £3,000 in his own recognizance upon his solemn promise. Finally they released him on 6 November on condition that he should give himself up if he had failed to arrange the exchange in three months and twenty days. On the same day Malet petitioned the Lords and they agreed that his wife and servants might be allowed to accompany him.[20]

In the time allowed to him Malet was able to obtain the King's warrant for the release of Sir John Temple from prison in Ireland, but was not able to satisfy the Lords about his date of release. On 18 January 1645 they therefore accorded him an extra month to complete the business.[21] Meanwhile Malet remained in Oxford. At last Sir John Temple reached London and on 3 February the Lords freed Malet from his bail and gave leave to his servant John Wingate to go and tell him of their order. From then onwards he was free of Parliamentary restraint, but the King commanded him to stay in Oxford and attend his service. His brothers, Bankes, Heath, Foster and Crawley, were already there and had all been made doctors of civil law by the university. The King had made Heath Chief Justice of King's Bench in place of Bramston, who dared not join him.[22]

Meanwhile the Parliamentary commanders became discredited by their failure to exploit the victory over the Royalists at Marston Moor. Cromwell seized the opportunity to force through the two Houses the Self Denying Ordinance which made members of both Houses resign their military commands and another ordinance which created the New Model Army to be paid out of national taxation under one commander, Sir Thomas Fairfax. These two steps laid the foundation of victory for the Parliamentary forces.[23]

Malet was continuously in the King's service at Oxford for a period of eighteen months.[24] We know very little of the circumstances because the records were later burned to avoid incriminating the Royalists. Almost certainly he acted in a judicial capacity. He probably acted as assistant in the Royalist Parliament at Oxford. It was a difficult time. By mid January 1645 many members of both Houses at Oxford were very short of money, having left their estates (sometimes in enemy hands) and receiving no income from their tenants. A substantial number had drifted away to Westminster and compounded for their estates.[25] Malet himself remained, although his estate was sequestered and his own rents from Exeter and Devon properties were unpaid either because the houses had been burned to the ground or by order of county committees or because tenants could not be brought to court.[26] The Royalists who remained at Oxford mostly wanted peace and some of them verged on disloyalty. The King was forced to arrest three of the peers and on 10 March 1645 he adjourned Parliament until October. The Oxford Parliament was no longer a help to him.[27]

That summer the tide of war ran heavily against the King. Fairfax defeated him at Naseby, smashed his Western army at Langport and recaptured Bristol.[28] On 24 November 1645 the two Houses disabled Malet from being a judge, as if he were actually dead, because they alleged he had 'advised and assisted the war against the Parliament'. Robert Heath of King's Bench, Robert Foster and Francis Crawley of Common Pleas, and Richard Weston, a baron of the Exchequer, suffered a similar fate. From then until the end of the reign the three common law courts each had only one judge who sat at Westminster.[29]

The Parliamentary army was now decisively larger than the Royalist army; it was better disciplined and supported by a more effective fund-raising organization. In the first three months of 1646 it reduced Devon and Cornwall, in May it captured the King at Newark and in June the garrison at Oxford surrendered. The terms of the capitulation, known as the Articles of Oxford, were unusually generous. They allowed the officers of the garrison to go free upon condition that they compounded for their estates.[30] Sir Thomas Fairfax had printed a supply of permits which allowed the bearers to pass the guards with 'servants, horses, armes, goods and all other necessaries'. He issued one of these passes to Malet on 24 June, four days after the surrender, and Malet lodged it with the committee for compounding at Goldsmiths' Hall in London. No similar copy reached the committee in respect of Lady Malet or John Malet. This is not necessarily proof that they were not there. It may have been simply that they had no estate for which to compound.[31]

It is not completely clear where Malet's family were during the early part of the Civil War. In September 1644, Jane, his wife, was in Westminster and the children were at Poyntington. We know this because Jane petitioned the House of Lords for a pass to go to Poyntington in that month.[32] In November of that year the Lords agreed to her going with Malet to Oxford when her husband was negotiating his exchange.[33] After the surrender of Oxford, Malet went back to live not at Poyntington but at Exeter, where he owned property.[34] By that time his personal estate had been plundered. A list of his assets contains no mention of furniture or pictures at Poyntington.[35] Sometime between September 1644 and late 1646 it would appear that continued living at Poyntington became impossible. Poyntington was only three miles from Sherborne Castle which became a key point in the struggle for the West. It was inevitable that the garrison at Sherborne should send out patrols to the surrounding villages when the Castle was not invested and that the besieging forces should billet those villages when it was. Malet's house at Poyntington survived the thinly spread Roundhead domination of Somerset in the early part of the war. There is circumstantial evidence that it was sacked between 1644 and 1646 and a probability that it was done by the forces under Fairfax which captured Sherborne Castle in August 1645. Family tradition says that the Roundheads took everything of value, including Lady Malet's wedding ring. Her portrait, painted after the Restoration, shows her wearing a black bone ring on the little finger of her left hand. This may have been a mourning ring rather than a mute protest at the robbery.[36]

Malet's eldest son, John, was still only twenty-three at the beginning of 1646.[37] He was at various times serving under arms in the Royalist garrisons at Oxford, Exeter, Sherborne and Bridgwater.[38] There is a contemporary portrait of him wearing a steel cavalry cuirass. Family tradition has it that he commanded a body of horsemen with which he constantly harassed the Roundheads, retiring at times to Ireland.[39]

On 3 June 1646, Malet's second son, Baldwin, is said to have been killed fighting at the age of nineteen. A hatchment in the parish church at Poyntington testifies to the man, the date and the cause:

BALDWIN MALET SECOND SONNE OF Sr THOMAS MALET DYED IN THE KING'S SERVICE THE 3d DAY OF JUNE An: Dni: 1646 IN THE TWENTIETH YEARE OF HIS AGE.[40]

The story of his death was embellished and handed down from one generation to another until it was finally committed by the rector to writing in 1870. He believed that Baldwin was killed in a local skirmish between the loyal villagers of Poyntington and a force of Roundhead soldiers.

The scene of the fiercely fought battle, in which [Baldwin] and a large number of combatants fell, is just beyond the limits of the parish (within the borders of Dorset), where are still to be seen many mounds marking the graves of those who fell in the contest. To this very day that battle-field is to the villagers of Poyntington and Oborne a place of dread as the shades of night draw on, and very few indeed of either village are bold enough to pass alone near to the spot where headless men and one headless woman are said to be seen in troops, about the time which Disraeli terms 'the witching hour of two'. And to this very day also my village children listen with trembling hearts and bated breath to the fireside tales in which are handed down, from generation to generation, the deeds of valour done by their village ancestors; and especially by that knight—the son of the great judge who lived in the big house—who is said to have leaped into battle over the gate dividing the two counties; leaping on horseback with all his armour on right into the midst of the fight, and, after killing more than a score, to have been within an hour brought back dead to his father's house, and, for fear of the plague, to have been buried the very next day.[41]

Nineteenth-century rectors tended to be enthusiastic but not always accurate historians. There is no other supporting evidence for the account, either in the parish registers or elsewhere. It is possible that Baldwin died fighting to defend his home in June 1646 and that Malet's house was not sacked until then. It is also possible that he died in June 1645 and that the house was sacked in the fighting that lead to the capture of Sherborne Castle by Fairfax's forces in August of that year.[42]

Malet's third son, Michael, was growing up. His fourth son, Thomas, must have seen military service at some time after the capture of Oxford, for he was apparently a major by 1662. Alice Malet, the fifth child, was still a spinster. Katharine, the sixth child, married Thomas Chafe of Sherborne. We know nothing about the remaining children, Zenobia and Elizabeth, at this period.[43]

Under the Articles of Oxford Malet was allowed to compound for his 'delinquency'. He put in his application to the committee for compositions at Goldsmiths' Hall on 24 September 1646, admitting that he had stayed in Oxford from the time when he was sent by the two Houses until the surrender of the garrison.[44] On 19 November he rendered to the committee a detailed statement of his estate. He is described at the time as being 'of the citty of Exeter'. There is no word of assets in Poyntington. He seems to have been deliberately vague in describing the land which he held in fee but it is clear that he did own and derive rents from a number of properties in Exeter itself and in Torrington and Honiton in Devon. The rents amounted in all to £93.11s.8d. per annum. He said that his personal estate had been plundered and all that remained were clothes and books worth £80. In addition he owed £800 to various creditors and the King owed him £750 in wages for his work as a justice of the Court of King's Bench. The committee accepted his statement and assessed his fine at £271.10s. He paid his debt on 15 December.[45]

While Malet was still in the Tower, another committee, the Committee for Advance of Money, set up to finance the Parliamentary war effort, had assessed him and his son John at £800, a twentieth part of their estate. When he had not discharged his debt by 16 September 1646, they ordered him to be brought in custody to London to pay it. Apparently he eluded them, because two further orders followed and then for a period he was respited.[46]

In 1646 the assizes were resumed in Somerset after an intermission during the Civil War,[47] and at the summer assizes in 1647 Malet's son John established the right of Malet's uncle Michael to the rents from the lease of considerable family properties in Somerset and Devon including the Manor of West Quantockshead with its 'mansion house' of St. Audries, amounting in all to a yearly rent roll of some £230 per annum. The judgement was confirmed in King's Bench and Michael Malet, who was too old to have taken part in the wars, began drawing the rent. Sir Thomas Malet, as his heir, had the reversion when he should die. This came to the attention of the Somerset county committee when he asked them to confirm the extent of his Somerset estate to the Committee for

Compounding in London. On 29 January 1648 they reported to London that he owned all these properties. Malet was asked to explain and he wrote a carefully worded memorandum for the committee for compounding explaining that it was his uncle Michael who drew the rents, that he knew nothing of his title to the properties at the time he made his composition and that his own succession to the reversion upon his uncle's death was not at all certain.[48] He persuaded Lord Fairfax to intervene on his behalf.[49] A fresh fine was set at £300. Four days later the committee found that instead of Sir Thomas holding the estate in reversion, he was actually in possession. They raised the fine to £600.[50]

Malet felt he had been unfairly treated. The business dragged on and in October he was given leave to go to London to argue his case. He was now sixty-six. The committee allowed him one month to pay the fine,[51] and somehow he found the money. Finally, in November 1648, the Lords and Commons passed an ordinance to absolve Sir Thomas Malet and John Malet from their delinquency on payment of £871.[52] Their assessment by the Committee for Advance of Money was then discharged.[53]

Malet was already hard pressed and could only have found the money by borrowing. In July 1649 he and his uncle Michael apparently raised a mortgage on properties in Devon, Exeter and Somerset, in order to pay for his composition. The properties in Somerset included the mansion house and estate at Poyntington which were the home of his uncle Michael.[54]

Meanwhile there had been a series of protracted negotiations between the beaten King, the two Houses and the Army. In August 1647 the army marched on London and expelled eleven of the Presbyterian majority in the House of Commons. In May 1648 a number of Presbyterian soldiers and a remnant of Cavaliers declared for the King. They were quickly suppressed by the New Model Army while the great mass of people in England looked on. The Scots crossed the border and Cromwell defeated them decisively at Preston. The Second Civil War was over. In December 1648 Colonel Pride expelled the Presbyterians from the House of Commons, leaving behind a subservient 'rump' which by resolution removed both the King and the House of Lords from the constitution. The trial and execution of the King was only an epilogue. Charles, who had failed at so much, achieved genuine greatness now. The fire of nostalgia would one day burn for his son.[55]

Soon after Michael Malet inherited the manor of West Quantockshead, Sir Thomas Malet's son John went to live at St Audries. His fighting was over. His father had compounded on his behalf with his enemies. It was time to settle down, to marry and bring up a family. Sometime prior to 1653 he married Florentia, the daughter of Sir John Wyndham of Orchard Wyndham. Her father had been a justice of the peace in Somerset and had died in 1649. Their first child cannot have been born before 1653 and they seem to have had children almost at the rate of one every year. In 1660 there were five still living. There was Baldwin, the heir, and William, the second child, who must have been born before 1655, the year that Anne, the third child, was buried at St. Audries. There was Elizabeth, born in 1656, another Anne, born in 1657, Katharine, born in 1658, and John, born in 1659.[56]

On 24 April 1650 Michael Malet, Sir Thomas's third son, was admitted as a student to the Middle Temple. His father was no longer a master of the bench but he got the benchers to agree that Michael should only pay twenty shillings for his admission, although so small a sum was without precedent. Michael cannot have been more than twenty-two or three. Five years later, on 25 May 1655, at the request of his father, he was 'of grace' called to the bar. The benchers agreed to shorten his period as a student. From then onwards he shared with a fellow member one of the smallest chambers for two in Middle Temple.[57]

Early in 1651 Malet's uncle Michael died. He was old, but he and Malet had been very close. Malet was his sole executor and residuary legatee, but much of his property had been mortgaged to pay for Malet's composition. Michael remembered the parish where he had passed his later years. He left forty shillings to the poor of Poyntington.[58]

Charles II had returned to Scotland in 1650 and there promised to establish Presbyterianism in Scotland and England. In return he persuaded a Scottish army to invade England and put himself at its head. But the combination of Cavaliers and invading Scottish Presbyterians alienated many who might have flocked to his colours. He was soundly beaten at Worcester and, dressed as a serving man, he found his way to the coast and eventually to France. Twice on his journey he stayed at Trent Manor, five miles from Malet's Poyntington. Thereafter, amid wrangling, impoverished courtiers, he spent a wretched life in exile awaiting an invitation to return.[59]

In the West Country and indeed in all England there followed ten years of financial and military oppression which united once more the moderate gentry who had opposed each other so bitterly during the First Civil War. When Oliver Cromwell died, the country became a prey to the 'weak but violent rule of soldiers, united indeed against civilians, but divided against themselves'. A number of judges were dismissed either because they opposed military rule or because they refused to take the oath ordered by the Rump Parliament. Others resigned. The country's administrative machinery was breaking down. In January 1660 General Monck, who commanded the army in Scotland, marched south on London.[60]

There was, of course, no king—at least not in England. The House of Lords had been abolished in 1649. The members of the House of Commons in 1660 were a small 'rump' of the original gathering which had been elected in 1640. They were not representative of national opinion and they were unpopular in the country. Monck had declared for a free Parliament, but he had no need to drive out the Rump by force. In late February he simply withdrew his guards from the Palace of Westminster and allowed the excluded members to enter. But before he did so, he secured from them a promise that they would vote for a dissolution and an election. The night that they returned the bells of the City rang out and the sky was lit by the light of a hundred bonfires. The Commons then proceeded to annul their engagement to be faithful to the Commonwealth without a king or House of Lords. Finally, they entered into the bill for dissolving Parliament a proviso saving the rights of the Lords. Samuel Pepys went to Westminster Hall on the day of the dissolution and found everyone happy and talking of a king.[61]

In the ensuing elections the competition for seats was strong. Generally, the electors chose candidates who would support Charles II's return. Malet's son, Michael, was elected for Milborne Port in Somerset. It was a town only three miles from his home at Poyntington.[62]

The Parliament that met on 25 April was, of course, not summoned by a king. It is known as the Convention Parliament of 1660. Some of the Rump of the Commons in the Long Parliament, supported by Presbyterian lords, had hoped to dominate its proceedings, perhaps to exclude any obvious Royalists who might be elected, and to impose stringent conditions for the return of monarchy. There had been some doubt whether the Lower House would permit the continued existence of the Upper. In the Commons, those who wanted the King back as soon and as freely as possible were in a majority and it was fairly quickly realized that the continued existence of the Lords and Royalist members in the Commons were indispensable prerequisites to his return. In the Lords, ten Presbyterian peers assembled on the first day and elected as their Speaker the Earl of Manchester. Three peers who had never sat before took their seats in the afternoon. Two days later there was a total of thirty-six and the Presbyterians were outnumbered. In the succeeding days there was a steady trickle of peers into the House and only those created during hostilities were excluded.[63]

On 1 May the Lords recalled that no writs of assistance had been issued and they sent for the Lord Chief Baron and the Master of the Rolls. On the following day they ordered 'Serjeant Mallet' to attend the House as an assistant. We do not know precisely when Malet reached the Lords from his distant home in the West Country, but he was certainly sitting on the lower woolsack a week later when the two Houses and the army had accepted the King's Declaration of Breda and invited him to rule over them once more. No doubt Malet accompanied the members of both Houses who went that day to the Palace Gate and to Temple Bar where Charles II was proclaimed King. Then there were royal salutes from the guns of the Tower and a joyous ringing of bells in the churches of London and Westminster. Once more the night sky was lit by countless bonfires. The nightmare of military oppression and anarchy was drawing to an end.[64]

On 25 May the King landed at Dover and on 29 May, his birthday, he reviewed the army at Blackheath and heard loyal addresses from both

Houses at Whitehall. John Evelyn wrote in his diary that day:

'I stood in the Strand & beheld it & blessed God: And all this without one drop of bloud.'[65]

In his train, the King brought with him two servants whose advice had profoundly influenced his father in the months immediately preceding the outbreak of civil war in 1642. Edward Hyde, knighted by Charles I, was now Lord Chancellor and Chancellor of the Exchequer to Charles II, and John Colepeper, appointed Master of the Rolls and created Lord Colepeper of Thoresway by Charles I, had continued in office under Charles II. As Lord Chancellor, Hyde lost no time in removing the judges of the Interregnum from the bench and within two days of Charles II's arrival in London he had appointed others more certain to support the royal interest.[66] He reappointed Malet as judge of the King's Bench. To the Court of Common Pleas he reappointed Sir Robert Foster who was with Charles I at Oxford and who was one of those disabled from sitting as judges 'as if they were actually dead' by the ordinance of 1645. (Despite this ordinance, Foster had managed to remain on tolerable terms with the Protector and his Council.)[67] Hyde also appointed to the Common Pleas his first cousin Robert Hyde, who as a serjeant-at-law had also been with Charles I at Oxford, and to be a baron of the Exchequer he appointed Thomas Leeke who had been cursitor baron until 1645.[68]

Hyde did not take immediate steps to fill the remaining vacancies on the bench of the courts of common law. It was important to appoint the right men, men of integrity and learning. There was scope, too, for appointing some men of this stamp who had held judicial office during the Interregnum. And so he took time. On 1 June Sir Orlando Bridgeman, who had supported Charles I during the Civil War, became Chief Baron of the Exchequer. In June Edward Atkins, who had been an unwilling judge during the Interregnum, became a baron of the Exchequer. In July Hyde appointed one more judge to each of the courts of common law. Among them was Thomas Twisden, a nephew of Sir Roger Twysden of Roydon Hall in Kent.[69] His uncle was still living there.[70] Malet himself was now seventy-eight. His imprisonment in the Tower and his privations thereafter had weakened his health. He had lost all or nearly all of his teeth. The daily routine of the courts had become a burden to him. He was not strong enough to preside over the Court of King's Bench as Lord Chief Justice of England and that post remained vacant.[71]

At this point it may be of interest to record what had happened to the other 'principal actors' of the Kentish petition of March 1642 during the Civil War. The Earl of Bristol joined the King but continued to work for peace. He was hated by the Parliamentarians and out of sympathy with the Royalists. In 1644 he withdrew from Oxford and after short periods at Sherborne and Exeter went overseas, where he died in 1653. Sir George Strode fought for the King at Edgehill and was wounded.

His estates were sequestered and when Charles I was defeated he, too, went abroad. He returned to London at the Restoration, but died soon afterwards. Richard Spencer supported the Royalists and then compounded for his estate. Sir Edward Dering joined the Royalist army but had no stomach for fighting. In 1644 he also attempted to come to a composition with Parliament, but he died in the same year before he could get back his estate. Sir Roger Twysden was advised by his Parliamentarian friends not to return to Kent. After an unhappy period spent largely in prison, he was allowed to go home in 1650 after he, too, had compounded. He never became reconciled either to the Parliamentarians or to the Court. When the Restoration came, Sir Thomas Malet was the only one of these six 'principal actors' who received any reward from his King.[72]

During the month of June it was decided that the men who sat in judgement upon Charles I should be brought to trial. The judges and law officers of the Crown met under the chairmanship of Sir Orlando Bridgeman, Chief Baron of the Exchequer, in Serjeants' Inn, Fleet Street, to determine the method of trial. There were at that time only four judges on the bench. The remaining three were Sir Thomas Malet of King's Bench and Sir Robert Foster and Sir Robert Hyde of Common Pleas. They went to great lengths to ensure that the conduct of the trial should be fair. They decided to try the prisoners at the Old Bailey sessions house at Newgate by a commission of gaol delivery. This involved issuing writs to the lieutenant of the Tower, where they were imprisoned, to deliver them to the sheriffs of the City of London and issuing writs to the sheriffs of the City to deliver them to Newgate. It was a complicated procedure and required commissions of gaol delivery to be sent to the judges and law officers and other magistrates for both Middlesex and Newgate. But before that trial could take place it was necessary for Parliament to decide who should be tried and who should be pardoned.[73]

The tide of popular sentiment now ran so strongly for Charles II that he could, had he wished, have broken many of the fetters that Lords and Commons were able to impose upon government. This was not in the character of the easy-going King and it was totally foreign to the strongly held views of his Lord Chancellor, Sir Edward Hyde. Hyde held ever in his mind the great days of monarchy in the days of Elizabeth and to this ideal his thoughts and writings continually returned.[74]

It was Hyde's ideal, transcending narrow jealousies, old grudges and factional discords, which informed the King's policies at this time. It was his wish that the two Houses should quickly pass a bill of indemnity and oblivion which would heal the wounds of civil war and allow England to become strong and united once more. He wanted all to be pardoned except the Regicides, that is the men who had condemned Charles I to death. But the Presbyterians who had supported the republicans in the First Civil War were less merciful than Charles II or Hyde who had suffered so much at their hands. All through June, July and most of August the wrangle went on. The Commons agreed to make only three exceptions in addition to the Regicides and on 29 August the bill became law. It was a great victory for Hyde.[75]

In the meantime, preparations went ahead for the summer assizes. When the judges met to choose their circuits, Malet, as one of the most senior, was allowed the longest and most lucrative of all, the Oxford circuit. He was to share it with Baron Turnor and they both received their commissions and patents on 10 July. Turnor had only been appointed to the Court of Exchequer three days before. The coming assizes would be difficult. There was still a great deal of lawlessness in the country. The bill for indemnity and oblivion had not yet become law and its passage would affect the whole conduct of the assizes. There were unfilled vacancies in the courts of common law and it was important that the assizes should be invested with the full majesty of judicial authority; yet if the Lords were still sitting, they would have need of judges as assistants. For all these reasons it was decided to postpone the assizes until September when the bill for indemnity and oblivion would be law and Parliament should be dissolved.[76]

The counties of the Oxford circuit were Berkshire, Oxfordshire, Herefordshire, Shropshire, Gloucestershire, Monmouthshire, Staffordshire and Worcestershire. It took thirty-two days from the opening of the first assize until the ending of the last. The daily allowances for the circuit amounted in all to over £200.[77] Malet and Turnor wasted no time in issuing the summons of assize to the sheriffs of these counties.[78] Until Parliament was dissolved, they took their turn acting as assistants in the Lords.[79] During this time the commissions of the peace of the eight counties had to be altered to include their names.[80] Not only Malet, but his two sons, John and Michael, had already been put in the commission of the peace for Somerset.[81]

We know very little of what took place in the Oxford circuit in the summer assizes of 1660 because most of the records no longer exist. We do know that the assizes opened at Reading on 4 September and ended at Stafford on 4 or 5 October. At Hereford the presentment of the grand jury reflected the unruly state of the times. They presented seven people for assaults which resulted in death, six people for speaking offensive words of the Sovereign or the book of common prayer and one rector for refusing to use the book in his parish. Then came an unusual amount of burglaries and cases of stealing livestock. The grand jury complained particularly about large taxes collected from the inhabitants and apparently misapplied, and about lack of proper accommodation for themselves. A bridge in Hereford and the streets at Leominster were in a poor state of repair after the neglect of the last tumultuous years.[82] This year Malet had no time for vacation at Poyntington when the assizes were over.[83]

On 9 October proceedings against the Regicides opened at Hicks Hall, Clerkenwell, and the commission of oyer and terminer was read to the grand jury which consisted of five baronets, three knights, nine esquires and three gentlemen. Malet was one of the judges on the bench there and the prisoners were committed for trial on the following day. Twenty-eight prisoners—all the Regicides that could be found—were tried at the bar of the Sessions House at the Old Bailey.[84] Again, Malet was one of the judges. By then he had become a popular legend, because of his courage and suffering. People all over England looked to him to 'do justice' to the Regicides. Popular feeling at this time is summed up in a letter written by Thomas Smith to a friend lodging with Secretary Nicholas at Whitehall:

'Judge Mallet (I dare say) will do them justice; and for mercy, God send it them in ye other world, for they can expect but little of it here.'

But like Croke before him, Malet had become old and tired defending the things he believed to be right.[85]

The conduct of the trial was scrupulously fair although there was never any doubt about the feelings of the spectators. Malet summoned all his experience as a 'Parliament man', stretching back over forty-five years to show that the Commons never had any jurisdiction, save to try their own members. He went on to show that if murder is a crime, then the greatest crime of all is the murder of the King, who is the father of his people. He quoted the great Coke in his support. But his speech was rambling and discursive; it lacked judicial incision. He must have disappointed many of his admirers. Perhaps, too, he disappointed his King who had held vacant the Chief Justiceship of the King's Bench for so long. By contrast, Foster of Common Pleas was firm and vigorous. It was the unhappy result of Malet's rectitude and suffering in defence of his King that at seventy-eight he should now be weak in body and confused in mind, while Foster, who was much the same age but had bowed to the wind, should still have his strength.[86]

Thomas Harrison, the first Regicide to be convicted, was drawn on a hurdle to the gibbet at Charing Cross on 13 October. Pepys saw the whole horrible sentence executed. Thereafter there was a daily procession of convicted prisoners to the same place. George Fox, the Quaker, saw the crowds gathered there to see the bowels of the Regicides burned. On the next morning Fox went to Malet's chamber as he was robing before taking his seat once more at the Old Bailey to continue the trial of the Regicides. Fox found Malet under strain and thought he was 'peevish and froward'.[87] Almost as soon as the trial was over Sir Robert Foster was appointed to the Court of King's Bench as Lord Chief Justice of England. It was probably a correct decision in the circumstances and it cannot have been entirely unexpected, but it must have been a blow to Malet.[88]

In November Parliament reassembled after the recess. Hyde filled the remaining vacancies in the courts of common law[89] and on the 24th of the month Malet wrote a petition to the King explaining that he had been 'much weakened both in person and fortune'. He said that he was no longer able to fulfil the duties of his office sitting long hours in draughts at Westminster Hall during the winter months. He asked to be excused attendance in court so that he could

> 'spend the more of the short remainder of his life (as by duty hee is bound) in prayers to Almighty God for the long continuance of your Majesty's prosperous reigne.'

He knew that he had not much longer to live.[90]

The King replied to Malet's petition that he would never require of anyone who had served him so faithfully to do anything 'beyond what there healthe and yeares shall enable them'. He kept Malet at his place as judge of King's Bench, with the fees normally attaching to the appointment, but excused his daily attendance in Westminster Hall.[91] Malet stayed at Westminster until the dissolution of the Convention Parliament in late December, sitting in King's Bench when he felt fit enough to do so.[92]

Charles II was crowned in Westminster Abbey on St. George's Day 1661 and Hyde, his Lord Chancellor, whom he raised to a baron after the dissolution, he now created Earl of Clarendon. The House of Commons that was elected to sit in May 1661 was mainly composed of landowners loyal to the King. Power went to its head and it sought to impose on a substantial dissenting minority its own articles of faith. By doing so it brought about the cleavage of society which Clarendon sought to avoid. Out of its own intolerance it created the division of 'Whig' and 'Tory' to replace the division of 'Roundhead' and 'Cavalier'. It was ironic that the measures which it introduced came to be known as the Clarendon Code.[93]

One of those excluded from the Act of Oblivion was Sir Henry Vane whose report to the House of Commons on 2 August 1642 had been largely instrumental in securing Malet's second and longer imprisonment in the Tower. He was committed for trial on a charge of treason at the Court of King's Bench. Malet was one of his judges. Vane was condemned to be hanged, drawn and quartered, but the King allowed him the privilege of being beheaded on Tower Green. For more than two hundred years after his death his headless ghost was said to haunt his home at Fairlawn, where once his father had invited Sir Roger Twysden to dinner in order to question him about the Kentish petition of March 1642.[94] Malet never rode circuit after the first post-Restoration assizes in the summer of 1660.[95] He is not mentioned at all in the *Lords Journals* during 1661, but his name does occur in the law reports.[96] In 1662 he is recorded as once more acting as assistant to the Lords during February and April; he took to the Commons the bill to reverse Strafford's attainder.[97] He certainly attended court during all four terms of that year, but rather infrequently.[98] He had, meanwhile, found an old deed by which the lands which he held in Devon and Somerset could not revert to him absolutely unless he paid £100 to the King. He asked the King for leave to pay it, wording his petition carefully so that his eldest son John should inherit the estates if he himself should die first. The King considered the petition in Council, but it was so long and complicated that he could only pass it to his Treasurer for advice. The Treasurer was equally at a loss and asked the help of the Attorney General, who put the issue into shorter, simpler language and recommended that the request be granted. The grant was finally authorized in Council in September.[99]

Malet's last reported appearance in court was in May 1663.[100] In June he received a complete dispensation from further attendance in court and on circuit by reason of his great age. He was given a pension of £1,000 per annum.[101] He received a fiat for a baronet's patent under the sign manual of Charles II dated 19 May. In recognition of the fact that he had voluntarily paid the maintenance of thirty foot soldiers in the army of Ireland for three whole years he was excused the normal payment of £1,095.[102] But a patent for his baronetcy never passed the Great Seal. His descendant Octavius Warre Malet suggests:

'It may have been that he thought it was not a sufficient requital for his sufferings and services, or on account of his advanced age and impoverished circumstances, or that he was a claimant to a barony (still in abeyance).'[103]

In fact, he was now relatively well off. Following his petition to the King in the previous year and after payment of the modest sum of £100 into the exchequer, he now held for himself and his heirs the following freehold properties:

The Manors of St. Audries, West Quantockshead, Brompton Ralph, Tolland, North Petherton, the Advowsons of the Church of West Quantockshead, and the Rectory of Otterford and other lands in St. Audries, West Quantockshead, Brompton Ralph, Tolland, North Petherton, Wembdon, Bridgwater, Langford, Binfield, Preston, Bindon, Milverton, Poyntington and Stowell in Somerset.

The Manor of Gittisham, and other lands in Gittisham, Honiton, Bradninch, Colyton, Raleigh [?Combe Raleigh], Oldiscombe, Vermantry, Awliscombe, Collwell and Offwell in Devon.[104]

Perhaps he was too old and tired to worry about baronetcies. One important task remained to him, to see that his worldly possessions were safely handed over to his family. He made his last will in May 1664. After commending his soul to God and his body to a Christian burial, he left to his 'loving wife Jane' all his property in Poyntington and Stowell in Somerset. His eldest son, John, was already established with his family at St. Audries, West Quantockshead. To him Malet left all his remaining property in Somerset, Devon and the City of Exeter. John was an active justice of the peace and was to become a member of Parliament and Recorder of Bridgwater. There were some small bequests which included five pounds for his 'very loving friend Mr. Fox the parson' who had come to live in Poyntington in 1643.[105]

He died on 19 December 1665 at the age of eighty-three and was buried in the churchyard of All Saints, Poyntington. His hatchment still hangs in the church to this day—next to that of his son, Baldwin, who 'died in the King's service'. It is emblazoned with his coat of arms. The crest is a griffin's head issuing out of a ducal coronet. Instead of his older family motto 'Ma force de en havlt', beneath his coat are the words 'Dieu voulant je suis content'. He had shown himself worthy of a proud and illustrious line. He was content with his lot.[106] Perhaps his most fitting epitaph was written over twenty years before:

'Mallet caryed himself slowtly and bravely.
Ye manner of it I knowe ye have heard.'[107]

Appendix I

Portraits of Mr. Justice Malet

I have been able to identify and locate with certainty only two original portraits of Mr. Justice Malet. One is an engraving published in 1642 and the other an oil painting done in 1661. Both are interesting: the first as a political comment and the second, not only for the fine execution of the original, but also because it gave rise to a number of copies at first, second, third and even fourth hand. Here is an account of those I have found.

The engraving published in 1642
This is in the British Library. It is by an unknown artist and measures $11\frac{3}{4} \times 8$ ins. It contains three quite separate pictures; each is a full-length caricature of the subject. Left is Judge Malet, centre is Archbishop Williams and right is Colonel Sir Thomas Lunsford, The shelf mark is 669 f 6 (71). It is described and reproduced in A. M. Hind (completed by Margery Corbett and Michael Norton), *Engraving in England in the 16th and 17th Century* (Cambridge 1952–64) III 356 and plate 201, and it is also listed in the *Catalogue of Prints and Drawings in the British Museum* 4 vols. (1870) I 246 no. 341. A copy by W. J. Smith exists in the Ashmolean Museum, Sutherland Collection, in Clarendon, 3 vols. (Oxford 1707), grangerized copy by Sutherland; collected 1795-1835 (grangerized version 1837) I 431.

The oil painting done in 1661
The original is in the collection of Colonel Sir Edward Malet Bt., OBE. It too is by an unknown artist. It is 48×42 ins. and dated 1661. The medium is oil on canvas. This portrait is reproduced in the plate section of this book.

The National Portrait Gallery has a short half-length copy of the original. It again is artist unknown, oil on canvas. It is 30×25 ins. and perhaps painted in the eighteenth century. It was bequeathed to the National Portrait Gallery by Miss Charlotte F. Gerard in 1888. It shows head and shoulders only and there is no coat of arms as in the original. It is inscribed 'Mallet/Aetatis suae 79/1661'. This version resembles the original more closely than any other copy. It must be presumed to have been done at first hand.

Both the above portraits are described in D. Piper, *Catalogue of Seventeenth*

Century Portraits in the National Portrait Gallery 1625-1714 (Cambridge 1963) 213, 214, but Piper confuses us by saying that in the original belonging to the Malet family Malet is seated with a scroll in his right hand. Malet is standing in Colonel Malet's painting and has no scroll in the copy in the Harvard Law School (see below).

A second copy exists in the Harvard Law School Library. It is undated and unsigned, but the painter is listed as 'John Bullfinch, English (d 1666)'. (In fact it was not the artist who died in 1666, but another subject of an original painting from which he made a copy.) It is a black and white wash painting on paper 13 × 9 ins. It is three-quarter length and depicts Malet in an armchair, right hand on arm of chair. The left hand is also visible and neither hand carries a scroll. It is a poor copy and shows little of the character in the original subject. The Harvard Law School acquired its copy from Sweet and Maxwell in Chancery Lane, London, in 1923. There is a small attached slip saying in ink 'Sr Thomas Mallet [*sic*] Judge dec 1663'. The composition of this copy is quite different from all the others and it is most unlikely that any of the other copies were derived from it. It resembles the original only in the head. It is possible that the rest was worked up afterwards.

A third copy exists in the Devonshire collections, Chatsworth, Bakewell, Derbyshire in Clarendon 3 vols. (Oxford 1707), grangerized by Bulfinch (or Bullfinch)—almost certainly he who painted the second copy—in volume I facing p. 542. It is an anonymous black and white pen and wash drawing 8 × 6¾ ins. c 1707 and is inscribed: 'Sir Thomas Mallet, Judge. This drawing is from the painting in Counsellor Mallet's hand in the Temple.' Here the composition is similar to that of the original painting and the drawing, like most of the pen and ink portraits in the Chatsworth copy, is surrounded by twin red lines.

A fourth copy (which is a copy of the third) exists in the Sutherland Collection, Ashmolean Museum, Oxford, in Clarendon 3 vols. (Oxford 1707) grangerized copy by Sutherland, collected 1795–1835 (grangerized version 1837). Here the subject looks much younger. The artist is W. N. Gardiner (1766–1814). The copy is a black and white pen wash drawing 8⅝ × 7½ ins. It is inscribed: 'Judge Sir Thomas Mallet. Drawing by W. N. Gardiner from the Devonshire Clarendon. Picture with Councellor Mallett, Middle Temple.'

A fifth copy (which is a copy of the fourth copy) also exists in the Ashmolean Museum in the same grangerized edition of Clarendon I, 382. It is a mezzotint by Samuel de Wilde (alias J. S. Paul 1748–1832), 9½ × 6¾ ins., described in the catalogue as: 'Mez. proof. before the plate was cleared—S de Wilde fecit. The original drawing by Gardner—quarto.' the mezzotint itself is endorsed: 'The only print that is of this head'—Mrs. A. H. Sutherland, *Catalogue of the Sutherland Collection*, 2 vols. (London 1837) I 614. One other print was probably made of the Samuel de Wilde version. In the Sotheby catalogue of the *Stowe Granger* (The Duke of Buckingham's collection of portraits), sold in 1849, there is the following entry (p. 96): '861 Judge Mallet 4to mezz, proof before any inscription and of which plate only one other plate was taken off before it was destroyed, see note in the autograph of the late Duke of Buckingham.'

Finally, there are two copies in the John Rylands University Library of Manchester in an Oxford 1807 edition of Clarendon, grangerized under the supervision of George John, 2nd Earl Spencer. One is a proof below which 'Judge Mallet' has been written in pencil; the other is the same portrait, also a proof, below which 'Sir Thomas Mallet' has been engraved. Both copies measure $6\frac{1}{2} \times 5$ ins. and both engravings are signed 'Robt. Cooper Sculpt', but there is no indication of date or source. They resemble most closely the de Wilde version. The references are I 758 and 1096.

I must thank Dr. John Baker of St Catharine's College, Cambridge, who drew my attention to the existence of most of these copies and first suggested their common derivation.

THE
PETITION

Of the Gentry, Ministers, and Commonalty of the County of

KENT.

Agreed upon at the Generall Affizes laft holden
for that County.

The Copie of which Petition being delivered to
Judge *Mallet* (who was for that Circuit)
and afterwards to the Earle of *Brifloll*.

Which Petition being concealed from
the Parliament by the Earle of *Briftoll* and the
faid Iudge *Mallet*, was for the fame,
both committed to the Tower,

March 28. 1642.

this may become by the hand of the Hangman

LONDON, Printed. 1642.

Appendix II

Kentish Petition of March 1642

The title page is reproduced by permission of the British Library and comes from the Thomason Tracts—E 142 (10). Note the endorsement in the handwriting of George Thomason: 'This was burned by the hands of yᵉ Hangman.' The ensuing text comes from the Lords *Journals* and is transcribed by permission of the House of Lords Record Office.

TEXT

To the Honourable House of Commons.

The humble Petition of the Gentry, Ministers, and Commonalty, for the County of *Kent*, agreed upon at the General Assizes for that County,

Most humbly sheweth,

That we cannot but take Notice how welcome to this Honourable House many Petitions have been, which yet came not from any assembled Body of any County, as this doth. We do hope to find as gentle and as favourable Reception of this, as any others have found of their Petitions; our Hearts witnessing unto us as good, as peaceable, and as pious Purposes as the best: These are therefore the true and ardent Desires of this County:

1. That you will please to accept of our due and hearty Thanks, for those excellent Laws which, by His Majesty's Grace and Goodness, you have obtained for us.
2. That all Laws against Papists be put in due Execution, an Account taken of their disarming, and that all Children of Papists may be brought up in the Reformed Religion.
3. That the solemn Liturgy of the Church of *England*, celebrious by the Piety of holy Bishops and Martyrs who composed it, established by the supreme Law of this Land, attested and approved by the best of all Foreign Divines, confirmed with Subscription of all the Ministers of this Land, a Clergy as learned and as able as any in the Christian World, enjoyed, and with holy Love embraced, by the most and best of all the Laity; that this holy Exercise of our Religion may, by your Authority, be enjoyed, quiet and free from

Interruptions, Scorns, Prophanations, Threats, and Force of such Men, who daily do deprave it, and neglect the Use of it in divers Churches, in Despight of the Laws established.

4. That Episcopal Government, as ancient in this Island as Christianity itself, deduced and dispersed throughout the Christian World even from the Apostolical Times, may be preserved, as the most pious, most prudent, and most safe Government for the Peace of the Church.

5. That all Differences concerning Religion and Ceremonies may be referred to a lawful, free, national Synod; and, as your Remonstrance promiseth, a general Synod of most grave, pious, learned, and judicious Divines, the proper Agents, whose Interest, Gifts, and Callings, may quicken them in that great Work, whose Choice to be by all the Clergy of the Land, because all the Clergy are to be bound by their Resolutions, and the Determinations of this Synod to bind us all, when you have first formed them into a Law; and this we take to be according to the ancient fundamental Law of the Land, confirmed by *Magna Charta*.

6. That some speedy and good Provision may be made (as by His Majesty hath been, and is by all good Men, desired) against the odious and abominable Scandal of schismatical and seditious Sermons and Pamphlets, and some severe Law made against Laymen, for daring to arrogate to themselves and to exercise the Holy Function of the Ministry, who some of them do sow their impious discontented Doctrines even in Sacred Places, by Abuse of Sacred Ordinances, to the advancing of Heresy, Schism, Prophaneness, Libertinism, Anabaptism, Atheism.

7. That, if the coercive Power of Ecclesiastical Courts, by Way of Excommunication, be already abrogated, or shall be thought fit so to be, that there be some other Power and Authority speedily established, for the suppressing of the heinous and now-so-much abounding Sins of Incest, Adultery, Fornication, and other Crimes, and for the recovering of Tithes, repairing of Churches, Probates of Wills, Church Assess, and Providings of Bread and Wine for the Communion, and Choice of Churchwardens and other Officers in the Church, and especially for Ministers who neglect the celebrating of the Holy Communion, and for Parishoners not receiving.

8. That the Professors of that learned Faculty of the Civil Law, without which this Kingdom cannot but suffer many Inconveniences, may not find Discouragement, and so desert their Studies and Professions.

9. That Honour and Profit, the powerful Encouragements of Industry, Learning, and Piety, may be preserved, without any further Diminution to the Clergy.

10. That you please sadly to consider the bleeding Wounds of our Brethren in *Ireland*, and with speedy Succours endeavour to preserve them; whereunto His Majesty hath promised a gracious Concurrence.

11. That you please to frame an especial Law for the regulating the

Militia of this Kingdom, so that the Subjects may know how at once to obey both His Majesty and the Houses of Parliament; a Law whereby may be left to the Discretion of Governors as little as may be; but that the Number of Arms, and what Measure of Punishment shall be inflicted on Offenders, may be expressly set down in the Act, and not left to any arbitrary Power; and that, according to the Precedent of former Laws, the Offenders may not be tried out of the County.

12. That the precious Liberties of the Subject (the common Birth-right of every *Englishman*) may be as in all other Points preserved entire, so in this also, that no Order, in either or both Houses, not grounded on the Laws of the Land, may be enforced on the Subject, until it be fully enacted by Parliament.

13. That His Majesty's Gracious Message of the 20th of *January* last, for the present and future Establishment of the Privileges of Parliament, the free and quiet enjoying of our Estates and Fortunes, the Liberties of our Persons, the Security of the true Religion professed, the Maintenance of His Majesty's just and regal Authority, the establishing of His Revenue, may be taken into speedy Consideration; the effecting whereof will satisfy the Desires of us His faithfull and loving Subjects.

14. That all possible Care may be taken, that the native Commodities of this Kingdom may have quick Vent; and that Cloathing and other Manufactures may be improved, wherein the Livelihood of many Thousands doth consist; and that Trade may be so balanced, that the Importation do not exceed the Portation, which otherwise will in Time prove the Consumption of the Kingdom.

15. That you please to frame up some Laws concerning Depopulations, Purveyance, Cart-taking, Delays in Justice, Traffick, Fishing on the Sea Coasts, Fulling-earth; that our Sea Forts may be repaired, and our Magazines renewed.

16. That you please to consider the general Poverty that seems to overgrow this Land.

17. Lastly, we beseech you to consider the sad Condition that we and the whole Land are in, if a good Understanding be not speedily renewed between His Majesty and the Houses of Parliament.

Our Hopes are yet above our Fears; secure them, we beseech you. GOD direct and bless your Consultations, for the removing of all Distrusts and Jealousies, and for renewing that Tie of Confidence and Trust, which is the highest Happiness, between our most Gracious Prince and us His most loving People.

And you shall have the daily Prayers of your humble Orators,

THE COMMONS OF KENT

It is desired, that whosoever do deliver forth any Copy of this Petition, that he testify the same to be a true Copy.

GENTRY.   MINISTERS.   COMMONS.

For the expediting of these Petitions; it is desired, That the Gentry, at their several Divisions, do agree upon amongst themselves to receive the Copies of all these Petitions, and all Subscriptions, between this and the *Easter Sessions* at *Maydestone;* and that all the Gentry of *Kent* do meet at *Blackheath* on *Friday* Morning, the 29th *April*, at Nine of the Clock in the Morning, from thence to accompany this Petition to the House.
—LJ IV 677a–678b.

NOTE. The copy of this Kentish petition, which was transcribed by the Earl of Bristol's servant, Theophilus Brown, and was handed over by the Earl to the House of Lords, is among the House of Lords Main Papers—HLRO Main Papers HL 28 Mar. 1642 (HMC 5 I 14b).

Appendix III

Probable Presence and Voting of Peers, 28 March 1642

The table overleaf does not include all the peers who dissented between 1 January and 28 March 1642; only the record of those likely to have been present on 28 March 1642. The 'pro-Parliamentarian' dissent of 15 March 1642 was not strictly pro-Parliamentarian but it was made by peers who were mainly pro-Parliamentarian at the time. There is no official list of peers present on 28 March 1642.

Probable Voting on 28 March	Estimated Maximum	Estimated Actual
F For the motion to imprison the Earl of Bristol.	21 votes	19 votes
A Against the motion to imprison the Earl of Bristol.	12 votes	10 votes
(D Actually dissented against the motion to imprison the Earl of Bristol.)		
W Waverer—voting uncertain.	9 votes	7 votes

[see over]

| Peer | Certainly present on | | | Days on which they dissented in 1642 | | | | | | | | | | | | Peers who joined the King | Probable vote 28 Mar |
| | | | | Pro-Royalist | | | | | | | Pro-Parliamentarian | | | | | | |
	25° Mar	26° Mar	28+ Mar	12 Jan	2 Mar	5 Mar	7 Mar	15 Mar	19 Mar	28 Mar	17 Jan	24 Jan	26 Jan	1 Feb	15 Mar		
Lord Keeper (Lord Littleton)	X	X	X								X					X	—
L. Admiral (Earl of Northumberland)	X	X	X										X	X	X		F
L. Chamberlain (Earl of Essex)	X	X	X									X	X	X	X		F
Marquess of Hertford	X	X	X													X	W
Earl of Bath	X	X	X		X	X		X	X	X	X	X				X	AD
Earl of Bedford	X	X									X	X	X	X	X		F
Earl of Bolingbroke	X	X	X										X	X	X		F
Earl of Bristol	X	X	X													X	—
Earl of Clare	X	X										X				X	W
Earl of Devonshire	X	X				X	X									X	A
Earl of Dover	X	X	X							X			X	X	X	X	AD
Earl of Holland	X	X	X								X		X	X	X		F
Earl of Huntingdon	X															X	W
Earl of Leicester	X		X								X		X	X	X	X	W
Earl of Lincoln	X	X									X		X	X	X		F
Earl of Monmouth	X	X	X		X	X				X		X	X	X	X		AD
Earl of Northampton	X	X			X		X					X				X	A
Earl of Pembroke	X	X	X								X	X	X	X			F
Earl of Peterborough	X	X									X	X	X	X	X		W
Earl of Portland	X	X	X		X	X				X	X	X	X			X	AD
Earl of Salisbury	X	X	X								X	X	X	X	X		W
Earl of Stamford	X	X	X								X	X	X	X	X		F
Earl of Warwick	X	X	X								X	X	X	X	X		F
Viscount Saye and Sele	X	X	X								X	X	X	X	X		F

Peer	Certainly present on			Days on which they dissented in 1642												Peers who joined the King	Probable vote 28 Mar
				Pro-Royalist							Pro-Parliamentarian						
	25° Mar	26° Mar	28+ Mar	12 Jan	2 Mar	5 Mar	7 Mar	15 Mar	19 Mar	28 Mar	17 Jan	24 Jan	26 Jan	1 Feb	15 Mar		
Lord Brooke	X	X	X								X	X	X	X			F
Lord Bruce of Whorlton	X	X				X	X	X	X	X		X					F
Lord Capell of Hadham	X	X	X		X									X		X	AD
Lord Cromwell	X	X										X				X	W
Lord Feilding of Newnham Paddockes	X	X									X	X					F
Lord Grey de Ruthyn	X	X	X		X	X	X		X	X	X	X	X	X			AD
Lord Grey of Werke	X	X									X	X	X	X	X		F
Lord Hastings	X	X	X			X	X	X							X	X	W
Lord Howard of Charlton	X	X	X			X		X		X	X	X	X	X			AD
Lord Howard of Escrick	X	X				X	X				X	X	X	X	X		F
Lord Kimbolton	X	X	X			X	X			X	X	X	X	X			F
Lord Mowbray	X	X	X	X	X	X			X		X	X	X	X	X		AD
Lord Paget	X	X				X	X									X	W
Lord Rich	X															X	A
Lord Robartes	X	X	X								X	X	X	X	X		F
Lord St John of Bletso	X	X	X								X	X	X	X	X		F
Lord Strange	X					X	X	X								X	W
Lord Savile	X	X	X								X	X	X	X		X	A
Lord Wharton	X	X									X	X	X	X			F
Lord Willoughby of Parham	X	X	X								X	X	X	X	X		F
TOTAL 44																	

Notes: ° Actually present according to the House of Lords original manuscript minutes.
+ Mentioned in the *Journals of the House of Lords* for 28 March.

THE KINGS

MAIESTIES

CHARGE

SENT TO ALL

THE JUDGES

OF

ENGLAND,

To be published in their respective Circuits,
By His Maiesties speciall Command.

London, Printed for *Laurence Blaiklock*,
Iuly 26. 1642.

Appendix IV

The King's Charge to the Judges, Summer 1642

The title page and the ensuing text are reproduced by permission of the British Library and come from the Thomason Tracts—E 108 (7).

TEXT

Charles R

Trusty and well-beloved, We greet you well. We call to mind that in former times the constant custome was, by the mouth of the Lord Keeper, for the time being, at the Court of Star-chamber, in the end of Trinity Terme, to put the Judges of Assize (shortly after to undertake their severall Circuits) in minde of such things as were then thought necessary for the present, for the good government of the Kingdome. This course in Our judgement We doe well approve of, That although We want the Opportunity, which We and Our Predecessors then had, of communicating Our thoughts to Our Judges, for the good of Our People, yet We doe still retaine the same care for the safety and prosperity of Our good Subjects. And much more, by how much the distempers and distractions of the present times, unhappily fallen, have given us more occasion. We have therefore thought it fit, to supply the defect by these Our Letters; wherein, besides the generall care of Our justice, committed to Us by God, and by Us delegated to Our Judges by Our severall Commissions, We recommend unto you in your Circuits, as We shall do to the rest of your Brethren in their severall Circuits, these particulars following.

First that you take care, by all the best meanes you can, to suppresse Popery in all those Counties whither you are to go, by putting the Lawes made against them in due execution: And that you take like care to give a stop to the over-hasty growth of Anabaptisme, and other Schismes, as farre as by the good Lawes of the Land you may; and to punish the Delinquents with an equall hand, and those specially of either sort whom you shall discover to bee seditious stirrers and movers of others to any Acts of disobedience to us, and our governement; And that in your Charge, and otherwise, as you shall have fit opportunity, you assure our good Subjects in our name, and in the word of a King, who calls God to witnesse, that by his gracious assistance we are constantly resolved to maintaine the true Protestant Religion, established by Law in this Church of *England*, in the purity thereof, without declining either to the right hand or to the left, as wee found it at our access to the Crown, and as it was maintained in the happy times of Queene *Elizabeth*, and King *James* our deare Father, both of happy memory, and therein both to live and die.

Secondly, You shall let Our People of those Counties know, That, according to Our Kingly duty and Oath, We are also constantly resolved to maintain the Lawes of this Our Kingdome; and by, and according to them to governe Our Subjects, and not by any Arbitrary power, whatsoever the Malevolent Spirits of any ill affected to Our Person or Government, have suggested, or shall suggest to the contrary. And that We shall also maintaine the just Priviledges of Parliament, as far as ever Our Predecessors have done, and as far as may stand with that justice which We owe to Our Crowne, and the honour thereof: But that We may not, nor will admit of any such unwarranted power, in either, or both Houses of Parliament, which in some things hath been lately usurped, not onely without, but against Our Royall Consent and Command. And We require and command you, as there shall be just occasion offered, in a legall way, that you take care to preserve Our just right in these cases.

Thirdly, We charge you, as you tender the peace of this Kingdom, in the Government whereof, according to the Lawes, you Our Judges of the Law have a principall part under Us, that you take care for suppressing of all Insurrections, if any such should happen, and of all Riots and unlawfull Assemblies under any pretence whatsoever, not warranted by the Lawes of this Land; and whosoever shall transgresse therein, that you let them know that they must expect that punishment which by the Law may be inflicted upon them, and at your hands We shall look for such an account herein, within your Circuit, as becometh the quality of the place wherein you serve Us.

Fourthly, because the distempers of the present times, unhappily stirred up & Fomented by some, under specious, but unjust pretences, & probable to stirre up loose & ungoverned people, under hope of impunity as farre as they dare to make a prey of Our good Subjects, We straitly charge and command you to take the best order you can in those Counties, That Rogues, Vagabonds, and other disorderly people may bee apprehended, dealt with and punished according to the Lawes, whereby the good and quiet people of our Kingdome may be secured, and the wicked and licentious may be suppressed: and Wee charge and command you to give it in charge in all the Counties whither you are sent by our Commissions, that Watches and Wards be straitly kept in all Parishes and places convenient, whereby the Lawes made against such disorders may be put in due execution.

Fifthly and lastly, you shall let Our people of those Counties know from Us, and by Our command, that if they shall professe unto Us, or unto you in Our stead, anything wherein they hold themselves grieved, in an humble and fitting way, and shall desire a just Reformation or reliefe, We shall give a gracious eare unto them, and with all convenience returne them such an answer as shall give them cause to thank Us for Our Justice and Favour: And when you shall have published Our cleare intentions to Our people in these things, lest at the first hearing they should not so fully apprehend Our sense therein, you shall deliver a copy of these Our letters to the Fore-man of the Grand-Jury, and to any other, if any one shall desire copies of these Our letters for their better information; And to the end that Our services in your Circuit may not suffer through the absence of Our learned Counsell, Our Will and Command is, that you assign in every place of your Sessions some of the ablest Lawyers who ride that Circuit to be of Counsell for Us, to assist in such Pleas of the Crown, that may bee most necessary for Our service in the execution and punishment of notorious Delinquents.

Of all these things We shall expect' that good account from you, as We shall from the rest of your Brethren Our Judges, to whom Wee have also written to the like purpose, of whose fidelity and good affections Wee are confident as becommeth Us to look for from you, and for you to render to Us, where in you have so great a trust committed,

Given at Our Court at Yorke, 4 July, 1642.

To Our trusty and wellbeloved the Judge or Judges of Assize for Our Counties of Kent, Surrey, Sussex, Hertford and Essex.

THE HUMBLE
PETITION
OF
The Commons of KENT,

Agreed upon at their Generall Aſſizes,

Preſented to His Majeſtie the firſt
of Auguſt. 1 6 4 2.

With certain Inſtructions from the County of
Kent to Mr *Auguſtine Skinner*, whereby the De-
ſires of the ſaid Countie may be preſented by
him to the Honourable Houſe of *Commons*.

With His Majeſties Anſwer to the
aforeſaid PETITION.

At the Court at York, Auguſt 4. 1 6 4 2.

LONDON:
Printed by ROBERT BARKER, Printer
to the Kings moſt Excellent Majeſtie: And
by the Aſſignes of JOHN BILL.
1 6 4 2.

Appendix V

Kentish Petition of July 1642 with Instructions to Augustine Skinner and the King's Answer.

The title page and the ensuing text are reproduced by permission of the British Library and come from the Thomason Tracts—E 112 (26) (1 Aug. 1642).

TEXT

To the Kings most Excellent Majestie

The Humble Petition of the Commons of Kent, agreed upon at their generall Assizes.

Most Gracious Soveraign,

We do, with all thankfulnesse acknowledge Your great Grace and favour towards us, and the whole Kingdom; In passing many good Laws for the benefit of Your Subjects, In promising to ease us of all our grievances; And graciously inviting us, by Your Letter directed to the Judge of our Assize, full of Love and Care for Your Peoples good, to Petition for redresse of them, promising a Gracious Answer; And we should with all humilitie have presented them to Your Majestie at this time, did not the present great distractions and apprehension of a Civill War (which we earnestly pray to God to divert) put us beyond all thought of other grievances. For prevention whereof, we have with all loyaltie of heart to Your Sacred Majestie, with all love and faithfulnesse to our Countrey, presented our humble advice in certain Instructions to one of our Knights of the Shire now here present with a Committee from the House of Commons, to be presented by him to that Honourable House: The Copie whereof we make bold to annex unto this Petition;

Most humbly desiring Your most Excellent Majestie, That if it shall please the Houses of Parliament to satisfie Your Majesties just desires in these particulars, That then Your Majestie would be graciously pleased to lay down Your extraordinary Guards, and cheerfully meet Your Parliament, in such a place where Your Sacred Majestie and each Member of both Houses may be free from tumultuary Assemblies.

And, as in all duty bound, we shall daily pray for Your Majesties long Life, and Prosperous Reign over us.

Instructions from the County of Kent to Master *Augustine Skinner, whereby the Desires of the said Countie may be presented by him to the Honourable House of Commons.*

Whereas a Committee from the House of Commons is now sent down to the Assizes, upon a credible Information (as they say) that something should be done to the Disturbance of the Peace of this Countie:

We, the Commons of *Kent*, require you Master *Augustine Skinner* (as our Servant) to certifie to that Honourable House, That you found the Countie in full Peace, and that there is no ground for any such Information, and that you desire, in our Names, to know the particulars of that Information (of which it seems you are ignorant, and the Informer) that this County may have full reparations in Honour against so scandalous an aspersion cast upon them; and that the Informer, of what quality soever, may receive condigne punishment. And that the House of Commons may understand our desires, not onely to preserve the Peace of this Countie, which (with Gods blessing, and the help of the good known Laws of this Kingdom) we are confident we shall maintain, but also of the whole Kingdom, being now in so great a distraction, that every Man stands at a gaze, to see what the event is likely to be. And well weighing what a great fire a small spark may kindle, abhorring and detesting the thought of a Civill War; We further require you to offer our humble advice, as Faithfull and Loyall Subjects to His Majestie, and good Patriots and Lovers of our Countrey, for setling the Distractions of these times. One principall means to effect it, we conceive will be to give His Majestie full satisfaction in His just Desires, in these four Particulars;

1. *In presently leaving the Town of* Hull *in the same State it was before Sir* John Hothams *entrance into it; And delivering His Majestie His own Magazine.*
2. *In laying aside the* Militia, *untill a good Law may be framed, wherein care may be taken as well for the Liberty of the Subjects, as the Defence of the Kingdom.*
3. *That the Parliament be adjourned to an indifferent place, where His Sacred Majestie, all the Lords and Members of your House of Commons may meet and treat with Honour, Freedom and Safetie.*
4. *That His Majesties Navie may be immediately restored to Him.*

Our Reasons are these.

1. For withdrawing your Garison out of the Town of *Hull*, we are perswaded your Fears and Jealousies of forraign Forces, of French, or Danes, or of the Papists at home (an inconsiderable Party, especially being disarmed) are long since vanished; the Magazine, or a great part of it being removed to *London*, we conceive Master Major of *Hull* may safely keep the Town as before.

2. For laying aside the Militia, we are free from Jealouses of Forraign Forces, so that you may have time enough to frame a lasting Law, which not withstanding, for fear of Inconvenience to the Subjects Liberty, you may, if you so think fit, make the Law a Probationer. Besides, His Majestie, if occasion should be, is vested with sufficient power to raise Forces for the Defence of the Kingdom, for which onely we are confident His Majestie will imploy them. And we should hold ourselves worse then Infidels, if, after so many protestations, to maintain The true Religion by Law established, The Subjects in the Liberty of their Persons and Propriety of their Goods, and The Priviledges of Parliament, and That He will govern us by the known Laws of the Land, we should not with full assurance beleeve Him and confide in Him.

3. For adjourning the Parliament to another place, His Majestie hath expressed the Reasons, That He was driven away by tumultuarie Assemblies, and that he cannot return thither with Honour and Safetie: And divers of the Lords are absent, who promise to return back to the House, when they may sit with the Libertie, and that condition that the Peerage of *England* formerly have done, secured from all menaces, or demanding any Account of their particular Votes, which We conceive to be against the Freedom of Parliament, which by Our Protestation We must maintain, and from tumultuarie Assemblies: These having been the occasions, as We beleeve, that of neer five hundred in the House of Commons, there are about one hundred and fourty left to sit there, and the greater part of the Lords gone away.

4. For the Restitution of the Navie, our Reason is, That the Neighbour Nations do take notice, that His Majesties Navie is detained from Him, which if not suddenly restored, may turn to His Majesties dishonour; whose honour, by our Protestation, we are bound to maintain.

5. Another means, we conceive, to settle the States and Mindes of the Subjects, is a free, generall, and large Pardon: which since His Majesty hath so graciously offered, we desire and expect to receive; and if any man do dislike it, he may be excepted, and the generality of the Subjects not hindered of their good, and His Majesties Grace and Goodnesse.

His Majesties Answer
To the humble Petition of the Commons of Kent, agreed
upon at their generall Assizes, and presented to
His Majestie the first of August.

At the Court at York this fourth of August, 1642.

His Majestie hath with great satisfaction in the Loyalty and Affection of the Petitioners considered this Petition, with the Instructions annexed to their Knight of the Shire, and hath expresly commanded me to return this His Answer, in these words:

That the Petitioners are not more eased and satisfied with the good Laws His Majestie hath passed, then His Majestie himself is pleased with that way of obliging His Subjects, neither hath He ever made the least Promise or Profession of repairing or redressing the grievances of His People, which he hath not been, and alwayes will be ready to perform.

His Majestie cannot blame the Petitioners to be apprehensive of a civill War, since the present distractions (grounded upon no visible cause, to which His Majestie could, or can yet apply a remedy) threaten no lesse confusion. But His Majestie doubts not, that the Petitioners and all His good Subjects, do well understand, That His Majesty hath left no way unattempted, which in Honour, or Wisdom could be consented to, to prevent that confusion.

That after so many Injuries and Indignities offered to Him, so many Combinations and Conspiracies against Him, He departed so much from His own Majestie, and the Justice due to it, That He required no other reparation, then to have His Town, Goods, and Navie (taken and kept by violence from, and against Him) to be restored to Him: The power of making Laws without Him, by the way of Ordinances (and that in particular, concerning the *Militia*) to be disavowed: And that a safe Place might be agreed on, where He might be present with His great Councell, for the composing all misunderstandings, and making the Kingdom happie.

That before any Answer returned to His Majestie (whilest with all patience and hope His Majestie forbore any Action or Attempt of Force, according to His Promise) Sir *John Hotham* issued out of *Hull* in the Night, burned the Houses, and murthered the Persons of his fellow Subjects (though he knew His Majestie quietly expected an Answer to His reasonable and necessary Demands) and hath since exercised most barbarous cruelty upon a Drummer then taken Prisoner by him.

That those Propositions made by His Majestie, and mentioned by the Petitioners in their Instructions, are dissented from, and His Majestie not suffered to enjoy what is as unquestionably His own, as any thing his Subjects can call most theirs, upon pretence there is some trust on foot to dispossesse His Majestie of them: Whether any such trust be derived from the Petitioners, themselves best know.

That a Generall is made to Command His Subjects against Him, and Forces already Marching with Cannon towards Him, under the Conduct of the Lord *Brook*, whilest all Labour and Endeavour is used to cut off all Succour and Supply from His Majestie, as from a Forraign Enemy.

When the Petitioners, and all other His Majesties Subjects have weighed this, and considered that these strange unheard of proceedings must be the effects of desperate Resolutions, and that all this calamity is brought upon this Nation, to wrest from His Majestie His Just Rights, when no sober man can see the want of any thing which is in His Majesties power to grant, and necessary for the peace and full happinesse of the Kingdom.

That when all encouragement is given, scandals raised, and provocations used to incense the People against His Majesty, and to publish Petitions and Declarations against the known Laws and established Government, The Petitioners, and all other His Majesties good Subjects (who out of a true sense of the Distraction and ruine the Common wealth must speedily fall into through these distempers, have prepared sober and moderate Petitions and Animadversions for the peace of the Kingdom) have been discountenanced, censured and imprisoned in a Lawlesse Arbitrary way, when no offence hath been committed by them, of which the Law hath taken notice: That all their Rights, Interests and Priviledges, which they were born to, by the good known Lawes, are taken from them, or subjected to an unintelligible Arbitrary power and resolution, which destroyes their confidence and assurance even in Innocencie itself; They will think it time to provide for their own security, by Assisting His Majestie for the defence of His Person, preservation of the true Protestant Religion, and maintenance of the Law of the Land, and Liberty of the Subject; of the which, as the Petitioners care is very eminent, and deserves all protection, thanks and estimation from His Majesty; So His Majesty will venture His Life and His Crown with them, in that Quarrell.

Lastly, lest any of the Petitioners may unjustly suffer for making or presenting this humble, dutifull and modest Petition to His Majestie; His Majestie declares, That He will with His utmost power and assistance protect and defend them against any power whatsoever, which shall question them for so doing; And to that purpose advertiseth them, That they are not obliged to yeeld Obedience to any Pursuivants, Sergeants, or Messengers, who shall endeavour to molest them for doing their Duty, and discharging their Consciences therein. And that the whole County of *Kent* may know His Majesties gracious acceptance of this expression of their Duty and affection unto Him: it is His Majesties pleasure, that this His Answer, together with the Petition and Instructions, be Read in all the Churches and Chappels of that County.

FALKLAND

Abbreviations

These abbreviations are used in the bibliography and notes:

AC	*Archaeologia Cantiana*
Add	British Library Additional Manuscript
AHR	*American Historical Review*
BL	British Library (all references beginning 669f are to Thomason Tracts, folio size)
CCC	*Calendar of the Proceedings of the Committee for Compounding with Delinquents—1643-1660,* 5 vols. (1889–93)
CHJ	*Cambridge Historical Journal*
CJ	*Journals of the House of Commons* [1547–1761], 28 vols. (1742 ff)
Clarendon	Edward Hyde, Earl of Clarendon, *The History of the Rebellion and Civil Wars in England* (references are to books and sections and to ed. W. D. Macray, 6 vols. (Oxford 1888) unless otherwise stated)
Cockburn	J. S. Cockburn, *A History of English Assizes 1558–1714* (Cambridge 1972)
CSPD	*Calendar of State Papers, Domestic*
CSPV	*Calendar of State Papers, Venetian*
Dering	Sir Edward Dering, *A Collection of Speeches Made by Sir Edward Dering Knight and Baronet in Matter of Religion* ...(1642)
D'Ewes (C)	*The Journal of Sir Simonds D'Ewes* [12 Oct. 1641—10 Jan. 1642], ed. W. H. Coates (New Haven, Conn. 1942)
D'Ewes (N)	*The Journal of Sir Simonds D'Ewes* [3 Nov. 1640—20 Mar. 1641], ed. W. Notestein (New Haven, Conn. 1923)
DNB	*Dictionary of National Biography,* ed. L. Stephen and S. Lee, 22 vols. (Oxford 1908–09)
E	British Library, Thomason Tracts, octavo size
EHR	*English Historical Review*
Everitt	Alan Everitt, *The Community of Kent and the Great Rebellion 1640–60* (Leicester 1966)

Firth	C. H. Firth, *The House of Lords during the Civil War* (1910)
Foss	Edward Foss, *The Judges of England* [1066–1864], 9 vols. (1848–64)
Gardiner	S. R. Gardiner, *History of England from the Accession of James I to the Outbreak of the Civil War 1603–1642*, 10 vols. (1883–84)
Glow	Lotte Glow, *House of Commons Committees and County Committees 1640–1644* ... 2 vols. (typescript PhD thesis Adelaide 1963)
Harl	British Library, Harleian Manuscript
HL	House of Lords
HLDJ	House of Lords, Original Manuscript Draft Journal
HLMS	Manuscripts of the House of Lords (new series), 12 vols. (1900 ff)
HLRO	House of Lords Record Office
HMC	Historical Manuscript Commission *Report*
JBS	*Journal of British Studies*
Jessup	F. W. Jessup, *Sir Roger Twysden 1597 1672* (1965)
Keeler	M. F. Keeler, *The Long Parliament 1640–1641* (Philadelphia 1954)
LJ	*Journals of the House of Lords* [1510–1829], 61 vols. (1767 ff)
LQR	*Law Quarterly Review*
Malet	Arthur Malet, *Notices of an English Branch of the Malet Family* (1885)
MT	*Middle Temple Records: Minutes of Parliament 1501–1703*, ed. C. T. Martin, 4 vols. (1904–05)
nd	no date
Nicholas	[Edward Nicholas], *Proceedings and Debates of the House of Commons 1620 and 1621* ... ed. T. Tyrwhitt, 2 vols. (Oxford 1766)
NPG	National Portrait Gallery
NRA	National Register of Archives
NRS	Wallace Notestein, F. H. Relf and H. Simpson, ed., *Commons Debates 1621*, 7 vols. (New Haven, Conn. 1935) (references in brackets after the volume number are to the diarist concerned)
PRO	Public Record Office (for group letters and class numbers see Bibliography pp. 206–7)
RCHM	Royal Commission on Historical Monuments (now Royal Commission on Ancient and Historical Monuments and Constructions)
Roberts	Clayton Roberts, *The Growth of Responsible Government in Stuart England* (Cambridge 1966)
Rushworth	John Rushworth, *Historical Collections of Private Passages of State* ... 7 vols. (1659–1701)
SAC	*Surrey Archaeological Collections*

Sanford	J. L. Sanford, *Studies and Illustrations of the Great Rebellion* (1858)
SANHS	*Somersetshire Archaeological and Natural History Society's Proceedings*
Spencer	*Articles of Impeachment of Richard Spencer Esq*, HLRO Parchment Collection HL 11 May 1642
SRS	*Somerset Record Society*
ST	W. Cobbett, T. B. Howell and others, ed., *Complete Collection of State Trials and Proceedings for High Treason and Other Crimes* ... 34 vols. (1809–28)
Strode	*Articles of Impeachment of Sir George Strode, Knight*, HLRO Parchment Collection HL 11 May 1642
Trevelyan	G. M. Trevelyan, *England under the Stuarts* (1949)
Wedgwood	C. V. Wedgwood, *The Great Rebellion, II: The King's War 1641–47* (1958)
Zagorin	Perez Zagorin, *The Court and the Country* (1969)

Notes to the Text

In these references I have cited sources:

either by one of the abbreviations on pages 158–60.

or by giving the author and title in full on the first occasion in each chapter and on subsequent occasions in the same chapter by citing the author's name only; if there would otherwise be ambiguity I have added the title in abbreviated form.

I have only included the abbreviations 'p', 'f' and 'm' for 'page', 'folio' and 'membrane' if it might be ambiguous to omit them.

GENERAL NOTE
Use of 'Kentish':
I have followed the example of earlier historians in referring to the petitions originating at Maidstone in 1642 as 'Kentish petitions'; this is strictly in accordance with the *Concise Oxford Dictionary* first meaning of the word 'Kentish', namely 'of Kent'. I am aware that 'Kentish' as applied to 'man' is a word of art signifying 'born West of the Medway in Kent' and, in order to prevent misunderstanding, I have generally in this book avoided the use of the adjective 'Kentish' in connection with people.

INTRODUCTION
1. See particularly R. C. Richardson, *The Debate on the English Revolution* (1977)—a historiographical survey; Lawrence Stone, *The Causes of the English Revolution 1529–1642* (1972); and Conrad Russell, ed., *The Origins of the English Civil War* (1973).
2. See Richardson, chapter 7 and references there.
3. See especially J. S. Morrill, *The Revolt of the Provinces* (1976). For the diversity of interests and communities, see 'Interest—Public, Private and Communal' by Ivan Roots in R. H. Parry, ed., *The English Civil War and After 1642–1658* (1970) 111–22.
4. *LJ* IV 677b; Dering 166.
5. See pp. 70, 78.

CHAPTER I—THE HOUR AND THE MAN

1. Diary of Sir Richard Hutton [1561?–1639] Cambridge University Library Additional MS 6863 f 80. The translation is by Dr. John H. Baker, St. Catharine's College, Cambridge. This refers to Malet at the time when he was created serjeant-at-law. See pp. 6, 7.

2. Gardiner VII 77–113.

3. Trevelyan 50.

4. H. G. Alexander, *Religion in England 1558–1662* (1968) 148–56; F. S. Siebert, *Freedom of the Press in England 1476–1776* (Urbana, Illinois 1952) 122–5.

5. J. H. Hexter, *The Reign of King Pym* (Cambridge, Mass. 1961) 77.

6. Gardiner VII 342–91, VIII 67–105, 199–223, 269–81.

7. Gardiner VIII 304–91, IX 1–55.

8. Gardiner IX 84–118, 165–217.

9. Zagorin 32–9, 74–5.

10. Zagorin 200–1; Esmé Wingfield-Stratford, *King Charles and King Pym 1637–1643* (1949) 8–10.

11. Gardiner IX 218–338.

12. Valerie Pearl, *London and the Outbreak of the Puritan Revolution 1625–1643* (Oxford 1961) 162–7, 210, 211; Siebert 203; D'Ewes (C) xx–xxiii; Zagorin 203–5.

13. *CJ* II 22b, 23a, 24b, 25a; D'Ewes (N) 5 and n20, 20 n7, 22 n19; Rushworth 3 i 30–4, 171; Pearl 214, 229.

14. Zagorin 228, 229; Clarendon III 67; D'Ewes (N) 282, 283 and n6. Samuel Butler, *Hudibras*, ed. A. R. Waller (Cambridge 1905) 44.

15. Everitt 86, 87; Rushworth 3 i 135–6; *CJ* II 67b.

16. Pearl 216–7; Zagorin 223 and n5, 224; *DNB*.

17. Gardiner IX 347, 378–83, 387–90.

18. Gardiner IX 375, 401, 402, 404; *CJ* II 184b, 185ab; Rushworth 3 i 298–300. However, the Bishop of Lincoln reported to the Lords that Pym asked for affairs to be put 'into such hands as *His Majesty* and the Parliament may confide in'—*LJ* IV 285b, 286b.

19. W. J. Jones, *Politics and the Bench* (1971) 139. *DNB*; Foss VI 294, 295; *CJ* II 203a; Gardiner VIII 278, 279; Sir John Coke the younger to Sir John Coke at Melbourne 14 July 1641—The collection of the Marquess of Lothian DL, Melbourne Hall, Derby. Cowper (Coke) MSS (HMC 12 Appendix II 288–9).

20. Chancery, patent rolls PRO C 66/2891 [mm not numbered] and Crown Office docket books PRO C 231/5 456, both 1 July 1641. There is no contemporary account of Malet's promotion to the Bench. The procedure at the time is described in Sir William Dugdale, *Origines Juridiciales* (1671) 97 and accounts of other promotions to the bench between 1620 and 1640 are contained in Jones, *Reports* 151, 247–8, 299, 358, 403, 415, 450 and in Sir James Whitlocke, *Liber Famelicus*, ed. J. Bruce (Camden Society 1858) 96–9.

21. Malet 1, 8, 17, 21, 49, 80.

22. MT I 409; Malet 57, 58. We know that Thomas Malet was born in about 1582, because of the hatchment in All Saints, Poyntington and the portrait described on page 137. There is no extant copy of Malachi's will and no trace of him in the Luxulyan parish register. Thomas Malet's grandfather, John Malet, lived at Wolley in Devon— his will PROB 11/52, s 37 (Lyon 37) proved 14 Nov. 1570.

23. MT I 409, 469. Malet's sponsor on admission was Chief Baron Peryam who bought his Little Fulford estate in Devon from Malet's uncle Robert—Malet 56.

24. *Return of the Names of Every Member Returned to Serve in Each Parliament (Official Return)* 2 vols. (1878) I xxxvii, 450b. A Thomas Malet of Tregony appears in the subsidy rolls for 1535 and 1543, and a Thomas Mallett was at the consistory court in 1556 where he was said to be aged forty and to have been resident at Tregony twenty years— Cornwall County Museum, Henderson MSS Calendars (c. 1930) X p. 118b. The bond on the administration of a will by Thomas Mallet of Cuby/Tregony approved at Bodmin in 1581 has unfortunately been lost. Malet's mother's family, the Trevanions, were well connected with Tregony. I am grateful to Mr. H. L. Douch, the Curator of the Cornwall County Museum, for this information. Tregony became Boscawen (now Lord Falmouth) property and the family muniments are at Tregothnan, near Truro.

25. In the 1614 Parliament Malet spoke out strongly against import duties or impositions levied without the authority of Parliament and against Bishop Neile who made a speech in the Lords implying that the Commons were disloyal to attack impositions—CJ I 473b, 501b. He did not graduate to his first committee for a public bill until the Addled Parliament had only seven days to run—CJ I 503b.

26. Malet's speeches in the 1621 Parliament are contained in the *Journals of the House of Commons*, in the book of committees and in the private diaries of ten members of the House of Commons, see CJ I, Nicholas, NRS generally, Appointment to committees for bills, see CJ I 527a, 534a, 536b, 551b (2), 567a, 582b, 600b, 602b, 607a, 652a; charges against Mompesson, CJ I 540a, 541a; charges against Bennett, CJ I 586b, 587a; NRS II (X) 310, 311, IV 245–247.

27. CJ I 473b, 543b, 618a; Nicholas I 130, 218, II 55, 56; NRS II (X) 176, V (Belasyse) 166, VI (Holland) 83 and n 3, 152.

28. For Malet's references to statute see the debates on:
    Westminster election—Nicholas I 212.
    Adjournment—NRS III (Barrington) 372.
    Goldsmith and Lepton—NRS II (X) 511 and n 2, VI (Z) 231–2.
    Lambe and Craddock—Nicholas II 362–3; NRS II (X) 543 and n 3, 544.
    For other references to precedent see Nicholas I 67, 99, II 149; NRS II (X) 142, III (Barrington) 228, IV (Pym) 106, 120, 404, V (Rich) 519; CJ I 528b.

29. *CJ* I 513a, 599b, 607a; NRS III (Barrington) 43, IV (Pym) 244, V (Smyth) 278. During the 1621 Parliament Malet was appointed steward and keeper of certain properties belonging to Westminster Abbey—Patent from the Dean and Chapter of Westminster Abbey to Malet 4 May 1621 NRA PP/AP/2 f 1.

30. Malet to Secretary Conway—PRO SP 14/146/82 14 June 1623 (*CSPD* 1619–23 608).

31. D. H. Willson, *The Privy Councillors in the House of Commons 1604–1629* (Minneapolis 1940) 80, 81; *Official Return* I 465b, 471a; William Weld to Philip Flemyng 16 Jan. 1626 PRO SP 16/523/14 (*CSPD* Addenda 1625–49 97).

I have only been able to find four occasions when Malet spoke in the 1625 Parliament:

Tuesday 21 June—S. R. Gardiner, ed., *Debates in the House of Commons in 1625* (Camden Society 1873) 8.

Wednesday 22 June—*CJ* I 800b.

Friday 8 July—*CJ* I 806b.

Tuesday 8 August—*CJ* I 813b; Gardiner, *Debates* 105

In the 1626 Parliament Malet was named to eight committees for bills—*CJ* 818a, 819a, 820a, 836a, 837a, 852b, 864b, 865b. On 1 June 1626 the business of Richard Fust's estate was committed to John Pym and Thomas Malet among others; they were both West Country men—*CJ* I 865b. In this Parliament Malet made a powerful speech advising the Commons not to act upon 'common fame' (widely held rumour) against the Duke of Buckingham, who was Conway's patron. Most of the lawyers of the House were against Malet on this issue—*CJ* I 847b.

While the 1626 Parliament was sitting Malet had the onerous duty of reader to the Middle Temple. It was role which, but for the plague, he should have fulfilled in the previous year. It involved responsibility for a learned after-dinner discussion on six separate occasions during the twelve-day period. He chose as the subject of his reading the statutes of jeofails enacted during the reigns of Henry VIII and Elizabeth (statutes 32 Hen.8,c. 30 and 18 Eliz. I, c.13). He brought to his task not only a lawyer's understanding but a legislator's practical experience, for it was those statutes which as a member of the Commons he had been committed to amend in the Parliament of 1621. He had the effort of clear thinking in a state of post-prandial repletion and under the watchful, practised eyes of the benchers. He had the strain of preparing his speeches beforehand and of acting as host at the lavish entertainment and feastings with which the readings were interspersed, a strain intensified by the importance of the guests and the burden of meeting the cost (a reader's expenses could be as much as £600). However, he quitted himself well and was finally admitted as an absolute and confirmed bencher at the next succeeding parliament of the Middle Temple on 28 April. His speech in the

Commons on common fame was six days before—MT II 701, 703, 705; Dugdale 203–10; *CJ* I 847b. There are notes from the reading in BL MS Hargrave 402 and Cambridge University Library MS Dd. 5. 50 (4) ff 27–40; Hh. 3. 7, ff 59–72.

On 4 September 1626 Malet was appointed by Queen Henrietta Maria to be her solicitor general. At Michaelmas and Lady Day he was entitled to receive his fee of £15 from the Queen's treasurer. Whether he would get it or not depended on the state of the royal finances—Patent, Queen Henrietta Maria to Malet 4 Sep. 1626, B. L. Stowe 142 35v, 36 (HMC 8 III 5).

32. Secretary Conway to Mr. Leigh, the mayor etc. of Newtown and the deputy lieutenant of the Isle of Wight—PRO SP 16/92/15–17 All 2 Feb. 1628 (*CSPD* 1627–28 541–2).

33. *DNB*; Sir George Croke, *Reports of Cases in King's Bench and Common Bench* [1582–1641] 3 vols. (1683–1792) III *Charles I* 295, 312, 337, 369. In 1633 Malet was elected by the masters of the bench to be treasurer and in effect principal officer of the Middle Temple—he held the post from 11 Oct. 1633 to 10 Oct. 1634—MT II 810, 824, 825, 843; Ingpen 28, 166–9.

34. Writ of summons. Chancery, petty bag series—PRO C 202/18/2/2.

35. A. Pulling, *The Order of the Coif* (1884) 14, 15, 16 and n 1, 33, 97; Sir Henry Chaundy, *The Historical Antiquities of Hertfordshire* 2 vols. (1826) I 156–7.

36. Besides reference at n 34 above see Sir William Jones, *Les reports de divers special cases cy bien in le Court de Banck le Roy, come le Common-Banck, Angleterre* [1620–1640] (1675) 360; Diary of Sir Richard Hutton *loc cit;* Common Pleas remembrance rolls PRO CP 45/281 m 11.

37. Croke III 531, 539, 540, 588; Serjeants' Inn records PRO 30/23/2/1 ff 40–2.

38. Exchequer, subsidy rolls PRO E 179/143/338 1641.

39. Malet to W. Hawkins 15 and 21 Dec. 1639. The collection of the Rt. Hon. Viscount De L'Isle VC, Penshurst Place, Kent, Sidney Papers 1160/89, 91 (HMC 77 De L'Isle VI 213, 214).

40. See quotations at the head of Chapters 1 and 9.

41. A knighthood normally followed elevation to the bench. Under the terms of a proclamation of James I (T. Rymer and R. Sanderson, *Foedera* 20 vols. (1704–32) XVII 488) Malet had to register his knighthood at the College of Arms within one month of his dubbing or forfeit the honour. His registration took place on 6 July 1641.—W. M. A. Shaw, *The Knights of England* 2 vols. (1906) II 209; Knights from the year 1633 to 1648 Harl 6832 77.

CHAPTER 2—WOOLSACK AND BENCH

1. *The Parliamentary Diary of Robert Bowyer 1606–1607* ed. D. H. Willson (Minneapolis 1931) 121.

2. There is no extant account of Malet's first coming to court as a judge, but I have described the custom of the time—Sir William Jones, *Les reports de divers special cases cy bien in le Court de Banck le Roy, come le Common-Banck, Angleterre* [1620–40] (1675) 151, 247, 248, 299, 415, 450. On one occasion at least during the reign of Charles I a judge treated his brothers to cakes and wine—Jones, *Reports* 415.

3. In Malet's time in Westminster Hall the form 'My Lord' was reserved for the Chief Justice sitting *en banc*; puisnes were 'Sir' even into the nineteenth century.

4. e.g. *LJ* IV 315a, 675b.

5. See, for instance, State Papers, Domestic, dockets SP 38/21/143 29 Sep. 1662 (*CSPD* 1661–2 498).

6. RCHM (England) *London* II *West* (1925) 121–3 and plate 180; John Stow, *The Survey of London* (Everyman 1956) 412–14.

7. British Museum Department of Prints and Drawings [Anon], *Westminster Hall, west end* [actually south], *with the Courts of Chancery and King's Bench in session.* (Line drawing seventeenth century). See plate.

8. Arthur Bryant, *The Story of England: Makers of the Realm* (1953) 178.

9. C. V. Wedgwood, *Thomas Wentworth, First Earl of Strafford 1593–1641* (1964) 337 *et seq.*

10. There is some confusion about the relative positions of the Courts of Chancery and King's Bench in Westminster Hall. This arises from a statement in Sir Thomas Smith, *De Republica Anglorum* (1583) 52:

    'In that hal be ordinarily seene 3 tribunals or judges seates.
    At the entrie on the right hande, the common place...
    At the upper ende of the hall, on the right hand, the kinges bench...
    And on the left hand sitteth the chauncellor...

    This was paraphrased by John Stow—*Survey* 416. King's Bench was on the left as viewed from the great entrance to the Hall and only on the right when viewed from the upper end of the Hall looking towards the entrance. This is confirmed by H. M. Colvin's authoritative *The History of the King's Works* 6 vols. (1963 ff) I plan III and by J. E. Powell and K. Wallis, *The House of Lords in the Middle Ages* (1968) illustration VIII, which is a reproduction of the same plan. W. J. Jones, *The Elizabethan Court of Chancery* (Oxford 1967) 6 falls into the trap set by Smith and Stow. He puts King's Bench on the same side as Common Pleas (when it was in fact on the other side) and Chancery in the south-west corner. A glance at any plan with a north point will show the south-west corner to be on the same side as Common Pleas. In short Jones has put King's Bench and Chancery in the same place. Catherine Drinker Bowen in *The Lion and the Throne* (1957) is so confused that she has put Chancery in the south-east corner on page 5 and in the south-west corner on page 120.

11. The other impeached judges besides Bramston and Berkeley were Chief Baron Davenport, Judge Crawley of the Common Pleas and Barons Trevor and Weston. Bramston and Davenport had both declared for Hampden on technical grounds—*LJ* IV 114b, 115ab, 116a; Gardiner VIII 279.

12. Foss VI 224; Rushworth 3 i 188r; *A Perfect Journall of the Daily Proceedings and Transactions in that Memorable Parliament Begun at Westminster the Third day of November 1640* 2 vols. (1656) I 37 [wrongly ascribed to 11 Feb. 1641]; Bulstrode Whitelocke, *Memorials of the English Affairs* (1682) 117. Dame Veronica Wedgwood refers to Berkeley as Lord Chief Justice. He never was.—C. V. Wedgwood, *The Great Rebellion I: The King's Peace 1637–1641* (1955) 431.

13. Colvin I plan III and n 10 above; Foss VI 211; *DNB*.

14. *Westminster Hall, west end*—; Colvin I plan III; E. W. Brayley, *Londiniana* 4 vols. (1828) I 209–12: *St. Hillaries Teares Shed upon All Professions from the Judge to the Pettyfogger* ([Jun] 1642)—E 151 (16); Hilary St. G. Saunders, *Westminster Hall* (1951) 158.

15. Chancery, patent rolls PRO C66/2891 [mm not numbered] and Crown Office docket books PRO C231/5/456 both of 1 July 1641; Foss VI 210. The form of words used in Malet's patent was in general use after January 1641, but did not become statutorily obligatory until the Act of Settlement in 1701—Sir William Holdsworth, *A History of English Law* 13 vols. (1922–52) VI 234.

16. Trinity Sunday was 20 June 1641. Formal business began on the Monday following and full term started on Friday 25 June 1641. The last legible entry in the King's Bench entry book of rules is dated 13 July 1641, but Trinity term was normally three weeks in length—PRO KB 125/75; C. R. Cheney, *Handbook of Dates for Students of English History* (1970) 68. In the fifteenth century the judges sat in Westminster Hall from 8–11 in the mornings—Sir John Fortescue, *De Laudibus Legum Angliae* (1660) 124. In the time of Sir Henry Spelman who died in 1641 they still did not sit in Westminster Hall in the afternoons—Sir Henry Spelman, *Reliquiae Spelmannianae* (Oxford 1698) 89. See also Holdsworth I 212–17, 226–31.

17. D. Veall, *The Popular Movement for Law Reform 1640–1660* (Oxford 1970) 31–2; *Harleian Miscellany*—ed. W. Oldys 8 vols. (1744–46) III 201.

18. We know that Malet must have received a writ of assistance, because he acted as assistant to the Lords, but no record of his writ exists either in the House of Lords or the Public Record Office. The Lords *Journals* and Chancery Crown Office docket books make it clear that writs were issued to assistants at the time—*LJ* V 263b and PRO C 231/5 p. 425. The quotation is taken from J. F. Macqueen, *A Practical Treatise on the Appellate Jurisdiction of the House of Lords and Privy Council* (1842) 36 n b.

19. Powell and Wallis 204; A. F. Pollard, *The Evolution of Parliament* (1926) 37–40.
20. *CJ* II 26a, 35a, 118a. It was a favourite trick of Pym to call for the doors of the Commons to be locked and the key placed on the table, when he wanted to heighten tension and make some wild rumour appear credible and serious.
21. HLMS X 11; *LJ* IV 95a, 101a, 172a.
22. *LJ* IV 354b.
23. M. Hastings, *Parliament House* (1950) 103, 104; Colvin I 501.
24. Sir William Dugdale, *Origines Juridiciales* (1671) 101. On 5 Nov. 1641 the Lords sat at 2 p.m. after their service and the Commons at noon—*LJ* IV 423a; D'Ewes (C) 87.
25. Sutherland Collection, Ashmolean Museum, Oxford: Clarendon 3 vols. (Oxford 1707) grangerized copy by Sutherland (grangerized version 1837) [Anon] [Charles I in Parliament] (engraving c. 1630) I 175.
26. HLMS X 3.
27. HLMS X 1; Foss VI 211, 343–8; Lord John Campbell, *The Lives of the Lord Chancellors and Keepers of the Great Seal of England* 8 vols. (1845–69). I 27 II 584–8; NPG [Edward Littleton, Baron Littleton of Mounslow 1589–1645 (Oil on canvas after Vandyke) and [John Finch, Baron Finch of Fordwich 1584–1660] (Oil on canvas after Vandyke).
28. De Maisse, *Journal* ed. G. B. Harrison and R. A. Jones (1931) 30; Nicholas II 106.
29. Catherine S. Sims, 'The Moderne Forme of the Parliaments of England', *AHR* LIII 2 (Jan. 1948) 296; H. Elsynge, *The Manner of Holding Parliaments in England* (1768) 111, 112; De Maisse 30. Nicholas II 106; Dugdale 101; Foss VI 231; *DNB*. Throughout the book 'on the Lord Keeper's right (left)' means on the right (left) as viewed by the Lord Keeper.
30. Sims 296–7; Elsynge 111, 112; M. F. Bond, *Guide to the Records of Parliament* (1971) 22.

All the engravings of the Lords chamber in the sixteenth and seventeenth centuries show what appear to be four masters in chancery occupying the lower woolsack facing the Cloth of Estate: behind them kneel four clerks, busy writing. Pollard puts the masters in chancery on the lower woolsack in the time of Elizabeth I—Charles I, Pollard 385. However, Henry Elsynge, who was Clerk of the Parliaments from 1621 until his death in the early 1630s, in 'The Moderne Forme of the Parliaments of England' wrote:

'The masters of the chancery sitt by the learned councell and on the outside of the woolsack towards the bishops. The Clerkes of the Crowne and Parliament sitt on the woolsacke crosse the middle of the House with a table before them to write on. And the Clerke of the Parliament hath one or two clerks who kneele behind the woolsack.'—Sims 296–7.

Elsynge is supported by T. Milles, *The Catalogue of Honor* (1610) 67, by Sir Simonds D'Ewes, *The Journals of All the Parliaments during the Reign of Queen Elizabeth* (1682) 59, and by his son Henry Elsynge, who has a slight variation for the positions of the masters in chancery: 'two on the same side and two on the other side, next the bishops'— Elsynge (1768) 111–12. I am inclined to believe that the two Elsynges, Milles and D'Ewes were right for all ordinary proceedings in 1641. When the sovereign occupied the throne there were more assistants than usual and there may have been a different arrangement.

31. Sims 296; Elsynge 110; *A Catalogue of the Dukes, Marquesses, Earles, Viscounts, Bishops, Barons that Sit in This Parliament Begun 3 of Nov* (3 Nov. 1640)—E 1091(1); W Carey 'The Present State of England' *Harleian Miscellany* 8 vols. (1744–46) III 200–1; Professor Elizabeth Foster wrongly says that 'barons occupied a second form behind the bishops'—Elizabeth R. Foster 'Procedure in the House of Lords during the Early Stuart Period' *JBS* V 2 (May 1966) 62.

32. Sims 296; see also [Anon] [Charles I in Parliament] (engraving c. 1630).

33. *LJ* IV 296 *et seq.*

34. A Lords *Journals* entry for 14 April 1641 reads 'Ordered, that the assistants attending this House are constantly to attend when this House sits' *LJ* IV 217a. See e.g. *LJ* IV 320b, 357b, 362a.

35. In the Lords and Commons *Journals* from mid 1641 to mid 1642, there is only one certain example of a message carried by a judge from Lords to Commons in term time and at a time when the common law courts were probably sitting. That was carried by Malet himself on Thursday 8 July 1641—perhaps an exception, because he was a newly appointed judge. There is a strong presumption that the judges were not normally in the Lords when the courts were sitting. They were certainly not there when they were riding circuit or during the period of licensed absence which followed the summer assizes. The records suggest that at least two were present on the woolsacks at other times during this period. On two occasions the judges withdrew in order to consider matters put to them by the Lords; this clearly indicates that they were present before the order was given—*LJ* IV 494a, 555b. Even during the heyday of the Star Chamber Court the Lords always made it clear that their business took precedence of other courts of law.

36. HLMS X, 3, 4;

37. eg *LJ* IV 293a, V 114a.

38. *LJ* IV and V generally.

39. Rushworth 3 i 130; *LJ* IV 115a.

40. e.g. The Lord Chief Baron was appointed assistant for the select

committee for a bill 'for the prevention of vexatious proceedings touching the order of knighthood'; this concerned the Court of Exchequer—*Statutes of the Realm* [to 1714 ed. T. E. Tomlins *et al*] 11 vols. (1810–28) V 131; *LJ* IV 331b. See also *LJ* IV 326b, 339b. Only one puisne ship-money judge seems to have been assistant to a committee between Malet's promotion and the recess and then only once —*LJ* IV 306b.

41. e.g. *LJ* IV 147b, 347a, 494a, 555b.
42. HLMS X 1, 3, 4; Bowyer 121. But see p. 54.
43. HLMS X 4; *LJ* IV 296–358. For examples of Malet as messenger see e.g. *LJ* IV 304b, 315a, 324a, 331b; *CJ* II 202a, 212b, 220a, 227a.
44. *LJ* IV 299b; Dugdale 102; Gardiner IX 404, 405.
45. *LJ* IV 296b, 297b; Zagorin 243, 244.
46. *LJ* IV 315a, 316b, 321b, 331a, 345a.
47. e.g. a.m. *LJ* IV 297a, 326b, 333a, 334a; p.m. *LJ* IV 302b, 305a, 316b, 332a.
48. E. R. Adair and F. M. Grier Evans, 'Writs of Assistance 1558–1700' *EHR* XXXVI 143 (July 1921) 362.
49. *LJ* IV 314b, 315a.
50. *LJ* IV 319a, 320b, 321b, 325b.
51. Zagorin 243.
52. *LJ* IV 330ab, 331a, 336b; Zagorin 243.
53. *LJ* IV 320a, 331a, 344b, 345a. The four counties were Gloucestershire, Worcestershire, Herefordshire and Shropshire.
54. *LJ* IV 311b, 316ab, 322a, 338b; Zagorin 243.
55. The bills for quieting and for the Welsh marches did not become law. The other three all received the royal assent on 7 Aug. 1641—*LJ* IV 349ab; *Statutes of the Realm* V 116–20 (16 Car I c 14, 15 and 16).
56. *CJ* II 194b. The charges against Bramston and Berkeley had already been read—*CJ* II 162a, 192b.
57. *LJ* IV 303a.
58. *CJ* II 197b.
59. *CJ* II 198a, 211a, 238b.
60. *CJ* II 200a. It never got a second reading.
61. *CJ* II 203ab.
62. *CJ* II 233b, 237b; *LJ* IV 341b.
63. *LJ* IV 305a, 309ab, 310b. The demand originated in the Ten Propositions of 24 June 1641. See p. 5.
64. Gardiner IX 263, 295, 375, 405, 414, 415.
65. *LJ* IV 304b, 324a, 331b, 339b, 347a.
66. Lotte Glow, 'The Manipulation of Committees in the Long Parliament 1641–1642' *JBS* V 1 (Nov. 1965) 46–7; *CJ* II 135a, 208a, 221b, 249b.
67. Firth 74–96.
68. Gardiner IX 353–6, 413, 414; *CJ* II 230b.
69. *LJ* IV 352ab, 356b, 357a; *CJ* II 246ab; Gardiner IX 417, 418.

CHAPTER 3—ASSIZE CYCLE

1. [Anon], *The Office of the Clerk of Assize* (1682) 1. This edition, as opposed to the shorter 1660 edition, is used as a source throughout the chapter.

2. Cockburn 153–87; W. J. Jones, *Politics and the Bench* (1971) 16–17; Thomas G. Barnes, *Somerset 1625–1640* (Oxford 1961) 91–7; *The Clerk of the Peace in Caroline Somerset* (Leicester 1961) 26–7.

3. Thomas G. Barnes, ed., *Somerset Assize Orders 1629–1640 SRS LXV* (Frome 1959) xiii–xvi; Cockburn 23–57; clerks of assize, south-eastern circuit, indictments—PRO ASSI 35/83/4 m3. There is a description of the commissions that were issued out of Chancery under the Great Seal of England to judges of assize in Cockburn 59–61. Malet's commission of oyer and terminer for this circuit was, in fact, issued on 25 June in anticipation of his promotion to the bench. There are sixty-five names on it and besides peers, officers of state, judges and serjeants, it included the clerk of assize and about eight working justices of the peace in each county. Only Weston and Malet were intended to try cases. The peers, officers of state and the other judges never sat. The rest of the commission sat in a supportive capacity and were ineligible to sit on the grand jury of their county—Chancery, entry books of commission (Crown Office) PRO C 181/5 ff 199, 203v, 204, 204v 25 June 1641; Blount's testimony to the Commons 29 March 1642 *CJ* II 502b. The commission of oyer and terminer, together with a patent of assize, a patent of association and commissions of gaol delivery for each of the counties in Malet's circuit are recorded in Chancery Crown Office docket books—PRO C 231/5/476 2 Aug. 1641. The commissions of the peace of these counties were amended to include Malet's name—PRO C 231/5/468, 472, 475 9–16 Aug. 1641. The commissions of gaol delivery are contained in the records listed at note 11 (p. 172). Only that for East Grinstead appears to be missing from the records of the summer assizes 1641.

4. *Clerk of Assize* 3. When Charles I gave his charge to the judges in 1642 he implied that the Lord Keeper had not given directions to the judges for some time before that—Appendix IV.

5. See the records listed at note 11 (p. 172). In 1642 summonses did not always follow the precept set out in *Clerk of Assize* 12–14, but were more often in two separate parts, dealing with assizes and gaol delivery. A good example is to be found in PRO ASSI 35/84/8 mm 17, 18.

6. *CJ* II 233b, 237b; *LJ* IV 341b. See also pp. 34, 35.

7. Compare the commission of the peace for Essex issued on 17 July 1641 (HMC 10 Appendix IV 507–8) with the list of justices among the assize indictments for Essex on 17 Aug. (PRO ASSI 35/83/3 mm 3, 3d).

8. In summer 1641 and winter and summer 1642 only about half the judges who went circuit obtained leave of absence and it is difficult

to detect a pattern. In the event only one judge rode each circuit except in the Norfolk circuit where Chief Justice Bankes (released late by the Lords in 1641) was supported by a serjeant—Cockburn 272; *LJ* IV 357a, 364a.

9. Barnes, *Assize Orders* xiv–xv; Cockburn 51; see also assize records at n 11 below.

10. Sir William Dugdale, *Origines Juridiciales* (1671) 102; Joan Parkes, *Travel in England in the Seventeenth Century* (Oxford 1925) 243–4.

11. The dates and places at which Malet presided at the assizes before the Civil War are shown below, together with the references to the records in the Public Record Office:

14 Aug 1641	Hertford, Herts.	ASSI 35/83/4
17 Aug 1641	Chelmsford, Essex	ASSI 35/83/3
23 Aug 1641	Maidstone, Kent	PRO 30/26/104 ff 14–29
26 Aug 1641	East Grinstead, Sussex	ASSI 35/83/8
30 Aug 1641	Kingston-upon-Thames, Surrey	ASSI 35/83/5
3 Mar 1642	Hertford, Herts.	ASSI 35/84/3
7 Mar 1642	Chelmsford, Essex	ASSI 35/84/10
12 Mar 1642	Southwark, Surrey	ASSI 35/84/6
17 Mar 1642	East Grinstead, Sussex	ASSI 35/84/10
22 Mar 1642	Maidstone, Kent	ASSI 35/84/11
14 Jul 1642	Hertford, Herts.	ASSI 35/84/4
18 Jul 1642	Chelmsford, Essex	ASSI 35/84/2
23 Jul 1642	Maidstone, Kent	ASSI 35/84/5
29 Jul 1642	East Grinstead, Sussex	ASSI 35/84/8
2 Aug 1642	Kingston-upon-Thames, Surrey	ASSI 35/84/1

Professor Alan Everitt says: 'The Maidstone assizes covered West Kent only . . . . . . For East Kent, the assizes were held at Canterbury . . .' Everitt 95 n 2. In fact this is not true of the three circuits that Malet rode. The Kent assizes were at Maidstone in summer 1641, winter 1642 and summer 1642 and they served the whole county on each occasion. Possibly Everitt is confusing assizes and quarter sessions. Kent was split for quarter sessions in the way he described.— Felix Hull, *Guide to the Kent County Archives Office* (Maidstone 1958) 1–2.

12. Parkes 13, 168, 185–224; T. F. Ordish, ed., *Roads out of London* (London Topographical Society 1911) 5; E. G. Box, 'Notes on Some West Kent Roads in Early Maps and Road-books' *AC* XLIII (1931) 95–7.

13. n 11 above; Ordish 5 and plate 1; Barnes, *Assize Records* xvii; Cockburn 65; Parkes 243–4; *Clerk of Assize* 23. We know that Malet travelled

on horseback and not by coach—HLDJ Braye 24 28 March 1642.
14. Barnes, *Assize Records* xvii; Cockburn 65; *The High Sheriff* (1961) 35, 42, 43; Dugdale 101.
15. PRO ASSI 35/83/4 m 18.
16. *CJ* II 35b, 69a; *LJ* IV 172a.
17. Cambridge University Library. The antiquarian collections of Thomas Baker Mm 1.45 31.
18. *CSPD* 1641–43 84; see generally records listed at n 11 above.
19. There is no record of any judge acting as assistant to the Lords from 14 August when the last judge was given leave to go circuit and 9 Sep. 1641 when the two Houses rose for an autumn recess—*LJ* IV 364a–396a. During the recess London and Westminster were hit by the plague so that there was every incentive to leave Westminster for the country.
20. Indenture 18 Jan. 1624 BL Egerton Charter 1608.
21. RCHM (England) *Dorset I West* (1952) 189; J. Fowler, *A Description of Sherborne Scenery* (Sherborne, Dorset 1936) 64–7. A court of survey 3 Oct. 1633 (Egerton 3007 f 87, 88 and Egerton roll 2099 m 1) lists certain fields and common rights which are shown in a tithe apportionment map of 1842 as belonging to the present 'Court House' close to the church—Somerset Record Office D/D/Rt 366 (1842).
22. *CSPD* 1619–23 608, 1623–25 338 etc; Malet 59.
23. R. A. Rebholz, *The Life of Fulke Greville, First Lord Brooke* (Oxford 1971) 300; Warwick County Record Office, Tomes, deeds of title, reference L3 Admington 21, 22, 34, 36, 37.
24. Indentures 10 May 1630 Somerset County Record Office DD SOG/794 and BL Egerton Charter 1609A; RCHM *Dorset West* 187–9. The site of this house can be identified with the present manor house by later leases in the Somerset Record Office—DD/SOG 830–53.
25. Indenture 18 Jan. 1624; court of survey 3 Oct. 1633.
26. Indentures 10 May 1630; court of survey 3 Oct. 1633; N. J. Hone, *The Manor and Manorial Records* (1912) 90. Many of the field names at Poyntington have remained the same from the seventeenth century to this day.
27. Malet to the Lords—HLRO Main papers HL 23 Aug. 1642 (HMC 5 I 44a).
28. MT II 825, 911, 912; J. Foster, ed., *Alumni Oxonienses 1500–1714* 4 vols. (Oxford 1891–92) vol. III 962a; John Hutchinson, *A Catalogue of Notable Middle Templars* (1902) generally; A. R. Ingpen, *The Middle Temple Bench Book* (1912) 194. John Malet was called to the bar in Middle Temple Hall on 9 July 1641. Three days later the Commons ordered all barristers to pay £10 by way of poll tax: he was un-lucky—*CJ* II 206b.
29. Malet 57–60; Michael Malet's will PRO PROB 11/215, s 50 (Grey 50): Proved 21 Mar. 1651.

30. J. E. Neale, *The Elizabethan House of Commons* (1949) 24–7; G. E. Aylmer, *The Struggle for the Constitution 1603–1689* (1968) 22–4; Barnes, *Somerset* 88–9.

   Two pieces of evidence point to Malet's 'dependence' upon the Earl of Bristol. Sir John Coke, the younger, writing to Sir John Coke of Melbourne, Derbyshire in April of the following year, said of the Earl of Bristol:

   'upon whom both the Judge [Malet] and Sir George Stroud have dependence.'—The collection of the Marquess of Lothian DL, Melbourne Hall, Derby. Earl Cowper (Coke) MSS 4 Apr. 1642 (HMC 12 Appendix II 311).

   This is positive and is supported indirectly by Sir George Strode's testimony to the House of Commons on 1 April 1642. He said that he gave Malet a copy of a petition and asked him to show it to the earl. He did not name the earl. Both of them knew which earl Strode meant—*CJ* II 507a.

31. Gardiner X 1–5; *LJ* IV 367b, 368a, 372b, 373a, 375ab, 379b, 384b–7a, 394b.

32. Gardiner X 14–18, 29–31; *CSPD* 1641–43 134; John Nalson, ed., *An Impartial Collection of the Great Affairs of State from the Beginning of the Scotch Rebellion in the Year 1639 to the Murther of Charles I* 2 vols. (1682–83) II 491, 492.

33. Gardiner X 32–79.

34. Dering 109.

35. Zagorin 261–9, 305; J. S. Morrill, *The Revolt of the Provinces* (1976) 31 ff.

36. Gardiner X 37, 38; *CSPD* 1641–43 193–7; *CJ* II 338ab, 339a, 340ab, 342a; D'Ewes (C) 263–6, 268–9, 270–3; Valerie Pearl, *London and the Outbreak of the Puritan Revolution 1625–1643* (Oxford 1961) 222, 223.

37. Gardiner X 117–25.

38. Gardiner X 128–33; *LJ* IV 500b, 501a, 502b; *CJ* II 367a.

39. Gardiner X 150, 152–60.

40. *CJ* II 370ab, 371a; *LJ* IV 506a; Nehemiah Wallington, *Historical Notices of the Reign of Charles I* [1630–46] ed. R. Webb 2 vols. (1869) II 1, 2.

41. *LJ* IV 537b–540b; *The Petition of the County of Essex to the House of Commons*... (18 Jan. 1642) E 131 (24); *Two Petitions of the Inhabitants of the County of Hertford*... (25 Jan. 1642) E 133 (15). Wallington 4. The Essex petition was delivered to the Commons on 20 January, the Middlesex petition on 24 January, and the two Hertfordshire petitions on 25 Jan. 1642—*CJ* II 387b, 391a, 393a.

42. *LJ* IV 537a–543a; Wallington II 4, 5.

43. Gardiner X 162–3; *LJ* IV 558ab, 563b, 564ab.

44. Gardiner X 165–7; *LJ* IV 580b.

45. *LJ* IV 573ab, 574b, 575ab, 579b, 587a, 589b, 611ab, 627b, 640ab, 647b, 648ab, 651ab, 652a; *CJ* II 440a, 441b, 449a, 455a, 469a, 476b, 497a, and sources quoted in n 46. See also HMC 5 I 6–15.

46. *CJ* II 412b, 421a, 422a, 423a, 424a, 425a, 428ab, 433a, 434a, 438a, 452b, 464a, 466b, 474ab, 480b(2), 491a, 503b.

47. Wallington II 2, 9, 31; Samuel Butler, *Hudibras* ed. A. R. Waller (Cambridge 1905) 44.

48. *CJ* II 389a. The ensuing Protestation Returns are held in HLRO.

49. *CJ* II 420b, 421a; *LJ* IV 570ab; *The Petition of the County of Northampton. together with the Two Petitions of the County of Kent* (8 Feb. 1642) E 135(36). The speech *Mr. Pym his Speech at a Conference of Both Houses concerning the Petition of the County of Kent* (8 Feb. 1642) E 200 (26) was never delivered.

    A description of the cavalcade coming up Fish Street Hill with this petition is given at Wallington II 8.9. It is clearly dated Tuesday 8 February, the day when this pro-Parliament petition was delivered to the two Houses. Dame Veronica Wedgwood uses Wallington's account to describe a later cavalcade led by Richard Lovelace and supporting the petition drafted at the March assizes.—Wedgwood 89–90 and n 86. Lovelace's cavalcade never got to Fish Street Hill; it was halted by a company of the London Trained Bands before London Bridge and only a small party was allowed to cross—*CJ* II 549ab; *Strange Newes from Kent concerning the Passages of the Kentish Men which Came to Westminster 29 April* [1642] E 145 (6).

50. *LJ* IV 609a; *CJ* II 451b; *ST* IV 141–52, 167–70; Pearl 148–50.

51. Rev. L. B. Larking, ed., *Proceedings Principally in the County of Kent . . .* (Camden Society 1862) xlii–xlvi; Everitt 92–4; Dering.

52. *LJ* IV 599b, 600b. One of the serjeants was a judge of assize. See Cockburn 272.

53. *LJ* IV 618b–20a.

54. *LJ* IV 612a.

55. PRO ASSI 35/84 3, 6, 10.

56. *LJ* IV 646a, 647a, 650a; *CJ* II 479ab, 481ab, 482a, 484a.

57. J. E. Neale, *The Elizabethan House of Commons* (1949) 426–9.

58. The journal of Sir Simonds D'Ewes Harl 163 60.

59. The assizes at East Grinstead began on Thursday 17 March—PRO ASSI 35/84/10 m 85. They would have lasted less than three full days. Malet rode into Maidstone on Saturday 19 March—see p. 34 and n 22 to that page.

CHAPTER 4—THE GREAT BUSINESS AT MAIDSTONE

(Names in brackets after *LJ*, *CJ*, Add and HLDJ references in this chapter refer to the men whose evidence to the appropriate House is the source of a statement in the text.)

1. *CJ* II 507a (Twysden). This chapter is concerned with the Maidstone

assizes March 1642. Dame Veronica Wedgwood says of these assizes (identified at Wedgwood 89):

> 'In Kent, a Royalist judge, Thomas Malet, had persuaded the grand jury at Maidstone to adopt a petition that all military power be restored to the King, and that Parliament remove from the vicinity of London to some place where members need fear no interference from the rabble.'—Wedgwood 83 and n 68.

It is at least questionable that Malet was a Royalist at this time (see p. 117). There is no evidence that Malet persuaded the grand jury to do anything except avoid discussing the petition in his presence. The worst he was accused of doing was concealing the petition from Parliament. Even contemporary pamphlets do not accuse him of more.

Dame Veronica is mistaken about the contents of the petition. The key lies in her footnote. She refers us to a page in the *Calendar of State Papers, Domestic* which contains not the Kentish petition of March 1642, but some instructions issued to Augustine Skinner, one of the knights of the shire, in July (see pp. 105–6). Dame Veronica has an excuse; the *CSPD* entry is wrongly dated—*CSPD* 1641–43 314. She gives an impression that the Kent petitioners of March 1642 were deliberately offensive, asking for trouble. The fact is that they were at great pains to submit something reasonable in concept, moderate and conciliatory in tone.

Perez Zagorin says 'A . . . . . significant outbreak of Royalist sentiment occured in Kent at the end of March' and goes on to talk of a Royalist petition—Zagorin 313, 314. He is quite wrong. No outbreak of Royalist sentiment took place in Kent in March. The March Kentish petition was Royalist neither in tone nor intent.

2. *Harleian Miscellany* ed. W. Oldys 8 vols. (1744–46) III 476; *DNB*. The incident that gave rise to this story was alleged to have taken place at Huntingdon assizes in 1619.

3. *DNB*; NPG [Anon] [Sir John Doddridge 1555–1628] (oil on canvas). Doddridge's reading took place in 1603—John Hutchinson, *A Catalogue of Notable Middle Templars* (1902) 75; Sir Thomas Smith, *De Republica Anglorum* (1583) 77; *The Clerk of Assize . . .* (1660) E 2139 (3) 4.

4. See plate section for J. H. Baverstock, *Some Account of Maidstone in Kent* (1832) sketch facing p. 10; Smith 77; Sir William Dugdale, *Origines Juridiciales* (1671) 101; *The Clerk of Assize* (1660) 4. There were about forty-five justices present—clerks of assize, south-eastern circuit, indictments PRO ASSI 35/84/11 mm 4, 4d, 3. A number of portraits of Malet exist. The most reliable for his dress and appearance in 1642 is reproduced in the caricature (see plate section). A full account of Malet's portraits appears at Appendix I, including some copies derived from the portrait reproduced in the plate section.

5. PRO Miscellaneous PRO 30/26/104 19 no 13.

6. *CJ* II 507a (Twysden); *LJ* V 18a (Dering's impeachment).
7. See relevant assize records listed at p. 172 n 11.
8. *William Lambarde and Local Government* ed. Conyers Read (Ithaca, New York 1962) vi.
9. *CJ* II 507a (Twysden, Strode); 'Sir Roger Twysden's Journal' ed. L. B. L[arking] AC I (1858) 202.

    Professor Alan Everitt says'... in response to Judge Malet's suggestion (for which there was apparently no precedent) that, instead of yeomen chosen by the sheriff, the gentry should offer themselves for the grand jury...'—Everitt 95. Everitt did not have the benefit of Dr. R. F. Hunnisett's work in sorting the assize records in the Public Record Office. Every one of the jurors at the preceding Maidstone assizes was a gentleman although none of them styled himself 'esquire'. See n 5 to this chapter. Malet was suggesting, not that the gentry should offer themselves, but that the grand jury should not be composed exclusively of minor gentry, that it should in fact contain some men of real consequence in the county. Brunton and Pennington point out that in theory 'esquire' was a title that could be acquired by office-holding and was not necessarily superior to 'gentleman' but in practice there was a clear social distinction—D. Brunton and D. H. Pennington, *Members of the Long Parliament* (1954) 4 n 1.
10. *AC* I 202.
11. J. H. Gleason, *The Justices of the Peace 1558–1640* (Oxford 1969) 116–22, 138–9.
12. PRO ASSI 35/84/11 mm 4, 4d, 3.
13. Chancery, entry books of commission (Crown Office) PRO C 181/5 221v–2v; *CJ* II 502b (Blount); Spencer; Answer of Richard Spencer Esq. to his impeachment HLRO Main Papers HL 21 May 1642 (HMC 5 I 24b).
14. These would be the justices who disapproved the proposals put forward on the preceding night. See p. 35 and *CJ* II 502 b (Blount).
15. *CJ* II 502b (Blount), 507a (Strode); *AC* I 202.
16. *CJ* II 502b (Blount), 507a (Strode); *DNB*; See also p. 174 n 30.
17. Blount later reported that ten justices left the bench to join the grand jury—*CJ* II 502b (Blount); Framlingham Gawdy's diary Add 14827 77 (Blount). A comparison of the grand jury list and the list of justices shows that only eight justices left the bench—PRO ASSI 35/84/11 mm 4, 4d, 3, 76.
18. The argument about 'packing' is advanced on p. 39.
19. *AC* I 202; L. B. Larking, ed., *Proceedings Principally in the County of Kent...* (Camden Society 1862) xxxix–xlvi.
20. *LJ* V 17b (Dering's impeachment); *The Office of the Clerk of Assize...* (1682) 31, 32.
21. *CSPD* 1641–43 349; *AC* I 202–3; *The Clerk of Assize* (1660) 7.
22. *AC* I 200; *CJ* II 197b. There is some confusion about the days on

which events occurred at these assizes. It stems from a statement in Twysden's journal '...whither I came on Tuesday, 21st March 1641–2, the assizes beginning the next day'.—*AC* I 200. Twysden made a mistake; the Tuesday was in fact 22 March. Jessup, his biographer, copies 'Tuesday 21 March' from the journal without checking it—Jessup 45. Everitt probably assumed that Twysden was more likely to be right about the day of the week than the date. He says that the gentry arrived in Maidstone on Monday 21 March, that they commenced their discussion about the proposed petition on the following day and that Malet made his suggestion about the composition of the grand jury on the Wednesday—Everitt 95. This conflicts with Twysden who makes it clear that the gentry arrived, supped and discussed the petition on the same day and that the assizes opened on the day following—*AC* I 200–2. From PRO records it is clear that the assizes began (and therefore the jurors were sworn) on Tuesday 22 March—PRO ASSI 35/84/11 mm 4, 5, 6 etc.

23. Everitt 44, 70–83; Jessup 42–3.
24. *AC* I 200; *DNB.*
25. *AC* I 200; *CJ* II 507a (Strode).
26. *AC* I 200, 201; D. C. Maynard, *The Old Inns of Kent* (1925) 197; PRO ASSI 35/84/11 mm 4, 4d, 3; *CJ* II 507a (Twysden).
27. Nehemiah Wallington, *Historical Notices of the Reign of Charles I* [1630–46] ed. R. Webb 2 vols (1869) II 8, 9; Everitt 94–5; *The Petition of the County of Northampton: Together with Two Petitions of the County of Kent* (8 Feb. 1642) E 135 (36).
28. *CJ* II 502b (Blount).
29. Spencer.
30. PRO C 181/5 221v–2v; See p. 171 n 3.
31. *AC* I 201–2.
32. Spencer.
33. *CJ* II 372b, 373a.
34. *AC* I 200.
35. J. M. Russell, *The History of Maidstone* (Maidstone 1881) 276–80; Baverstock sketch, plate section; PRO 30/26/104 24 no 19; PRO ASSI 35/84/11 m 6 etc; Cockburn 314.
36. PRO ASSI 35/84/11 mm 78–108.
37. *LJ* V 19a (Dering's impeachment).
38. Strode; *CJ* II 502b (Blount); *LJ* V 18a (Dering's impeachment).
39. PRO ASSI 35/84/11 m 76; PRO 30/26/104 f 19 no 13.
40. Everitt 138, 154; *DNB.*
41. *AC* I 203; *The Clerk of Assize* (1660) 7; PRO ASSI 35/84/11 m 79.
42. *AC* I 203; Add 14827 76 (Browne).
43. *AC* I 203.
44. *AC* I 203, 204; Jessup 5, 42. The quotation is from clause 17 of the petition. See Appendix II.

45. *AC* I 204; Jessup 47.
46. *CJ* II 507a (Piers).
47. *AC* I 204.
48. Sir John Coke the younger to Sir John Coke at Melbourne 4 April 1642. The collection of the Marquess of Lothian DL, Melbourne Hall, Derby. Cowper (Coke) MSS (HMC 12 Appendix II 311).
49. The names of the nineteen jurors are contained in PRO ASSI/35/84/11 m 76.

    Of the nineteen on the jury nine protested against the petition—*CJ* II 502b (Blount); Sir John Coke the younger to Sir John Coke at Melbourne 4 April 1642

    Dering and Strode were impeached for framing the petition. Hamond supported the petition—*CJ* II 511b; Palmer was a Royalist—pp. 32, 38, 99. There could only have been six other jurors who voted for the petition.

    Blount was on the jury and against the petition. On 29 March 1642 he handed to the Commons a note containing the signatures of the nine who voted against it. Soon afterwards, on the same day, the Commons summoned eight other jurors to attend them (Amherst, Broadnax, Fance, Hardres, Oxinden, Lennard, Cattlett and Roper). There is a strong presumption that these eight were the balance of the jury who voted with Blount against the petition. Amherst later joined the county committee for Kent—*CJ* II 502b, 503a; Everitt 154.

    There is no conclusive evidence about which Oxinden served on the grand jury. Henry Oxinden of Barham was unable to accompany Livesey's petition although a number of his friends wanted him to support them; from the tenor of a letter written on 6 Feb. 1642 it would appear that he was ill—Dorothy Gardiner, ed., *The Oxinden Letters 1607–1642* (1933) 287–8. He was again ill in April/May, although he had wanted to accompany a petition to Parliament on that occasion, too. Dorothy Gardiner assumes that his undated letter referred to Dering's petition—Gardiner, *Oxinden Letters* 297 and n. He may well have been talking about Blount's petition which reached Parliament five days later. The views in his letters are not inconsistent with his having opposed Dering's petition on the grand jury. Henry Oxinden of Deane approved the Grand Remonstrance and Henry Oxinden of Great Maydeacon was later a Parliamentary captain. Either of these could have been the Oxinden who served on the grand jury—Gardiner, *Oxinden Letters* 254; Everitt 153.
50. *CJ* II 502b (Blount).
51. *CJ* II 503a (Blount); Strode.
52. *LV* IV 675b (Jones).
53. *CJ* II 503a (Blount). Although no single witness spells out the fact, it is clear that the issue of a petition was raised in open court in the presence of the judge both before and after it was drafted. The

first occasion is recorded by Twysden at *AC* I 203 and the second at *CJ* II 503a (Blount). At neither time did the judge allow it to be discussed in his presence.

54. Sir John Coke the younger to Sir John Coke at Melbourne 4 April 1642.
55. *LJ* V 18b (Dering's impeachment); Strode; Spencer.
56. *AC* I 204–5.
57. Jessup 48.
58. *AC* I 205; *CJ* II 507a (Twysden); *LJ* IV 676a (Jones).
59. Add 14827 77v (Blount).
60. *LJ* V 18b (Dering's impeachment); Strode. Professor Everitt is mistaken in saying that Pope was the clerk of assize—Everitt 98. He was neither clerk of assize nor was he an associate. See p. 37 and n 35 to this chapter.
61. *LJ* IV 678ab (Kentish petition). See Appendix II.
62. Add 14827 75v, 76 (White), 77v (Blount); *LJ* V 18b (Dering's impeachment).
63. Add 14827 77v (Blount); Sir John Coke the younger to Sir John Coke at Melbourne 4 April 1642; *LJ* IV 678b (Kentish petition). *The Journals of the House of Commons* say that the meeting would take place on 23 April, but this is incorrect—*CJ* II 503a (Blount).
64. T. F. Ordish, ed., *Roads out of London* (1911) 7.
65. *The Clerk of Assize* (1660) 25; *The Office of the Clerk of Assize* (1682) 35.
66. HLDJ Braye 24 28 Mar. 1642 (Malet); *LJ* IV 678b (Malet); *CJ* II 507a (Strode); Strode.
67. *CJ* II 507a (Strode). Pope is wrongly described as 'Cope' at *LJ* IV 678b.
68. HLDJ Braye 24 28 Mar. 1642 (Malet); *LJ* IV 678b (Malet).
69. *LJ* IV 677a–8b. See Appendix II, clauses 11 and 12.
70. *LJ* IV 651ab, 652a; *CJ* II 485a; Zagorin 292.
71. Jessup 138–44; Everitt 70–83, 89, 90.
72. *AC* I 210.
73. The journal of Sir Simonds D'Ewes Harl 163 65; *CJ* II 513a.
74. *LJ* IV 721a.
75. *CJ* II 510ab (Cropley).
76. *CJ* II 549b (Lovelace).
77. D'Ewes wrote that 'Anthonie Haiman' was reported to the Commons because he got hands for the petition—Harl 163 63v; but the Commons sent for 'Mr. Anth. Hammon'—*CJ* II 511b.
78. *AC* I 210–11.

CHAPTER 5—MONDAY 28 MARCH

1. Gardiner X 182.
2. The journal of Sir Simonds D'Ewes Harl 163 50v; *LJ* IV 674b.
3. D. H. Pennington in his 'A Day in the Life of the Long Parliament'

History Today III (1953) 681 says there were four tiers of benches on Tuesday 16 November 1641. He was probably unaware of the two prints of the House of Commons chamber in 1640. The one in the British Museum Print Room shows the Short Parliament in session, while the one in the Duchy of Cornwall records depicts the Long Parliament in session and reads

A MORE PERFECT PLATFORM THEN HITHERTO HATH BIN PUBLISHED OF THE LOWER HOUSE OF THIS PRESENT PARLIAMENT

Assembled at Westminster, the third day of November, 1640 and in the 17 yeere of his Majesties happie raigne

With the names of the lords spirituall and temporall of the upper House as also the knights, citizens and burgesses of the counties, cities and boroughs of England and Wales, and barons of the ports of the Lower House

> LONDON
> PRINTED by E P for Nicholas Bourne,
> and are to be sold at his shop at the
> South Entrance of the Royal Exchange
> 1641.

In fact the Duchy of Cornwall picture of the Long Parliament (as opposed to the title and names) is the same as that of the Short Parliament in the British Museum. Both show five rows of members and not four as Pennington suggests. Both are interesting because they are the first to give any reliable guide to the architectural detail of the Commons chamber.

I am grateful to Mr. H. M. Colvin CBE, Reader in Architectural History at Oxford University, for drawing my attention to the Duchy of Cornwall version which is reproduced in the plate section. Earlier prints of the Commons chamber are not consistent in the number of rows they depict. My authority for the position of the mace is a line drawing done by Drapentier sometime between 1625 and 1649—Ashmolean Museum, Oxford, Sutherland Collection. Sutherland's grangerized copy of Clarendon 3 vols. (1707) collected 1795–1835 completed 1837 I 141. For evidence that the mace lay on the table when the speaker was in the chair see D'Ewes (N) 210, 211, 368, 380.

4. *CJ* II 500b, 501a; Harl 163 50v, 51v.
5. Sanford 295–6; Harl 163 50v, 51v, 52v; J. Forster, *The Debates on the Grand Remonstrance...* (1860) 283.
6. Sanford 296; D'Ewes (N) xii.
7. Sanford 295; D'Ewes (N) xiii.
8. Harl 163 52v.
9. Forster 282.

10. D'Ewes (C) xxviii n 32, 58; *CSPD* 1641–43 190.
11. Harl 163 52v.
12. Harl 163 57v; there is also confirmation that Moore collaborated with D'Ewes at D'Ewes (N) x, xii.
13. *CJ* II 501b.
14. HLDJ Braye 24 28 Mar. 1642. See also n 15 below.
15. *CJ* II 501b; Framlingham Gawdy's diary Add 14827 75, 75v, 76, 76v.
16. *CJ* II 501 ab; Forster 283–5; Sanford 295–6. The ultimate aurhority for the normal places occupied by members of the Long Parliament is the manuscript diary of Sir Simonds D'Ewes (Harl 162–6). This is only partly in print and the rest takes a great deal of time to decipher. Successive historians have usually, therefore, been partly dependent on the researches of their predecessors. The first attempt to place some of the members from D'Ewes's notes was made in the *Edinburgh Review* in 1846. Then John Forster published an article in 1858 and was followed by J. L. Sanford a few months later (*Studies and Illustrations of the Great Rebellion* (1858) 295–6). J. Forster incorporated his version into his *The Debates on the Grand Remonstrance* (1860) 283–5. These two succeeded in placing still more members. (They also put Sir Walter Erle on different sides of the chamber.) D. H. Pennington, 'A Day in the Life of the Long Parliament' *History Today* III (1953) 681–8 appears to be the most recent to indulge in this exercise.
17. Clarendon III 241.
18. *CJ* II 501a; Add 14827 75v 76; *LJ* IV 675b, 676a. It is not completely clear whether a Mr. White gave the last part of this evidence or whether Framlingham Gawdy wrote 'Whyte' when he meant 'Jones', to whom he had referred earlier.
19. *CJ* II 501a; Add 14827 76.
20. *CJ* II 501a.
21. *CJ* II 478b.
22. *DNB;* Keeler; J. Forster, *The Statesmen of the Commonwealth of England* 5 vols. (1840) III 242–3. The first person who made any attempt to group the various shades of opinion among the Parliamentarians was Professor J. H. Hexter, *The Reign of King Pym* (Cambridge, Mass. 1961), who differentiated between the war, middle and peace groups in the period after the oubreak of the Civil War. Lotte Glow in her typescript PhD thesis of 1963 (Glow 70–4) used the same grouping to distinguish opposition groups before as well as after the outbreak of war but she added to these three groups a fourth group, the administrators, who, she says, were 'non-political members who did not take a public stand on the major issues of the day'. Two years later in 'The Committee-men in the Long Parliament August 1642—December 1643', *Historical Journal* VIII I (1965) 13, she suggested that they were 'impartial administrators'. I am unconvinced that this

fourth group ever existed except in the sense that the individuals who composed it were undoubtedly administrators ignored by Hexter and noticed by Miss Glow. As we shall see, John Wilde and George Peard, whom Miss Glow labelled 'administrators', were every bit as political as some of Pym's closest adherents. I have used the word 'moderate' to describe those who belonged to the 'peace' group of Professor Hexter before the Civil War; some of them who became Royalists later were still numbered among the Country opposition on 28 March 1642.

23. *CJ* II 501ab.

24. *CJ* II 501b.

25. The courts were not sitting at the time. It was certainly Malet's duty to be present in the Lords—see p. 12. The evidence that Malet was present on the woolsack in the Lords on this morning is circumstantial, but convincing. When the Commons asked for a conference with the Lords at which Malet should be present, the Lord Keeper, after consulting the Lords, replied at once to the messengers from the Commons that 'Mr Justice Malet shall be present at it'—*LJ* IV 675b. Had Malet not been present the Lord Keeper would have replied either that the Lords would send for him or that the Lords would reply by messengers of their own.

26. De Maisse, *Journal* ed. G. B. Harrison and R. A. Jones (1931) 30; from 15 Feb. 1642 the Lord Keeper's chaplain said prayers—*LJ* IV 586b. The benches of the bishops were hard against the wall—Harl 163 68v. In the expression 'on the right hand side of the chamber' the words 'as viewed by the Speaker' are implied. See also p. 2 n 29.

27. Only serjeants and masters in chancery were used as messengers by Lords to Commons 1 Mar.—8 Apr. 1642 inclusive—*LJ* IV 620b–707b.

28. *LJ* IV 674b; cf *LF* IV 633b, 634a, 640ab, 642a, 643ab, 658b, 659b, 663a, 664b.

29. On 9 Feb. 1642 there were 67 peers absent; on 2 April 1642 there were 69 absent—*LJ* IV 571 ab, 693 ab.

30. On 26 March there were 37 peers present according to the House of Lords original manuscript minutes. No manuscript minutes exist for the period 28 Mar.—16 Dec. 1642. The evidence about voting on 28 Mar. 1642 is circumstantial. I have taken the list of peers present on 25 and 26 Mar. 1642, the last two days on which are original manuscript minutes to record the presence of peers. I have added to this list all those who were reported in the journal, those who were placed on the committee for the Kentish petition and those who protested against the motion to consign the Earl of Bristol to the Tower on 28 March, but I have estimated that there were probably about 36 peers present on 28 March. I have deduced the way that the peers actually voted on 28 Mar. 1642 from the way that they protested against motions in the Lords during the weeks

immediately before and from information about the lives of individual peers. Very few of the peers likely to have been present on 28 March did not declare themselves by entering official protests on a number of occasions. J. E. T. Rogers, ed., *A Complete Collection of the Protests of the Lords* 3 vols. (Oxford 1875) is misleading because it only gives the protests for which dissenting peers advanced reasons in writing. There were many others for which reasons were not advanced in writing including the protest of 28 Mar. 1642. A list of how peers dissented from motions in the Lords between 1 Jan. and 28 Mar. 1642 and how they probably voted on 28 Mar. 1642 is contained in Appendix III.

The waverers at this stage are fairly easy to identify. Lord Keeper Littleton eventually fled with the Great Seal after a spell of psychosomatic illness. Hertford, Huntingdon and Strange never declared their hand by dissent, but eventually sided with the King. Leicester, Hastings, Cromwell and Paget had sided more or less with the popular party till now; eventually they, too, sided with the King. Clare and Salisbury continued to waver.

31. *LJ* IV 646b and Appendix III. De Maisse 30.
32. *LJ* IV 674b, 675a; Catherine S. Sims, 'The Moderne Forme of the Parliaments of England' *AHR* LIII 2 (Jan. 1948) 300; HLMS X 4; W. Hakewill, *The Manner How Statutes are Enacted in Parliament by Passing of Bills* (1641) 71.
33. HLMS X 4; Sims 300; [PRO] *Guide to the Contents of the Public Record Office* 2 vols. (1963) I 10; Hakewill 5, 71; Lord John Campbell, *The Lives of the Lord Chancellors and Keepers of the Great Seal of England* 8 vols. (1845–69) I 27; *LJ* IV 675a; Keeler.
34. Sims 300; *LJ* IV 675b.
35. HLMS X 4; *LJ* IV 675b.
36. HLMS X 4.
37. *LJ* IV 675b.
38. *The Parliamentary Diary of Robert Bowyer 1606–1607* ed. D. H. Willson (Minneapolis 1931) 232 *et seq*; *Diary and Correspondence of John Evelyn* (including Nicholas correspondence) ed. H. B. Wheatley 4 vols. (1906) IV 99; HLMS X 5.
39. HLMS X 3, 4, 5.
40. H. M. Colvin, *The History of the King's Works* 6 vols. (1963ff) I 495 and Plan III; E. W. Brayley and J. Britton, *The History of the Ancient Palace and Late Houses of Parliament at Westminster* (1836) 418–20; Hilary St. George Saunders, *Westminster Hall* (1951) 22.
41. *CJ* II 501a.
42. D'Ewes (C) 117.
43. *A Worthy Speech Made by Master Pym to the Lords concerning an Information against the Lord Digby* (31 Dec. 1641) E 199 (49). The speech was never delivered, but the form of words rings true. D'Ewes (C) 363 n 16.

44. Pym's handling of the accusation against Strafford and of 'the Incident' during the King's visit to Scotland are typical examples of his technique—D'Ewes (N) 27–9, (C) 21 n 13.

45. *LJ* IV 676a; *CJ* II 501ab; HMC 5 I 14b; It would appear that there was no evidence implicating Strode until after the Commons had asked for a conference with the Lords. See n 46 below. The Earl of Bristol produced a copy of the petition to the Lords in the afternoon—*LJ* IV 677a.

46. HLDJ Braye 24 28 Mar. 1642. There is a discrepancy between the original manuscript journal (from which the printed *Journals of the House of Lords* are derived) and the original manuscript draft journal for this day. The original manuscript journal reports that Malet was only interrogated by the Lords once in the afternoon. The original manuscript draft journal makes it clear that he was questioned both in the morning and afternoon sessions. The account in the manuscript draft journal must be the correct one for even the manuscript journal reports that the Lords sent for Strode before dinner; their questioning of Malet about him was designed to see whether they *should* send for him. The manuscript draft journal reported events in chronological order; the manuscript journal tended to play down differences of opinion and this one was resolved during the course of the day.

47. HLDJ Braye 24 28 Mar. 1642.

48. Appendix III; *LJ* IV 678b; *DNB*.

49. *DNB*; J. H. Hexter, *The Reign of King Pym* (Cambridge, Mass. 1961) 78 n 31. C. V. Wedgwood, *The Great Rebellion I: The King's Peace 1637–1641* (1955) 131; C. E. Wade, *John Pym* (1912) 255; Evelyn ed. Wheatley 93.

50. *LJ* IV 676a; *CJ* II 501b. The Commons *Journals* report that it was Sir Edward Leech and not Serjeant Finch who acted as messenger with Serjeant Ayloff. It is assumed here that the Clerk of the Parliaments was more likely to be right.

51. *CJ* II 501b.

52. *CJ* II 501b; 'Sir Roger Twysden's Journal' ed. L. B. L[arking] *AC* I (1858) 211, 212.

53. *CJ* II 501b; *LJ* IV 676a.

54. Glow 17 and n 28, 18.

55. *DNB*; Keeler, Glow 227, 228, 229 and n 105, 361, 362; *CJ* II 501b. Strictly Dover was considered not a Kent constituency but a cinque port. Sir Henry Vane the younger was not added to the committee until Oliver Cromwell proposed him on 31 Mar. 1642, although his name appears in the original list of committee members in the journals—*CJ* II 506b; Harl 163 56v. Professor Keeler wrongly records Sir Henry Heyman as member for Rye; Brunton and Pennington show him as plain Henry Heyman. He was baron for Hythe, knighted on 7 July 1641 and created a baronet in the following month—Keeler; D. Brunton and D. H. Pennington, *Members of the Long Parliament*

(1954) 217, 234; *Return of the Names of Every Member Returned to Serve in Each Parliament (Official Return)* 2 vols. (1878) 497. *DNB* says wrongly that Robert Reynolds was knighted in 1618. He was knighted in 1660.—MT III 1146, 1147, Keeler, *Official Return* 496.

56. HLDJ|Braye 24 28 Mar. 1642; c.f. *LJ* IV 678b.

57. HLDJ Braye 24 28 Mar. 1642; *LJ* IV 678b.

58. *LJ* IV 678b, 679a; HLMS X 2; Sims 296. Professor J. S. Cockburn says: 'Everitt is mistaken in asserting that following the March petition Malet J was sent to the Tower.'—Cockburn 239 n 1. In fact Professor Everitt was right. Malet went to the Tower twice: 28 March: *LJ* IV 679a, 711b, V 12a, 35b; 6 August: *LJ* V 268b, 337b, 652a etc. See also Clarendon V 52, 426; Gardiner X 181.

CHAPTER 6—RETRIBUTION

1. *CSPV* 1642–43 35.

2. *CJ* II 502b, 503a. An example of the publicity given to the Kentish petition of March 1642 outside Parliament is to be found in a contemporary news pamphlet, which reported that 'there was like to be a great insurrection thereupon within the said county.' There never was the slightest danger of an insurrection until the two Houses began to harry the petitioners—*A Perfect Diurnall of the Passages in Parliament from the Twenty-Eighth of March 1642 to the Fourth of April* [Apr. 1642] E 202 (1).

3. *CJ* II 502b, 503a; the journal of Sir Simonds D'Ewes Harl 163 53v; Framlingham Gawdy's diary Add 14827 77, 77v.

4. *CJ* II 503a; Harl 163 53v.

5. *LJ* IV 488b, 497b; *CJ* II 473b, 506b.

6. *LJ* IV 683a; *CJ* II 505b.

7. *CJ* II 506a; Everitt 107, 108.

8. *CJ* II 507a; Harl 163 57v.

9. *CJ* II 507a; Harl 163 57v.

10. *CJ* II 507a, 508a; Harl 163 57v. D'Ewes thought that Dr. Piers was a physician.

11. *LJ* IV 687b.

12. 'Sir Roger Twysden's Journal' ed. L. B. L[arking] AC I (1858) 212–13.

13. *AC* I 212.

14. *LJ* IV 685a; *CJ* II 506a.

15. *LJ* IV 693a, 701a; *CJ* II 513a.

16. *LJ* IV 699a; *CJ* II 511b.

17. *LJ* IV 709a; *CJ* II 513a.

18. Harl 163 86.

19. *CJ* II 558b; Add 14827 95

20. *CJ* II 503a.

21. *CJ* II 510a.

22. *CJ* II 511b.

23. *CJ* II 513a, 518b, 526b; Everitt 144.
24. *AC* I 213.
25. Harl 163 63v; *CJ* II 511b. See p. 45 and n 77 to that page.
26. Harl 163 65.
27. *CJ* II 513a. D'Ewes reported incorrectly that the issue was referred to the Committee for Irish Affairs—Harl 163 65v.
28. *LJ* IV 701a.
29. *LJ* IV 710b.
30. *LJ* IV 717a.
31. *CJ* II 513b, 514b; *LJ* IV 703ab; E 202 (1) wrongly ascribed to 31 Mar. 1642.
32. *CJ* II 514b.
33. *CJ* II 516b, 518a; Harl 163 66v 67.
34. Harl 163 68v, 68; *DNB*; Keeler.
35. *CSPV* 1642 43.
36. *CJ* II 546b.
37. *LJ* IV 699a, 701a.
38. *LJ* IV 711b.
39. *LJ* IV 721a, V 9b, 40a; HMC 5 I 18b.
40. *LJ* V 6ab.
41. *LJ* IV 718b, 719a; See also Appendix III and p.|183 n 29.
42. Catherine S. Sims, 'The Moderne Forme of the Parliaments of England' *AHR* LIII 2 (Jan. 1948) 298.
43. *LJ* V 7ab, 8b; *CJ* II 536a, 537a, 538a, 539b; Harl 163 85v.
44. *CJ* II 550b; Glow 361–2; Keeler; *DNB*. Lotte Glow does not include Sir Thomas Bowyer among the 100 most active committee men (eight committees or more) in the Long Parliament between November 1640 and July 1642—Glow 361–2; Professor Keeler says that he was named to twenty-three committees in that period—Keeler 113a.
45. *CJ* II 552a, 555b, 556a, 577a; *LJ* V 69b, 70a, 72b, 73a; On Robert Reynolds see p. 186 n 55.
46. 'Sir Roger Twysden's Journal' ed. L. B. L[arking] *AC* II (1859) 179, 180; *CJ* II 517a, 520ab.
47. *CJ* II 533b.
48. *CJ* II 535a; Harl 163 82v.
49. *CJ* II 536b, 537ab; Harl 163 85v, 86, *LJ* V 9a.
50. *LJ* V 17b–19b; Harl 163 86v.
51. *LJ* V 18a.
52. *CJ* II 503a.
53. *LJ* IV 678a, V 18ab. See also Appendix II.
54. *LJ* V 17b, 18b, 19ab; Harl 163 86v.
55. Harl 163 83v.
56. *CJ* II 543b.
57. *CJ* II 549b; Add 14827 88v; Harl 163 99.
58. *CJ* II 549b; Harl 163 99.
59. *CJ* II 556b, 559a, 565a; Add 14827 93, 93v.

60. *LJ* V 58b, 59ab, 60a; *CJ* II 565b.
61. *LJ* V 17b–18b; Strode; Spencer.
62. *CJ* II 486a, 512b; Strode; Spencer.
63. Strode; Spencer.
64. *LJ* V 60b; 61a; *CJ* II 568a.
65. Petitions of Strode and Spencer HLRO main papers HL 13 May 1642 (HMC 5 I 23a); *LJ* V 62b; *DNB*. Chaloner Chute became Speaker of the House of Commons in January 1659, but he died very soon afterwards.
66. The answers of Strode and Spencer HLRO main papers HL 21 May 1642 (HMC 5 I 24b).
67. The answers of Strode and Spencer; *CJ* II 479ab; *LJ* IV 646a.
68. The answers of Strode and Spencer.
69. The answers of Strode and Spencer; *CJ* II 507a.
70. *CJ* II 622b; *LJ* V 131a.
71. *AC* I 213.

CHAPTER 7—REACTION
1. Everitt 100.
2. *CSPV* 1642–43 35, 36.
3. *LJ* IV 678a. See Appendix II.
4. See pp. 28–9.
5. *LJ* V 17b.
6. Spencer; Strode.
7. HMC 5 I 21b; *LJ* V 44ab.
8. *CSPV* 1642–43 35.
9. 'Sir Roger Twysden's Journal' ed. L. B. L[arking] *AC* I (1858) 213, 214.
10. *CJ* II 518b, 519a; the journal of Sir Simonds D'Ewes Harl 163 69v.
11. *CSPV* 1642–43 35, 36, 39.
12. Everitt 100–2.
13. *CSPV* 1642–43 55.
14. 'Sir Roger Twysden's Journal' ed. L. B. L[arking] *AC* II (1859) 180.
15. He later delivered the Kentish counter-petition to the Commons.
16. Harl 163 99, 99v; *CJ* II 537b. Professor Everitt says that Lovelace flourished Blount's petition 'on his sword's point'—Everitt 102 and n 2. I cannot find a 'sword's point' in the folios he quotes in his footnote to this page—Harl 163 99, 99v. 'Mr Browne' was probably Richard Browne, baron for New Romney.
17. *CSPV* 1642–43 55, 38.
18. Harl 163 63v, 65.
19. *CJ* II 545b, 546a; *LJ* 25ab; Esmé Wingfield-Stratford, *King Charles and King Pym 1637–1643* (1949) 11–13.
20. *Newes from Black-heath* . . . (29 Apr. 1642)—E 144 (13); *Strange Newes*

from Kent . . . (29 Apr. 1642)—E 145 (6); *CSPD* 1641–43 316; *CJ* II 549a, 550a; Gordon Home, *Old London Bridge* (1931) 85 and n 3, 91–2, 127–30, 173–9; Harl 163 98v; Framlingham Gawdy's diary Add 14827 88, 88v. The captain's name is given as 'Bunch' in E 145 (6) but the text of this pamphlet is badly spelt, even by the standards of the day. There was a trained band captain called Sir James Bunce and the captain at bridge foot was almost certainly he—Valerie Pearl, *London and the Outbreak of the Puritan Revolution 1625–1643* (Oxford 1961) 313.

21. *CJ* II 549ab; Harl 163 98v; Add 14827 88, 88v.
22. *CJ* II 549b; Harl 163 99, 99v; Add 14827 88v; *AC* II 180.
23. *CJ* II 549b, 550a; Harl 163 99v; Add 14827 88v. c.f. the account in *CJ* II 537b.
24. *CJ* II 550a; Harl 163 99v. Framlingham Gawdy says incorrectly that Boteler was committed to the Tower—Add 14827 88v.
25. *LJ* V 34a; *CJ* II 550b, 551b.
26. *CJ* II 556b; Keeler.
27. *CSPV* 1642–43 55.
28. *CSPV* 1642–43 55.
29. Endorsement on Blount's petition HMC 5 I 21b.
30. *LJ* V 44ab; *To the Lords and Commons: The Petition of Many of the Inhabitants of Kent* (5 May 1642)—BL 669 f 5 (13).
31. *CJ* II 558a; Add 14827 94v, 95. D'Ewes reported that a Mr. Henry Blount presented the petition—Harl 163 107v.
32. *LJ* V 44b.
33. HMC 5 I 21b; *CJ* II 558a.
34. *CJ* II 568a, 579a, 628b, 629a, 661b; Add 14827 156.
35. *CJ* II 629a. HLRO Main Papers HL 17 June 1642 (HMC 5 I 296b).
36. Keeler; *CJ* II 635b; Harl 163 187v.

CHAPTER 8—PAPER WARFARE

1. Clarendon V 366.
2. *LJ* IV 679a, V 35b.
3. Margaret Irwin, *That Great Lucifer* (1960) 212; H. Hulme, *The Life of Sir John Eliot 1592–1632* (1957) 362–5; Norman Lloyd Williams, *Sir Walter Raleigh* (1962) 211, 212. It is through Sir Thomas Malet that posterity knows that Sir Walter Raleigh spoke with a broad Devonshire accent until his dying day—John Aubrey, *Brief Lives* ed. O. L. Dick (1958) 154, 255.
4. *CJ* II 411a, 426b.
5. *CJ* II 467a, 478ab, 479a.
6. *LJ* IV 639b, 642a.
7. *CJ* II 339a, 351b.
8. *LJ* IV 678b, 705a, 711b.

9. Sir John Conyers to the Lords 9 May 1642 HMC 5 I 22a; *LJ* V 56b, 118b.

10. *LJ* IV 172b; *DNB.*

11. *LJ* IV 522b, V 44b, 45ab, 49b, 50a. Two out of twelve did not go to the Tower.

12. Rev. E. H. Bates-Harbin, ed., *Quarter Sessions Records for the County of Somerset* II *Charles I 1625–1639 SRS* XXIV (1908) 266; *Sermon Preached in the Tower by the Bishop of Bath and Wells* [William Pierce] (24 Apr. 1642) E 155 (21).

13. *LJ* IV 423b, 424a, 561b, V 56b.

14. *CJ* II 554a; *LJ* V 19b.

15. *LJ* V 56b, 117b, 118b; HMC 5 I 22a.

16. *LJ* IV 616a, 653b, 659a, 703b, 705ab; Clarendon V 51. On 19 March the Lords ordered that Benyon be bailed, but the Commons objected and he remained in custody. On 8 April he was condemned to two years at Colchester, but he continued in the Tower while a civil action against him was pending in the Lords. He had still not reached Colchester Gaol on 30 June 1642—*LJ* V 168b.

17. *LJ* IV 543b, V 48ab; *CJ* II 560b; *DNB.*

18. Bristol to the Lords HLRO main papers HL 7 and 8 Apr. 1642 (HMC 5 I 16b); *LJ* IV 705a, 711b.

19. Sir John Coke the younger to Sir John Coke at Melbourne 4 April 1642—the collection of the Marquess of Lothian DL, Melbourne Hall, Derby. Cowper (Coke) MSS (HMC 12 Appendix II 311).

20. *LJ* IV 721a, V 5ab, 6a, 12a, 35b, 37a; Bristol to the Lords HLRO main papers HL 19 April 1642 (HMC 5 I 18a).

21. *LJ* V 35b, 37a.

22. Easter term began on Wednesday 27 April—King's Bench (plea side) entry books of rules PRO KB 125/77; J March, *Reports: or, New Cases* [King's Bench and Common Pleas 1639–42] (1675) 204–11; See *LJ* V generally for the period 27 April–23 May 1642.

23. See generally *LJ* and *CJ* for this period.

24. *LJ* IV 706a; *CJ* II 515a, 518a.

25. *LJ* IV 709b, 710a, 717a, 718a, 719b, 720ab; *CJ* II 522a, 527ab, 528ab.

26. Gardiner X 187–90.

27. Gardiner X 190–4.

28. Gardiner X 194–6; *LJ* V 76b, 77a.

29. Foss VI 252; Clarendon V 346.

30. *LJ* V 68ab; *CJ* II 575b.

31. Clarendon V 203 and n 1; *LJ* V 80a; Lord John Campbell, *The Lives of the Lord Chancellors and Keepers of the Great Seal of England* 8 vols. (1845–69) I 22; II 592–9.

32. Firth 113–15; Gardiner X 196; *A Speech Made by John Earl of Bristol in Parliament concerning Accommodation* (20 May 1642) E 200 (43).

33. *The Declaration or Remonstrance of Parliament* (19 May 1642) E 148 (17); *LJ* V 73a.

34. *His Majesties Answer to a Book Entituled, The Declaration of the Lords and Commons of 19 May* (21 May 1642)—E 150 (29).

35. *LJ* V 97b–99a.

36. Roberts 113–14; Corinne C. Weston, *English Constitutional Theory and the House of Lords 1556–1832* (1965) 23–8.

37. *LJ* V 124ab.

38. *LJ* V 113ab, 122b, 123a, 124ab.

39. *LJ* V 65a, 108a, 114a.

40. *LJ* V 152a; *CJ* II 634a; *The Truest and Most Reall Relation of the Apprehension of Three Rebels in Ireland, viz. the Lord Maguire, Collonel Read, Captain MacMallion*—[June 1642]—E 151 (13): Aidan Clarke, *The Old English in Ireland 1625–1642* (1966) 160–1, 190, 206.

41. *LJ* V 154a, 182a; Receipt for sixteen parcels of papers from Malet—HLRO Main Papers HL 6 July 1642 (HMC 5 I 35b).

42. *ST* IV 653–754.

43. *St. Hillaries Teares Shed upon All Professions from the Judge to the Petty Fogger . . .* ([Jun] 1642) E 151 (16).

44. Rushworth 3 i 630–5, 637, 638.

45. Gardiner X 201–11; *LJ* V 123b, 186a; *CSPD* 1641–43 344.

CHAPTER 9—THE LAST CIRCUIT

1. Sir John Sackville to Sir Robert Foster PRO SP 16/491/107 9 Aug. 1642 (*CSPD* 1641–43 368).

2. *CJ* II 635b, 641ab; *LJ* V 164a, 166a.

3. *The King's Majesties Charge Sent to All the Judges of England* (4 July 1642)—E 108 (7). See also *CSPD* 1641–43 349–50. The text is given in full at Appendix IV. The Thomason Tract version is preferred to the State Paper version because it purports to be a copy of the letter actually addressed to Malet.

4. *LJ* V 188a, 190a, 192b, 198b, 199b.

5. Clerks of assize, south-eastern circuit, indictments PRO ASS1 35/84/4.

6. *CJ* II 671b; the journal of Sir Simonds D'Ewes Harl 163 272; Keeler; *DNB*. In the Commons *Journals* above, John Harrison is called 'Sir John', but he appears to have been plain 'Mr.'

7. Harl 163 272v.

8. *CJ* II 671b, 672a; Harl 163 272v.

9. The two Houses did not require the judges to publish the votes and declarations of both Houses that commissions of array were illegal until 20 July—*CJ* II 681b, 682ab; *LJ* V 222b.

10. F. M. Page, *History of Hertford* (1959) 77–9; Zagorin 325–8; *CJ* II 597a, 602b, 951b, 961b.

11. Zagorin 325–8; Alfred Kingston, *Hertfordshire during the Great Civil War* (1894) 11–14; Page 78, 79.

12. E 108 (7).

13. *A Perfect Diurnall of the Passages in Parliament from the 18th of July to the 25th 1642* [July 1642]—E 202 (23) entry for 23 July 1642;

A Perfect Diurnall or the Proceedings in Parliament from 18 of July to the 25 of the Same 1642 [July 1642]—E 202 (24) entry for 23 July 1642.

14. *To the King. The Humble Declaration of the County of Essex* (18 July 1642) BL 669 f5 (66); R. O. Coller, *The People's History of Essex* 2 vols. (Chelmsford 1861) I 108, 109; *CJ* II 622a.

15. PRO ASSI 35/84/2 mm 3, 3d, 4. R. O. Coller was the fooled historian. He wrote that the declaration 'was drawn up by the grand jury'— Coller I 108. Coller did not have access to the assize records (in the sense that they had not yet been sorted), but he must have noticed that only seven grand jurors at most signed the petition. There is some doubt whether a seventh was actually a grand juror.

16. *CJ* II 682a.

17. *CJ* II 655a; Harl 163 258v; *LJ* V 186b.

18. Everitt 107, 108.

19. *LJ* V 213b, 214a; *CJ* II 675b, 676a; Harl 163 273v 274; Framlingham Gawdy's diary Add 14827 161, 161v.

20. *CJ* II 681b, 682ab, 683a; *LJ* V 222b; *CSPD* 1641–43 358.

21. Harl 163 288v ⎫Both accounts say that Marten reported from
22. Add 14827 166v.⎭the Committee for Defence, but see pp. 194–5 n 63.

23. *CJ* II 685b, 686ab, 687a.

24. PRO ASSI 35/84/5; *CJ* II 686ab, 687a.

25. Jessup states 'when the judge opened the proceedings he found his court reinforced by a large committee sent down by the House of Commons'—Jessup 57. They had not yet arrived when the proceedings opened—the journal of Sir Simonds D'Ewes Harl 164 258. The Commons *Journals* omit Sir Peter Wroth from the list of members sent down to Maidstone—*CJ* II 686ab. Sir Roger Twysden and a contemporary pamphlet include him—'Sir Roger Twysden's Journal' ed. L. B. L[arking] *AC* II (1859) 181, 182; *Instructions from the Honourable House of Commons Assembled in Parliament to the Committee in Kent* (13 Aug. 1642) E 111 (13). The seventeen include Wroth.

26. 'Sir Roger Twysden's Journal' ed. L. B. L[arking] *AC* I (1858) 200, 204.

27. *CJ* II 686ab; E 111 (13); *AC* II 181, 182.

28. *CJ* II 686b, 687a.

29. *AC* II 183.

30. This statement is based on the commission of the peace issued on 21 Feb. 1640—Chancery, patent rolls PRO C 66/2859 mm 28d, 27d; on the list of justices of the peace for the preceding assizes—PRO ASSI 35/84/11 mm 4d, 4, 3; on the changes recorded in Chancery, Crown Office docket books—PRO C 231/5; and on the list of justices for these assizes, where it is legible—PRO ASSI 35/84/5 mm 1–3.

31. Harl 164 258.

32. *AC* II 183.

33. *CJ* II 698a; J. Cave-Browne, *The History of the Parish Church of*

All Saints, Maidstone (Maidstone nd [1889]) 29.

34. J. M. Russell, *The History of Maidstone* (Maidstone 1881) 112, 113, 191.

35. *CJ* II 698a.

36. *A Perfect Diurnall of the Passages in Parliament from the 1 of August to the 7 . . . 1642* [Aug. 1642]—E 202 (30) entry for 5 Aug. 1642; *A Perfect Diurnall of the Passages in Parliament from the 8th of August to the 15th 1642* [Aug. 1642]—E 202 (8) entry for 8 Aug. 1642; *A True Relation of Certaine Speciall and Remarkable Passages from Both Houses of Parliament, since Monday the 15 of August till Friday the Nineteenth 1642* [Aug. 1642]—E 112 (36). Everitt's account suggests that the Commons committee was sent to Maidstone because Barrell preached a fiery assize sermon—Everitt 105. This is incorrect. The committee was ordered to Maidstone on Friday 22 July—*CJ* II 686ab; it arrived after the assizes were opened on Saturday 23 July—Harl 164 258; *AC* II 181, 183; and the sermon was preached on Sunday 24 July—*CJ* II 698a.

37. Harl 164 258; *AC* II 183.

38. Harl 164 258; *AC* II 183; *A Perfect Diurnall of the Passages in Parliament from the 1 of August to the 8 of August 1642* [Aug. 1642]—E 202 (31) entry for 2 Aug. 1642; *A Perfect Diurnall of the Passages in Parliament from the First of August to the Eighth 1642* [Aug. 1642]—E 202 (32) entry for 4 Aug. 1642; *Some Speciall Passages from London, Westminster, York, Hull, Holland, Denmark, Portsmouth and Divers Other Parts of England since the First of August to the Ninth 1642* [Aug 1642]—E 109 (35) entry for 2 Aug. 1642.

39. Harl 164 258, 258v.

40. *AC* II 184.

41. *AC* II 184; E 111 (13).

42. *AC* II 184, 185.

43. Harl 164 258v.

44. *AC* II 185.

45. *AC* II 185, 186; Harl 164 258.

46. *AC* II 186; and p. 192 n 30.

47. *The Petition of the Commons of Kent Presented to His Majestie . . . with His Majesties Answer, August 4, 1642* E 112 (26). The full text of this petition together with the instructions to Augustine Skinner and the King's answer are given in Appendix V.

48. E 112 (26); Rushworth 3 i 642.

49. *AC* II 186, 187.

50. *AC* II 187; E 112 (26).

51. BL 669 f 5 (66); Charles I to Malet 31 July 1642—NRA PRC/I. For full text see pp. 108–9.

52. E 112 (26): Rushworth 3 i 642, 643.

53. PRO ASSI 35/84/8.

54. *CJ* II 700b; E 112 (26); Note that the instructions . . . to Augustine

Skinner at *CSPD* 1641–42 314 are wrongly dated April. A report of the Maidstone proceedings reached the House of Commons on Monday, 1 August, but business was heavy. In the event it was decided to postpone debate on the Maidstone Assizes until the following day—*CJ* II 699a, 700b.

55. Harl 164 258, 258v.

56. E 109 (35) entry for 2 Aug. 1642; E 202 (31) entry for 2 Aug. 1642.

57. *CJ* II 700b. See n 63 below.

58. PRO ASSI 35/84/1.

59. The *General Index to the Journals of the House of Lords vols. I–X* (1836) 361 wrongly refers to a 'copy of a warrant from His Majesty requiring the attendance of Justice Malett' at *LJ* V 264b. The warrant at *LJ* V 264b was intended for the Lord Chief Justice (the Chief Justice of the King's Bench) whose command from the King to attend him in York is reported on the previous page of the *Journal*—*LJ* V 263b; it is written from Beverley and commands the addressee to 'repair hither to us'. I am grateful to Mr. H. S. Cobb, Deputy Clerk of the Records, House of Lords, for pointing out that in the journal there is wording in the margin against the entry for the Lord Chief Justice, which is repeated against the entry for the warrant. The King's letter to Malet is in National Register of Archives PRC/1 and calendared in HMC 5 I 313b; it commanded him to repair to his own home (i.e. to Somerset).

60. Sir Richard Onslow to Denzil Holles *LJ* V 264ab and HLRO main papers HL 5 Aug. 1642 (HMC 5 I 41a).

61. *LJ* V 250a–270a; *CJ* II 698b–708b; HLRO Parchment collection HL, B2 Book of Orders and Ordinances (both Houses) 20 Oct. 1641–25 Oct. 1642.

62. *CJ* II 700b.

63. Clarendon says that the warrant was issued by 'the Houses or some committee'—Clarendon V 426; it was, for reasons already explained, more probably the latter. The Commons *Journals* record two matters as referred to the Committee for the Defence of the Kingdom on 2 Aug. 1642—*CJ* II 700b. This was a committee of the Commons alone, appointed on 14 Aug. 1641 and it included a number of moderate members who later became Royalists—*CJ* II 257a; Glow 247, 270. The Committee for the Safety of the Kingdom was a joint committee of both Houses appointed on 4 July 1642; it was composed of determined Parliamentarians who could be counted upon for ruthless action— Glow 270; *LJ* V 178ab; *CJ* II 651b. Marten is quoted as reporting from the Committee for the Defence of the Kingdom to the Commons on 22 July 1642 about a plot at the coming Maidstone Assizes—Harl, 163 288v; Add 14827 166v. He was not a member of the Committee for Defence, but he was a member and spokesman of the Committee for Safety e.g. Harl 163 258. It was to Holles, or failing him, Hampden

that Onslow's letter was addressed; neither Holles nor Hampden were members of the Committee for Defence, but they were both members of the Committee for Safety. When they received Onslow's letter the Commons referred the size of the armed escort for Malet to the Committee for Defence, but Sir Philip Stapleton, when he reported their action to the Lords, said that the business had been referred to the Committee for Safety—*CJ* II 704b; *LJ* V 264b. On 6 May 1643 Holles reported to the Commons that Malet had been committed to the Tower 'by authoritie of the committee of Lords and Commons appointed for the safetie of the kingdom'—Harl 164 382. All this suggests that the Commons members of the new Committee for Safety took over the functions hitherto performed by the old Committee for Defence and were sometimes called by the old title. See also Glow 367.

64. *LJ* V 263a. Lord Mandeville was also known as Lord Kimbolton.
65. Sir Richard Onslow to Denzil Holles—5 Aug. 1642.
66. H. E. Malden, 'The Civil War in Surrey 1642' *SAC* XXII (1909) 105, 106; Earl of Onslow, 'Sir Richard Onslow 1603–1664' *SAC* XXXVI (1925) 62, 63.
67. Thomas G. Barnes, ed., *Somerset Assize Orders 1629–1640 SRS* LXV (Frome 1959) xv n 2; Cockburn 272; Foss VI 252, 258, 324, 325.
68. *LJ* V 264b.
69. Malden 105; Onslow 60–2; *DNB*; Keeler; HMC 11 Appendix V (Dartmouth I) 3; *LJ* V 264ab.
70. The original letter from Sir Richard Onslow to Denzil Holles in HLRO Main Papers HL is undated. In HMC 5 I 41a the date attributed to it is 5 Aug. 1642, but the sole purpose of this date is to connect it with the relevant entry in the *Lords Journals* for that date (*LJ* V 264ab). It could not have been written on that date. There was not time on 5 August for Malet to adjourn the assizes at ten in the morning, to receive the warrant, to return to his lodging, to argue with Onslow, for Onslow to write a letter, for the letter to travel to the House of Commons, to be debated there and to be the subject of a message to the Lords half way through the same morning's business. The letter must have been written on 4 August.

CHAPTER 10—ASSIZE AT ARMS

1. G. E. Aylmer, *The King's Servants: The Civil Service of Charles I 1625–1642* (1961) 386.
2. *CJ* II 698a; *A Perfect Diurnall of the Passages in Parliament from the 8th of August to the 15th 1642* [Aug. 1642]—E 202 (8) entry for 8 Aug. 1642; see also p. 102 and p. 193 n 36.
3. 'Sir Roger Twysden's Journal' ed. L. B. L[arking] *AC* II (1859) 183. The journal of Sir Simonds D'Ewes Harl 164 258, 258v.
4. *CJ* II 709b, 728a.
5. *AC* II (1859) 189, 190; *CJ* II 700b, 704a, 712b, 735b, 758b, 761a.

Twysden was at Charing Cross from 5 to 24 August.

6. *LJ* V 263b, 264b; See p. 194 n 59.

7. Campbell, Lord John, *Lives of the Lord Chief Justices of England from the Norman Conquest to the Death of Lord Tenterden* 3 vols. (1849–57) I 406.

8. *LJ* IV 115a, V 263b; *The Autobiography of Sir John Bramston* ed. Lord Braybrooke (Camden Society 1845) 83, 84.

9. Aylmer 386; Foss VI 258, 286, 299, 368, 374, 375; DNB; *LJ* V 198b, 404b, 405a, 446b; *CJ* II 811b, 812a, 850b.

10. It was in Launceston, Cornwall, that the sheriff protected by his guard read the King's proclamation against the militia and the warrant to execute the commission of array—*LJ* V 275ab.

11. *LJ* V 275a, 582b; *True Newes from Somersetshire* ([6 Aug.] 1642)—BL 669 f 6 (62).

12. See e.g. *Diary of Henry Townshend of Elmley Lovett 1640–1663* ed. J. W. Willis-Bund 2 vols. (Worcs Historical Society 1915–16) II 68; *CJ* II 710b.

13. Clarendon V 346; Cockburn 272; *Two Petitions; the One to the King of the Grand Jury at the Assizes in Southampton; the Other to the Justices of the Peace at the Assizes at Bury St Edmunds* (30 July 1642) E 112 (9); G. Bankes, *The Story at Corfe Castle* (1853) 135; Foss VI 252, 253; *LJ* V 582b.

14. Rushworth 3 i 646–7; *LJ* V 124ab.

15. Gardiner X 214; Clarendon V 417–9; Dr. Bastwick denounced the bishops as the enemies of God in a book he published in 1637. He was sentenced in Star Chamber to lose his ears, to be fined £5,000 and to be imprisoned for life. This savage sentence contributed substantially to the unpopularity and eventual abolition of the Star Chamber Court. In November 1640 he was released by order of both Houses and entered London in triumph in the following month.

16. Gardiner X 214–18; Warwick Castle was the property of Lord Brooke.

17. Trevelyan 186–93; Dorothy Gardiner, ed., *The Oxinden Letters 1607–1642* (1933) 312.

18. Peter Verney, *The Standard Bearer* (1963) 205.

19. Irene Coltman, *Private Men and Public Causes* (1962) 11.

20. *CJ* II 704b. The title of the committee is wrongly reported in *CJ*. See pp. 194–5 n 63.

21. Sir Richard Onslow to Denzil Holles HLRO main papers HL 5 Aug. 1642. (HMC 5 I 41a). The letter was actually written on 4 August—see p. 195 n 70.

22. *CJ* II 704b; *LJ* V 264ab.

23. Sir John Sackville to Sir Robert Foster PRO SP 16/491/107 9 Aug. 1642 (*CSPD* 1641–43 368).

24. N. G. Brett-James, *The Growth of Stuart London* (1935), maps of London in 1603 and 1660 facing pp. 78 and 124. The evidence that Malet was brought south of the river to London Bridge is circumstantial.

This was the shortest route, for the Thames describes a great serpentine arc to the north. It was also the normal route and, in fact, constituted the first twelve miles of the Portsmouth road from London—T. F. Ordish, ed., *Roads out of London* (1911), plate 5. The route north of the river lay in Middlesex, but it was the sheriff of Surrey whose help the Commons enlisted to bring Malet to London—*CJ* II 704b. If the Commons had wanted help from the sheriff of Middlesex they would have said so. When the Commons brought the prisoner Beeling from Haverfordwest they ordered 'the sheriffs of the several counties through which they are to pass' to see him and his fellow prisoners safely conducted—*CJ* II 506b.

25. A contemporary news pamphlet reports that 'Judge Mallet was brought to towne by the sherriffe, and a great company of horse out of Kent'—*A Perfect Diurnall of the Passages in Parliament from the 1 of August to the 8 of August 1642* [Aug. 1642] E 202 (31) entry for 6 August. The only known troop of Parliamentary horse in Kent at that time was commanded by Colonel Sir Edwin Sandys and there is a strong presumption that either he or one of his officers commanded Malet's escort.

26. W. Rendle, *Old Southwark and Its People* (1878), map of Southwark 1542 facing title page, 23–4, 92; W. Rendle and P. Norman, *The Inns of Old Southwark* (1888), map of Southwark 1746 facing page 1, 202–3, 270, 271; The Ashmolean Museum, Oxford, Department of Western Art. John Norden, *Civitas Londini* [bird's eye view of London] (engraving 1600).

27. *LJ* V 268b.

28. *LJ* V 288a.

29. See n 1 and 23 to this chapter.

30. Clarendon V 425, 426.

CHAPTER 11—EPILOGUE: WAR AND PEACE

1. PRO SP 29/445/44 17 Sep. 1660 (*CSPD* Addenda 1660–70 649).

2. Malet to the Lords HLRO main papers HL 23 Aug. 1642 (HMC 5 I 44a); *LJ* V 337b.

3. *CJ* II 716b, 717a, 720b, 722b: *LJ* V 289a, 291a.

4. *CJ* II 733a.

5. Everitt 111–16; *CJ* II 721b.

6. *CJ* II 744b–746b; *LJ* V 332b, 333ab; *The Petition of the County of Kent Presented to Parliament, Wherein They Disclaim That Late Petition Sent to his Majestie* (30 Aug. 1642) E 115 (1).

7. *CJ* II 745b; Everitt 116; On Tuesday 6 Sep. 1642 a considerable quantity of arms, ammunition and saddlery was found in 'Judge Mallett's house in Kent'; this was probably the place where Malet lodged during the assizes—*True and Remarkable Passages from Several Places in This Kingdome from Munday the Fifth of September to Saturday the 10 of September 1642* [Sep. 1642] E 116 (28) entry for 6 September.

8. *LJ* V 341b; Clarendon VI 21.

9. Malet to the Lords HLRO main papers HL 25 Nov. 1642 (HMC 5 I 58a).

10. Malet to the Lords HLRO main papers HL 17 March 1643 (HMC 5 I 77a); *LJ* V 652a.

11. Malet to the Lords HLRO main papers HL 29 April 1643 (HMC 5 I 83a); *LJ* VI 22a, 23a, 24a.

12. *CJ* III 73b; the journal of Sir Simonds D'Ewes Harl 164 384. See pp. 194–5 n 63.

13. *LJ* V 268b.

14. *CJ* III 73b, 74b, 75a; *LJ* VI 35b, 36a; Harl 164 384, 384v.

15. Alfred H. Burne and Peter Young, *The Great Civil War: A Military History of the First Civil War 1642–1646* (1959) 44–6, 77–97.

16. *LJ* VI 177b, 178a; *CJ* III 202a.

17. Rev. E. H. Bates-Harbin, ed., *Quarter Sessions Records for the County of Somerset* III *Commonwealth 1646–1660* SRS XXVIII (1912) xx.

18. *CJ* III 567a; *LJ* VI 646a; Draft order for the exchange of Justice Mallet HLRO main papers HL 24 July 1644 (HMC 6 I 19b). A note in Macray's edition of Clarendon says that Malet was exchanged 'for Mr. Michell and his son and Captain Halling on July 22 1642'—Clarendon V 426 second n 1. No exchange took place at this time.

19. Lady Malet to the Lords HLRO main papers HL 18 Sep. 1644 (HMC VII 27a); *LJ* VI 709a.

20. *LJ* VII 26b, 29a, 43a, 45b, 49ab; Malet to the Lords HLRO main papers HL 6 Nov. 1644 (HMC 6 I 34b); *CJ* III 666ab, 670b.

21. *LJ* VII 148a.

22. Malet to the Committee for Compounding PRO SP 23/191/661 24 Sep. 1646 (CCC II 1511); *LJ* VII 169b, 179b; A. à Wood, *Fasti Oxonienses* (1721) 26–7.

23. J. P. Kenyon, *The Stuarts* (1966) 91.

24. Somerset county committee to the Committee for Compounding PRO SP 23/191/647 29 Jan. 1648 (CCC II 1511). At some stage Malet came into the possession of a gilt badge depicting the head and arms of Charles I. These badges were common at the time and appear to have been widely reproduced. They were used by the Royalist forces as a badge and under the Commonwealth as a sign of Royalist sympathies. Malet's badge measures 1.85 × 1.55 in. It is cast and chased and may have originated from a piece or pieces by Thomas Rawlins. See plate section.

25. S. R. Gardiner, *History of the Great Civil War 1642–1649* 3 vols. (1886–91) II 57, 58, 484.

26. A particular of Sir Thomas Malet's estate PRO SP 23/191/663 19 Nov. 1646 (CCC II 1511).

27. Gardiner, *Civil War* II 58, 135 and n 1.

28. Trevelyan 220–2.

29. *LJ* VIII 6a, 7b; Foss VI 220, 221, 222.
30. Trevelyan 223; Kenyon 91; Joshua Sprigge, *Anglia Rediviva* (1647) 260–83.
31. Pass issued by Sir Thomas Fairfax to Malet PRO SP 23/191/665 24 June 1646 (CCC II 1511).
32. Lady Malet to the Lords HLRO main papers HL 18 Sep. 1644 (HMC 6 I 27a).
33. *LJ* VII 49b.
34. Proceedings of the Committee for Compounding PRO SP 23/3/298 and SP 23/191/637, 638 21 Nov. 1646 (CCC II 1511).
35. A particular of Sir Thomas Malet's estate 19 Nov. 1646.
36. Octavius Warre Malet, 'Memoir of Sir Thomas Malet' *SANHS* XX (1874) ii 111. The portrait of Lady Malet (1661) in the collection of Colonel Sir Edward Malet Bt., OBE shows her wearing a black bone ring, but not on her wedding finger (see plate section). Her daughter Alice who died in 1661 left her a mourning ring in her will—PRO PROB 11/309, s 76 proved 23 May 1661.
37. J. Foster, ed., *Alumni Oxonienses 1550–1714* 4 vols. (Oxford 1891–92) III 962a.
38. Somerset county committee to the Committee for Compounding 29 Jan 1648.
39. Letter to the author by Colonel Sir Edward Malet Bt., OBE nd [1974].
40. Hatchment in the parish church of All Saints, Poyntington (see plate section).
41. Rev. J. Heale, 'Poyntington' *SANHS* XVI (1870) ii 68, 69.
42. The early register used to be in a terrible state having been found on rubbish heaps on the floor of the church in 1844 and 1875. The pages have been skilfully repaired, but many entries are missing through decay. The register is now in the Dorset County Record Office (P 198/RE 1). The entry above that for Baldwin Malet reads:

'William Hannam aged 92 years [?was buried] Aprill the 23d 1645.'

The entry for Baldwin Malet reads:

'Bal . . . sonne of Sr Tho Mallett . . . buried June the . . .'

There is a gap after 'Mallett' of about two inches where some remark could have been inserted about it (though it might have contained his age). There has been wording here but the faint marks that remain are illegible and the ultra violet light reveals no more. The entry following is illegible.

A transcript of the parish register by Canon Mayo in 1889 (Dorset Record Office D 103/1) gives the date of Baldwin Malet's death as June 1645. In the transcript the entry after that for Baldwin Malet reads:

'Jone ? wife of Nicho Jacu . . .'

and gives the date 'June 28 1645'. In the original register the parchment has rotted away at the bottom. There could have been several further entries before the next page starts with the burial of Alice Harvie on 9 December 1646. I am grateful to Miss Holmes, the Dorset County Archivist, for this information. It does suggest that Baldwin's death may have been in 1645 and not 1646. However, the Brown MSS (Somerset Record Office SAS C/1193/5/4) gives the date of Baldwin's death as '3rd June 1646 in the 20th year of his age'. Rev. John Collinson, *The History and Antiquities of the County of Somerset* 3 vols. (Bath 1791) II 377 gives the same date but a different version, but Collinson is notoriously unreliable. Since the inscription is painted, it could easily have become illegible at some time in its history. Finally, there is no supporting evidence either in the parish register or in Canon Mayo's transcript of it that Baldwin Malet was killed in the way that Rev. Heale describes. No bishop's transcripts of the parish register appear to have survived.

43. Malet 59, 60, 138; Thomas Chafe's will PROB 11/309, s138 (Laud 138) dated 22 June 1662, proved 12 Nov. 1662.

44. Pass issued by Sir Thomas Fairfax to Malet 24 June 1646; Malet to the Committee for Compounding PRO SP 23/191/661 24 Sep. 1646 (CCC II 1511).

45. A particular of Sir Thomas Malet's estate 19 Nov. 1646; Proceedings of the Committee for Compounding 21 Nov. 1646; Malet to the Committee for Compounding PRO SP 23/191/645 14 Feb. 1648 (CCC II 1511).

46. Proceedings of the Committee for Advance of Money Assessment PRO SP 19/63/23 18 Sep. 1643; Proceedings /5/102 16 Sep. 1646; Proceedings /5/112 2 Oct. 1646; Proceedings /5/115 14 Oct. 1646. See also *Calendar of the Proceedings of the Committee for Advance of Money 1642–1656* 3 vols. (1888) I 247.

47. Cockburn 241, 272.

48. A particular of Sir Thomas Malet's estate PRO SP 23/191/657–9 [Feb. 1648] (CCC II 1512); Somerset county committee to Committee for Compounding PRO SP 23/191/647 and 649 29 Jan. 1648 (CCC II 1511).

49. Lord Fairfax to John Ash PRO SP 23/191/655 5 Feb. 1648 (CCC II 1512).

50. Somerset county committee to the Committee for Compounding PRO SP 23/191/653–4 21 Feb. 1648. (CCC II 1512); Proceedings of the Committee for Compounding PRO SP 23/4/179 and 181 21 and 25 Feb. 1648. (CCC II 1512.)

51. Proceedings of the Committee for Compounding PRO SP 23/5/11 5 Oct. 1648 (CCC II 1512).

52. Draft pardon for Sir Thomas and John Malet HLRO main papers HL 2 Nov. 1648 (HMC 7 I 60a); *LJ* X 574b; *CJ* VI 40a.

53. Proceedings of the Committee for the Advance of Money PRO SP

19/7/186 25 July 1649 (*Calendar of the Proceedings of the Committee for Advance of Money 1642–1656* 3 vols. 1888 I 247).

54. Indenture 25 July 1649—BL Egerton Charter 742. For confirmation that the missing release was almost certainly a mortgage see mortgages of the same properties raised in 1691 and 1694—Somerset Record Office DD/SOG 804, 806.

55. Trevelyan 230–40.

56. Malet 60, 61. John's third child, Anne, was buried at West Quantockshead in 1655 and a number of his children were born there between 1656 and 1664. (Transcript of West Quantockshead Parish Register [1558–1684] and *SANHS* XVI (1870) ii 39.) It is thus almost certain that John was living at St. Audries in 1655 and unlikely that he was there much before, because his first two children were not born there.

57. MT III 1014, 1015, 1080, 1098, 1214. Baldwin Malet, Michael's elder brother, was killed on 3 June 1645 or 1646 in his twentieth year. See p. 200 n 42.

58. Michael Malet's Will PRO PROB 11/215. s 50 (Grey 50) proved 21 Mar. 1651.

59. Trevelyan 246–8; Richard Ollard, *The Escape of Charles II* (1966) 69 ff, 80, 88, 94, 101–2, 105.

60. David Underdown, *Somerset in the Civil War and Interregnum* (Newton Abbot 1973) 175–88; Trevelyan 273; Cockburn 245; Godfrey Davies, *The Early Stuarts 1603–1660* (Oxford 1959) 253.

61. Davies 253–6; Firth 268, 275, 276.

62. *Return of the Names of Every Member Returned to Serve in Each Parliament* (*Official Return*) 2 vols. (1878) I 515.

63. Firth 282–4; Godfrey Davies, *The Restoration of Charles II 1658–1660* (Oxford 1955) 339.

64. *LJ* XI 6b, 9b, 18b, 19a; Davies, *Restoration* 345–6.

65. Davies, *Restoration* 351–4; *The Diary of John Evelyn* ed. E. S. de Beer 6 vols. (Oxford 1955) III 246.

66. Foss VII 69, 70, 125–7.

67. Crown Office docket books PRO C 231/7/1 31 May 1660; *LJ* VIII 7b.

68. Foss VII 135, 136, 140, 141.

69. Foss VII 2–4, 10, 12, 13, 54, 55, 60, 61, 176, 179–182, 186. Neither Twisden nor Twysden is misspelt.

70. Jessup 100–5.

71. Malet to Charles II PRO SP 29/21/111 24 Nov. 1660 (*CSPD* 1660–61 363); compare the portrait of Malet in 1661 with the version of 1642, both reproduced in the plate section.

72. *DNB*.

73. *LJ* XI 32ff; Sir J. Kelyng, *Report of Divers Cases in Pleas of the Crown* [1662–1669] (1708) 7ff; Entry book of commissions PRO C 181/7 1 and 3 (12 Charles II).

74. Arthur Bryant, *King Charles II* (1931) 114, 115.

75. Bryant 116, 117.

76. *Diary of Henry Townshend of Elmley Lovett 1640–1663* ed. J. W. Willis-Bund 2 vols. (Worcs Historical Society 1915–16) I 55; *By the King a Proclamation concerning the Times of Holding This Summer Assizes* (23 July 1660) BL 669 f 25 (59); Chancery Crown Office docket books PRO C 231/7/33 entry for 10 July 12 Charles II.

77. BL 669 f 25 (59). cf. Thomas G. Barnes, ed., *Somerset Assize Orders 1629–1640* SRS LXV (Frome 1959) xiv–xv: Cockburn 25.

78. Writ. Clerks of assize, south-eastern circuit, indictments PRO ASSI 5/1/3 mm not numbered 11 July 12 Charles II.

79. e.g. *LJ* 97b, 112a, 138a.

80. PRO C 231/7/36 entry for 6 Sep. 12 Charles II and /39 entry for 12 Sep. 12 Charles II.

81. M. C. B. Dawes, ed., *Quarter Sessions Records for the County of Somerset IV Charles II 1666–1677* SRS XXXIV (1919) xiv.

82. BL 669f 25 (59); PRO ASSI 5/1/3 mm not numbered entry for 6 Sep. 12 Charles II.

83. Malet could well have left for London before his circuit was ended in order to get back for the trial of the Regicides.

84. Bryant 124; *ST* V 985, 986, 987, 994.

85. Thomas Smith to Joseph Williamson PRO SP 29/445/44 17 Sep. 1660 (*CSPD* Additional 1660–70 649)

86. *ST* V 1030; *The Indictment Arraignment Tryal and Judgement at Large of Twenty-Nine Regicides the Murtherers of His Most Sacred Majesty King Charles I of Glorious Memory* (1714) 63; Bryant 124.

87. Bryant 124; *The Journal of George Fox* ed. Norman Penney (1924) 190.

88. There is some confusion in Foss VII about when Sir Robert Foster was promoted to be Chief Justice of King's Bench. He is shown on p. 9 as being appointed on 1 October 1660 and on p. 98 as being appointed on 21 October 1660. 21 October is correct—Chancery, patent rolls PRO C 66/2954 16; Sir T. Siderfin, *Les Reportes des Divers Special Cases, Bank le Roy, Co Ba & L'Exchequer* [1657–70] 2 parts in 1 vol. (1683–84) I 3.

89. *LJ* XI 176b; Foss VII 10, 12. One of the judges appointed in November 1660 was Wadham Wyndham who was an uncle to Malet's daughter-in-law, Florentia—Malet 61; H. A. Wyndham, *A Family History 1410–1688* (Oxford 1939) Genealogy II. See p. 126.

90. Malet to Charles II PRO SP 29/21/111 24 Nov. 1660 (*CSPD* 1660–61 363).

91. Warrant of Charles II 3 Dec. 1660 BL Sloane 856 25v.

92. Sir C. Levinz, *Reports of Cases in the Court of King's Bench and Common Pleas* [1660–96] (1702), 7, 8.

93. *DNB*; Trevelyan 283 ff. The judges attended the coronation feast in Westminster Hall—*The Form of His Majesties Coronation Feast to*

be Solemnised at Westminster Hall (23 April 1661) BL 669 f 27 (15). Michael Malet was once more elected member for Milborne Port— *Official Return* I 527.

94. Violet A. Rowe, *Sir Henry Vane the Younger* (1970) 233–42; *The Tryal of Sir Henry Vane Kt at the King's Bench Westminster June the 2d and 6th 1662* (1662) 96; *ST* VI 119–202.

95. Cockburn 274, 275.

96. Levinz 22; J. Keble, *Reports, King's Bench, at Westminster* [1661–79] 3 vols. (1685) I 72, 114; Sir T. Raymond, *Reports, King's Bench, Common Pleas and Exchequer* [1660–83] (1696) 19, 21, 24, 31, 41.

97. *LJ* XI 387a, 419b.

98. Hilary:Levinz 52; Easter:Levinz 64; Trinity:Keble I307; Michaelmas: Levinz 81, 82, 84.

99. Malet to Charles II PRO SP 29/97/30 24 April 1662 (*CSPD* 1663–64 565); warrant for a grant Charles II to Attorney General PRO SP 29/53/97 [April] 1662 (*CSPD* 1661–62 356)
Charles II to Lord Treasurer PRO SP 44/13/109 24 April 1662 (*CSPD* 1661–62 348).
Secretary of State to Lord Treasurer PRO SP 29/97/30 24 Apr. 1662 (*CSPD* 1663–64 565)
Lord Treasurer to Attorney General PRO SP 29/97/30 6 May 1662 (*CSPD* 1663–64 565)
Attorney General to Lord Treasurer PRO SP 29/97/30 16 May 1662 (*CSPD* 1663–64 565)
Lord Treasurer to Charles II PRO SP 29/97/30 [1662] (*CSPD* 1663–64 565)
Warrant for a grant and Charles II to Attorney General PRO SP 44/7/259–262 10 and 24 Sep. 1662 (*CSPD* 1661–62 483).
Grant to Malet PRO SP 38/21/143 29 Sep. 1662 (*CSPD* 1661–62 498)
Note that the above documents calendared in *CSPD* 1663–64 are wrongly dated 1664 in that calendar.

100. Raymond 77; Keble 507.

101. Memorandum PRO SP 29/75/159 June 1663 (CSPD 1663–64 188); Siderfin I 150.

102. Sir Charles Warre Malet, *Papers on the Subject of Sir Charles Warre Malet's Application for Precedency in the Order of Baronets according to the Ancient Patent of Charles the Second* (Salisbury, England 1805) 15–17; fiat for the patent of baronetcy to Malet NRS FH/P/1 19 May 1663.

103. Octavius Warre Malet, 'Memoir of Sir Thomas Malet' *SANHS* XX (1874) ii 112.

104. Apart from one or two properties mentioned in Malet's will (n 105, over), all the properties are listed in the draft warrant described in n 99 above. A further draft Charles II to Attorney General PRO SP 29/97/30.1 dated 18 Charles II [1666] (*CSPD* 1663–64 565) confirms

that the properties described were in fact granted to Sir Thomas Malet by letters patent under the Great Seal on or about 10 Oct. 14 Charles II [1662].

105. Malet's Will PRO PROB 11/319, s 28 (MICO 28) proved 2 Feb. 1666; Malet 59, 61; F. W. Weaver, *Somerset Incumbents from the Hugo MSS* (Bristol 1889) 169.

106. Sir Thomas Malet's hatchment in the parish church of All Saints, Poyntington—see illustration; O. W. Malet 112. The work 'assignato' on the hatchment should be 'assignatorum'. The armorial bearings painted on the hatchment are: Quarterly 1 & 4 *azure* 3 escallops *or* 2 & 3 *gules* 2 demi-lions guardant *or* impaled with paly of six *argent* and *sable* on a fess *gules* 3 molets *or*; there is no mark of cadency. His arms in the centre window on the south side of Middle Temple Hall are: *azure* three escallops *or* a crescent charged with a label of three points for a difference. There is no crest—A. R. Ingpen, ed., *The Middle Temple Bench Book* (1912) 185, 415; Sir William Dugdale, *Origines Juridiciales* (1671) 225. His arms put up before the Civil War in the 'compasse window' of the Hall in Searjents' Inn, Chancery Lane, and now in the north window of the Common Room of the Law Society Hall, are similar to those in Middle Temple Hall, but there is no mark of cadency—Serjeants' Inn records PRO 30/23/2/1 f 53; Dugdale 334; F. S. Eden, 'Heraldic Painted Glass at the Law Society's Hall, London' *Law Society's Gazette* XXV (Oct. 1928) 267. I am indebted to Dr. John Baker of St. Catharine's College, Cambridge for pointing out these variations.

107. Sir John Sackville to Sir Robert Foster PRO SP 16/491/107 9 Aug. 1642 (*CSPD* 1641–43 368).

Bibliography

This list includes works which have contributed something to the content of the book. Accounts written within sixty years of the event have been listed as primary sources.

I PRIMARY SOURCES

A *Manuscripts*

In the collection of Colonel Sir Edward Malet Bt., OBE and lodged in the strongroom of the National Register of Archives

PRC/1	Professional: correspondence
FH/P/1	Family history: patents of nobility
PP/AP/2	Personal: appointments

In the collection of the Marquess of Lothian DL, Melbourne Hall, Derby
Cowper (Coke) MSS

In the collection of the Right Honourable Viscount De L'Isle, VC, Penshurst Place, Kent.

Sidney Papers

In the British Library

Add	14827	Framlingham Gawdy's diary
	32093	Sir Alexander Malet's MSS
	41581	Dansey papers
Egerton	3007	Heath and Verney papers XXX [1512–1812]
—charters	742	relating to Exeter and Poyntington [1649]
	1608–1610	relating to Poyntington [1624–30]
—rolls	2098–2100	relating to Poyntington [1607–37]
Hargrave	402	Law readings at the Middle Temple
Harleian	163, 164	The journal of Sir Simonds D'Ewes
	6832/19	Knights from the year 1633 to 1648

| Sloane | 856 | Copies of letters, warrants etc. of Charles II |
| Stowe | 142 | Earl of Ashburnham's MSS |

In the Cambridge University Library

Dd	5.50	Law readings at the Middle Temple [1626–39]
Hh	3.7	Law readings at the Middle Temple [1623–26]
Mm	1.45	The antiquarian collections of Thomas Baker (1656–1740), late Baker 34
Additional	6863	Diary of Sir Richard Hutton [1561?–1639]

In the House of Lords Records Office
Original manuscript minutes HL
Original manuscript draft journal (HLDJ) Braye 24 [4 Mar.–1 Apr. 1642]
Parchment collection HL
Main Papers HL

In the Public Record Office, London

PRO	30/23	Serjeants' Inn records
	/26	Miscellaneous
ASSI	5	Clerks of assize, Oxford circuit, indictments
ASSI	35	Clerks of assize, South-Eastern circuit, indictments
C	66	Chancery, patent rolls
C	181	Chancery, entry books of commissions (Crown Office)
C	202	Chancery, petty bag series
C	231	Chancery, Crown Office docket books
CP	45	Common Pleas, remembrance rolls
E	179	Exchequer, subsidy rolls
E	372	Exchequer, pipe office, pipe rolls
KB	125	King's Bench (plea side) entry books of rules
PROB	11	Prerogative Court of Canterbury, registered copy wills
SP	14	State Papers, Domestic, James I
SP	16	State Papers, Domestic, Charles I
SP	19	State Papers, Domestic, Interregnum, Committee for the Advance of Money
SP	23	State Papers, Domestic, Interregnum, Committee for Compounding with Delinquents

SP   29   State Papers, Domestic, Charles II
SP   38   State Papers, Domestic, docquets
SP   44   State Papers, Domestic, entry books
In the Cornwall County Museum and Art Gallery
                         Henderson MSS Calendars c. 35 vols.
                         (c. 1930)
In the Dorset County Record Office
D   103/1   Canon C. H. Mayo Transcript of
                         Poyntington Parish Register (1889)
P   198/RE 1   Poyntington   Parish   Register
                         (1618–1713)
In the Somerset County Record Office
DD   SOG/793–853   Poyntington deeds
D/D/Rt   366   Poyntington tithe apportionment
                         (1842)
SAS   C/1193/5/4   Brown MSS (1889)
In the Warwick County Record Office
Tomes, deeds of title reference L3 Admington 21, 22, 34, 36, 37
In St. Andrew's Church, West Quantockshead, Somerset
Transcript of West Quantockshead Parish Register [1558–1684]

B   *Printed calendars, registers, reports*

Bloom, Rev. J. Harvey, *The Cartae Antiquae of Lord Willoughby de Broke*
   4 vols. (Hemsworth, Yorks 1900)
Calendar of State Papers, Domestic 1619–23, 1623–25, 1627–28, 1629–31,
   1633–34, 1641–43. Addenda 1625–49, 1660–61, 1661–62, 1663–64, 1670
   with addenda 1660–70
Calendar of the Proceedings of the Committee for Advance of Money 1642–1656
   3 vols. (1888)
*Calendar of the Proceedings of the Committee for Compounding with Delinquents
   1643–1660* 5 vols. (1889–93)
Calendar of State Papers, Venetian 1640–42, 1642–43
Foster, J., ed., *Alumni Oxonienses 1500–1714* 4 vols. (Oxford 1891–92)
General Index to the Journals of the House of Lords vols. I–X (1836)
Hind, A. M., (completed by Margery Corbett and Michael Norton) *Engraving
   in England in the 16th and 17th Century* 3 vols. (Cambridge 1952–64)
Historical Manuscripts Commission
   Reports 5, 6, 7, 8, 10, 11, 12
      45 *Buccleuch (Montagu House)* III
      77 *De L'Isle and Dudley* VI
Manuscripts of the House of Lords (new series) 12 vols. (1900ff)
Middle Temple Records: Minutes of Parliament 1501–1703 ed. C. T. Martin
   4 vols. (1904–05)
Piper, D., *Catalogue of the Seventeenth Century Portraits in the National Portrait
   Gallery 1625–1714* (Cambridge 1963)

Return of the Names of Every Member Returned to Serve in Each Parliament 2 vols. (1878)

Sutherland, Mrs. A. H., *Catalogue of the Sutherland Collection* 2 vols. (1837)

Statutes of the Realm [to 1713 ed. T. E. Tomlins *et al.*] 11 vols. (1810–28)

C   Printed tracts and pamphlets

Catalogue of the Pamphlets . . . Collected by George Thomason, 1640–61 [in the British Museum] ed. G. K. Fortescue 2 vols. (1908)

The references in quotation are:

    Octavo size   E . . .
    Folio size   BL 669 f . . .

Thomason Tracts, where listed below, are taken from the short title in the catalogue.

Harleian Miscellany . . . ed. W. Oldys 8 vols. (1744–46)

A Catalogue of the Dukes, Marquesses, Earles, Viscounts, Bishops, Barons that Sit in This Parliament Begun 3 Nov (3 Nov. 1640)—E 1091 (1)

A Catalogue of the Names of the Knightes, Citizens, Burgesses and Barons for the Ports for the House of Commons, for This Parliament, Begun 3 Nov (3 Nov. 1640)—E 1091 (2)

A Perfect Journall of the Daily Proceedings and Transactions in That Memorable Parliament Begun at Westminster the Third Day of November 1640 2 vols. (1656)

Hakewill, W., *The Manner How Statutes Are Enacted in Parliament by Passing of Bills* (1641)

A Worthy Speech Made by Master Pym to the Lords concerning an Information against the Lord Digby (31 Dec. 1641)—E 199 (49). The speech was never delivered.

The Petition of the County of Essex to the House of Commons . . . (18 Jan. 1642)—E 131 (24)

Two Petitions of the Inhabitants of the County of Hertford . . . (25 Jan. 1642)—E 133 (15)

The Petition of the County of Northampton. Together with Two Petitions of the County of Kent (8 Feb. 1642)—E 135 (36)

Mr. Pym His Speech at a Conference of Both Houses concerning the Petition of the County of Kent (8 Feb. 1642)—E 200 (26) (never delivered)

The Petition of . . . the County of Kent 25 Mar. (1642)—E 142 (10)

A Perfect Diurnall of the Passages in Parliament from the Twenty Eighth of March 1642 to the Fourth of April [Apr. 1642]—E 202 (1)

Sermon Preached in the Tower by the Bishop of Bath and Wells [William Pierce] (24 Apr. 1642)—E 155 (21)

Newes from Blackheath concerning the Meeting of Kentish Men . . . (29 April 1642)—E 144 (13)

Strange Newes from Kent concerning the Passages of the Kentish Men Which Came to Westminster 29 April (29 April 1642)—E 145 (6)

To the Lords and Commons. The Humble Petition of Many of the Inhabitants of Kent . . . (5 May 1642)—BL 669 f 5 (13)

The Declaration or Remonstrance of Parliament (19 May 1642)—E 148 (17)

A Speech Made by John Earl of Bristol in Parliament concerning an Accommodation (20 May 1642)—E 200 (43)

His Majesties Answer to a Book Entituled the Declaration of the Lords and Commons of 19 May (21 May 1642)—E 150 (29)

The Truest and Most Reall Relation of the Apprehension of Three Rebels in Ireland, viz the Lord Maguire, Collonel Read, Captain MacMallion [June 1642]—E 151 (13)

St. Hillaries Teares Shed upon All Professions from the Judge to the Petty Fogger . . . ([June] 1642)—E 151 (16)

The King's Majesties Charge Sent to All the Judges of England (4 July 1642)—E 108 (7)

To the King. The Humble Declaration of the County of Essex (18 July 1642)—BL 669 f 5 (66)

A Perfect Diurnall of the Passages in Parliament from the 18th July to the 25th 1642 [July 1642]—E 202 (23)

A Perfect Diurnall of the Proceedings in Parliament from 18 July to the 25 of the Same 1642 [July 1642]—E 202 (24)

Two Petitions; the One to the King of the Grand Jury at the Assizes in Southampton; the Other to the Justices of the Peace at the Assizes at Bury St. Edmunds (30 July 1642)—E 112 (9)

The Petition of the Commons of Kent Presented to His Majestie with His Majesties Answer 4 Aug (1 Aug. 1642)—E 112 (26)

True Newes from Somersetshire ([6 Aug.] 1642)—BL 669 f 6 (62)

A Perfect Diurnall of the Passages in Parliament from the 1 August to the 7 1642 [Aug. 1642]—E 202 (30)

A Perfect Diurnall of the Passages in Parliament from the 1 of August to the 8 of August 1642 [Aug. 1642]—E 202 (31)

A Perfect Diurnall of the Passages in Parliament from the First of August to the Eighth 1642 [Aug. 1642]—E 202 (32)

Some Speciall Passages from London, Westminster, York, Hull, Holland, Denmark, Portsmouth and Divers Other Parts of England since the First of August to the Ninth 1642 [Aug. 1642]—E 109 (35)

Instructions from the Honourable House of Commons Assembled in Parliament to the Committee in Kent (13 Aug. 1642)—E 111 (13)

A Perfect Diurnall of the Passages in Parliament from the 8th of August to the 15th 1642 [Aug. 1642]—E 202 (8)

A True Relation of Certaine Speciall and Remarkable Passages from Both Houses of Parliament, since Monday the 15 August till Friday the Nineteenth 1642 [Aug. 1642]—E 112 (36)

The Petition of the County of Kent Presented to Parliament, Wherein They Disclaim That Late Petition Sent to his Majestie (30 Aug. 1642)—E 115 (1)

True and Remarkable Passages from Several Places in This Kingdome from Munday the Fifth of September to Saturday the 10 of September 1642 [Sep. 1642]—E 116 (28)

The Clerk of Assize . . . (1660)—E 2139 (3)

By the King a Proclamation concerning the Times of Holding This Summer Assizes (23 July 1660)—BL 669 f 25 (59)

The Indictment Arraignment Tryal and Judgement at Large of Twenty-Nine Regicides the Murtherers of His Most Sacred Majesty King Charles I of Glorious Memory (1714)

The Form of His Majesties Coronation Feast To Be Solemnised at Westminster Hall (23 April 1661)—BL 669 f 27 (15)

The Tryal of Sir Henry Vane Kt at the King's Bench Westminster June the 2d and 6th 1662 (1662)

The Office of the Clerk of Assize (1682)

Elsynge, H., *The Manner of Holding Parliaments in England* (1768)

D   *Printed books and modern periodicals*

Aubrey, John, *Brief Lives* ed. O. L. Dick (1958)

Barnes, Thomas G., ed., *Somerset Assize Orders 1629–1640 SRS* LXV (Frome 1959)

Bates-Harbin, Rev. E. H., ed., *Quarter Sessions Records for the County of Somerset* II *Charles I 1625–1639 SRS* XXIV (1908) III *Commonwealth 1646–1660 SRS* XXVIII (1912)

Bowyer, Robert, *The Parliamentary Diary of* . . . *1606–1607*, ed. D. H. Willson (Minneapolis 1931)

Bramston, Sir John, *The Autobiography of* . . . ed. Lord Braybrooke (Camden Society 1845)

Butler, Samuel, *Hudibras* ed. A. R. Waller (Cambridge 1905)

Clarendon, Edward Hyde, Earl of, *The History of the Rebellion and Civil Wars in England* (Oxford various editions)

Cobbett, W., ed., *The Parliamentary History of England* [1066–1803] 36 vols. (1806–1820)

Cobbett, W., T. B. Howell and others, ed., *Complete Collection of State Trials and Proceedings for High Treason and Other Crimes* . . . 34 vols. (1809–1828)

Croke, Sir George, *Reports of Cases in King's Bench and Common Bench* [1582–1641] 3 vols. (1683–1792)

Dawes, M. C. B., ed., *Quarter Sessions Records for the County of Somerset* IV *Charles II 1666–1677 SRS* XXXIV (1919)

De Maisse, *Journal* ed. G. B. Harrison and R. A. Jones (1931)

Dering, Sir Edward, *A Collection of Speeches Made by Sir Edward Dering Knight and Baronet in Matter of Religion* . . . (1642)

D'Ewes, Sir Simonds, *The Journals of All the Parliaments during the Reign of Queen Elizabeth* (1682)

D'Ewes, Sir Simonds, *The Journal of* . . . [3 Nov. 1640–20 Mar. 1641] ed. W. Notestein (New Haven, Conn. 1923)

D'Ewes, Sir Simonds, *The Journal of* . . . [12 Oct. 1641–10 Jan. 1642] ed. W. H. Coates (New Haven, Conn. 1942)

Dugdale, Sir William, *Origines Juridiciales* (1671)

Evelyn, John, *The Diary of* . . . ed. E. S. de Beer 6 vols. (Oxford 1955)

Evelyn, John, *Diary and Correspondence of* . . . (including Nicholas correspondence) ed. H. B. Wheatley 4 vols. (1906)

Fortescue, Sir John, *De Laudibus Legum Angliae* (1660)

Foster, Elizabeth R., ed., *Proceedings in Parliament 1610* 2 vols. (New Haven, Conn. 1966)

Fox, George, *The Journal of* . . . ed. Norman Penney (1924)

Gardiner, Dorothy, ed., *The Oxinden Letters 1607–1642* (1933)

Gardiner, S. R., ed., *Debates in the House of Commons in 1625* (Camden Society 1873)

Gerard, Thomas, *The Particular Description of the County of Somerset 1633* ed. Rev. E. H. Bates-Harbin *SRS* XV (1900)

Ingpen, A. R., ed., *Master Worsley's Book* (1910)

Ingpen, A. R., ed., *The Middle Temple Bench Book* (1912)

Jones, Sir William, *Les Reports de divers Special Cases cy bien in le Court de Banck le Roy, come le Common-Banck, Angleterre* [1620–40] (1675)

Journals of the House of Commons [1547–1761] 28 vols. (1742 ff)

Journals of the House of Lords [1510–1829] 61 vols. (1767 ff)

Keble, J., *Reports, King's Bench, at Westminster* [1661–79] 3 vols. (1685)

Kelyng, Sir J., *Report of Divers Cases in Pleas of the Crown* [1662–69] (1708)

Larking, L. B., ed., *Proceedings Principally in the County of Kent* . . . (Camden Society 1862)

Levinz, Sir C., *Reports of Cases in the Court of King's Bench and Common Pleas* [1600–96] (1702)

March, J., *Reports: or, New Cases* [King's Bench and Common Pleas 1639–42] (1675)

Milles, T., *The Catalogue of Honor* (1610)

Nalson, John, ed., *An Impartial Collection of the Great Affairs of State from the Beginning of the Scotch Rebellion in the Year 1639 to the Murther of Charles I* 2 vols. (1682–83)

[Nicholas, Edward,] *Proceedings and Debates of the House of Commons in 1620 and 1621* . . . ed. T. Tyrwhitt 2 vols. (Oxford 1766)

Notestein, Wallace, F. H. Relf and H. Simpson, ed., *Commons Debates 1621* 7 vols. (New Haven, Conn. 1935)

Ogilby, John, *Britannia* (1675)

Ordish, T. F. ed., *Roads out of London* (London Topographical Society 1911) [reprints from Ogilby, John, *Britannia* (1675)]

Raymond, Sir T., *Reports, King's Bench, Common Pleas and Exchequer* [1660–83] (1696)

Read, Conyers, ed., *William Lambarde and Local Government* (Cornell 1962)

Relf, F. H., ed., *Notes of the Debates in the House of Lords* . . . *1621, 1625, 1628* (Camden Society 1929)

Rogers, J. E. T., ed., *A Complete Collection of the Protests of the Lords* 3 vols. (Oxford 1875)

Rushworth, John, *Historical Collections of Private Passages of State* . . . 7 vols. (1659–1701)

Rymer, T. and R. Sanderson, ed., *Foedera* 20 vols. (1704–32)

Siderfin, Sir T., *Les reports des divers special cases, Bank le Roy, Co Ba & L'Exchequer* [1657–70] 2 parts in 1 vol. (1683–84)

Sims, Catherine S., 'The Moderne Forme of the Parliaments of England' *AHR* LIII 2 (Jan. 1948)

Smith, Sir Thomas, *De Republica Anglorum* (1583)

Spelman, Sir Henry, *Reliquiae Spellmannianae* (Oxford 1698)

Sprigge, Joshua, *Anglia Rediviva* (1647)

Stow, John, *The Survey of London* (Everyman 1956)

Townshend, Henry, *Diary of . . . of Elmley Lovett 1640–1663* ed. J. W. Willis Bund 2 vols. (Worcs Historical Society 1915–16)

Twysden, Sir Roger, 'Sir Roger Twysden's Journal' ed. L. R. L[arking] *AC* I (1858) *AC* II (1859)

Wallington, Nehemiah, *Historical Notices of the Reign of Charles I* [1630–46] ed. R. Webb 2 vols. (1869)

Whitelocke, Bulstrode, *Memorials of the English Affairs* (1682)

Whitelocke, Sir James, *Liber Famelicus* ed. J. Bruce (Camden Society 1858)

Wood, A. à, *Fasti Oxonienses* (1721)

E   *Paintings, drawings and engravings*

In the collection of Colonel Sir Edward Malet Bt., OBE
  [Anon], [Sir Thomas] Malet (1582–1665] (¾ length oil on canvas 1661)
  [Anon], Jane Lady Malet, [wife of above] (head and shoulders, oil on canvas c. 1661)
In the Devonshire collections, Chatsworth, Bakewell, Derbyshire
  Clarendon 3 vols. (Oxford 1707) grangerized copy by Bulfinch:
  [Anon], *Sir Thomas Malet, Judge* (drawing 1795–1814 from a painting of unknown date) I 542
In the Sutherland Collection, Ashmolean Museum, Oxford
  Clarendon 3 vols. (Oxford 1707) grangerized copy by Sutherland, collected 1795–1835, (grangerized version 1837):
  [Anon], [Charles I in Parliament] (engraving c. 1630) I 175
  de Wilde, Samuel [alias J. S. Paul], *Sir Thomas Malet* (mezzotint nd) I 382
  Smith, W. J., [Sir Thomas Malet, Archbishop Williams and Colonel Sir Thomas Lunsford] (facsimile drawing from the engraving of the same subject in the British Library I 431)
  Drapentier, *The House of Commons* [chamber] (line drawing 1625–49) I 141
  Gardiner, W. N., *Judge Sir Thomas Mallett* (black and white pen and wash drawing 1795–1814) I 382

Also:

Bocquet, [Sir George Strode 1583–1663] (sketch from a portrait by Glover c. 1642) C 11 42.

Norden, John, *Civitas Londini* [bird's eye view of London] (engraving 1600) B I 793

Visscher, C. J., [Long view of] *London* [from the south] (engraving 1616)

In the British Library:

[Anon], [Sir Thomas Malet, Archbishop Williams, and Colonel Sir Thomas Lunsford] (1642) 669 f 6 (71)

In the British Museum, Department of Prints and Drawings:

[Anon], *Westminster Hall, west end* [actually south] *with the Courts of Chancery and King's Bench in session* (line drawing seventeenth century)

In the Duchy of Cornwall Records:

[Anon], *A more perfect platform then hitherto hath bin published of the Lower House of this present parliament assembled at Westminster, the third day of November 1640* . . . (engraving 1641)

In the National Portrait Gallery:

[Anon], [Sir John Doddridge 1555–1628] (oil on canvas nd)

[Anon], [John Finch, Baron Finch of Fordwich 1584–1660] (oil on canvas after Vandyke nd)

[Anon], [Edward Littleton, Baron Littleton of Mounslow 1589–1645] (oil on canvas after Vandyke nd)

[Anon], [Sir Thomas] *Mallet* [1582–1665] (oil on canvas nd)

In the John Rylands University Library of Manchester:

Clarendon 3 vols. (Oxford 1807) grangerized copy by George John 2nd Earl Spencer finished in 1822:

Cooper, Robert, *Sir Thomas Mallet* (engraving nd) I 758 and 1096

In the Harvard Law School Library, Cambridge, Mass.

[Anon], [Sir Thomas Mallet 1582–1665] (black and white wash painting) nd)

In the Westminster City Collection, Westminster City Library:

Carter, John, *East View in the Painted Chamber* (1788)

Hollar, Wenceslaus, [View of Westminster Palace from the river] (engraving 1647) and [View of New Palace Yard from the east] (engraving 1647).

II SECONDARY SOURCES

A *Unprinted material*

Enright, B. J., *Public Petitions in the House of Commons* (typescript 1960) (HLRO)

Glow, Lotte, *House of Commons Committees and County Committees 1640–1644* . . . 2 vols. (typescript PhD thesis Adelaide 1963)

Mallet, Mathilde, *Origin of the Name of Mallet and the Various Ways of Writing It* (typescript 1933) (Somerset Archaeological and Natural History Society Library, Taunton Castle)

Williams, O. C., *The Topography of the Old House of Commons* (typescript nd) (Ministry of Works Library)

B   *Printed books*

[Anon], *Descent of the House of Malet from William Malet to the Present Day (nd)*

[Anon], *Old Serjeant's Inn Chancery Lane* (Law, Union and Rock Insurance Company 1912)

Alexander, H. G., *Religion in England 1558–1662* (1968)

Aylmer, G. E., *The King's Servants: The Civil Service of Charles I 1625–1642* (1961)

Aylmer, G. E., *The Struggle for the Constitution 1603–1689* (1968)

Bankes, G., *The Story of Corfe Castle* (1853)

Barnes, Thomas G., *Somerset 1625–1640* (Oxford 1961)

Barnes, Thomas G., *The Clerk of the Peace in Caroline Somerset* (Leicester 1961)

Baverstock, J. H., *Some Account of Maidstone in Kent* (1832)

Bell, A. H., *Some Account of the Parish of Poyntington* (Yeovil 1928)

Bond, M. F., *Guide to the Records of Parliament* (1971)

Bowen, Catherine D., *Francis Bacon* (1963)

Bowen, Catherine D., *The Lion and the Throne* (1957)

Brayley, E. W., *Londiniana* 4 vols. (1828)

Brayley, E. W. and J. Britton, *The History of the Ancient Palace and Late Houses of Parliament at Westminster* (1836)

Brett-James, N. G., *The Growth of Stuart London* (1935)

[British Museum], *Catalogue of Prints and Drawings . . .* 4 vols. (1870)

Brunton, D., and D. H. Pennington, *Members of the Long Parliament* (1954)

Bryant, Arthur, *King Charles II* (1931)

Bryant, Arthur, *The Story of England: Makers of the Realm* (1953)

Burne, Alfred H. and Peter Young, *The Great Civil War: A Military History of the First Civil War 1642–1646* (1959).

Campbell, Lord John, *The Lives of the Chief Justices of England from the Norman Conquest to the Death of Lord Tenterden* 3 vols. (1849–57)

Campbell, Lord John, *The Lives of the Lord Chancellors and Keepers of the Great Seal of England* 8 vols. (1845–69)

Cave-Browne, J., *The History of the Parish Church of All Saints, Maidstone* (Maidstone nd [1889])

Chauncy, Sir Henry, *The Historical Antiquities of Hertfordshire* 2 vols. (1826)

Cheney, C. R., *Handbook of Dates for Students of English History* (1970)

Clarke, Aidan, *The Old English in Ireland 1625–1642* (1966)

Cockburn, J. S., *A History of English Assizes 1558–1714* (Cambridge 1972)

Coller, R. O., *The People's History of Essex* 2 vols. (Chelmsford 1861)

Collinson, Rev. John, *The History and Antiquities of the County of Somerset* 3 vols. (Bath 1791)

Coltman, Irene, *Private Men and Public Causes* (1962)

Colvin, H. M., *The History of the King's Works* 6 vols. (1963 ff)

Davies, Godfrey, *The Early Stuarts 1603–1660* (Oxford 1959)

Davies, Godfrey, *The Restoration of Charles II 1658–1660* (Oxford 1955)

Dictionary of National Biography ed. L. Stephen and S. Lee 22 vols. (Oxford 1908–09)

Everitt, Alan, *The Community of Kent and the Great Rebellion 1640–1660* (Leicester 1966)

Firth, C. H., *The House of Lords during the Civil War* (1910)

Forster, J., *The Debates on the Grand Remonstrance . . .* (1860)

Forster, J., *The Statesmen of the Commonwealth of England* 5 vols. (1840)

Foss, Edward, *The Judges of England* [1066–1864] 9 vols. (1848–64)

Fowler, J., *A Description of Sherborne Scenery* (Sherborne, Dorset 1936)

Gardiner, S. R., *History of England from the Accession of James I to the Outbreak of the Civil War 1603–1642* 10 vols. (1883–84)

Gardiner, S. R., *History of the Great Civil War 1642–1649* 3 vols. (1886–91)

Gleason, J. H., *The Justices of the Peace 1558–1640* (Oxford 1969)

Hargreaves-Mawdsley, W. N., *A History of Legal Dress in Europe* (Oxford 1963)

Hastings, M., *Parliament House* (1950)

Hexter, J. H., *The Reign of King Pym* (Cambridge, Mass. 1961)

Holdsworth, Sir William, *A History of English Law* 13 vols. (1922–52)

Home, Gordon, *Old London Bridge* (1931)

Hone, N. J., *The Manor and Manorial Records* (1912)

Hull, Felix, *Guide to the Kent County Archives Office* (Maidstone 1958)

Hulme, H., *The Life of Sir John Eliot 1592–1632* (1957)

Hutchinson, John, *A Catalogue of Notable Middle Templars* (1902)

Irwin, Margaret, *That Great Lucifer* (1960)

Jessup, F. W., *Sir Roger Twysden 1597–1672* (1965)

Jones, W. J., *The Elizabethan Court of Chancery* (Oxford 1967)

Jones, W. J., *Politics and the Bench* (1971)

Keeler, M. F., *The Long Parliament 1640–1641* (Philadelphia 1954)

Kenyon, J. P., *The Stuarts* (1966)

Kingston, Alfred, *Hertfordshire during the Great Civil War* (1894)

Macqueen, J. F., *A Practical Treatise on the Appelate Jurisdiction of the House of Lords and Privy Council* (1842)

Malet, Arthur, *Notices of an English Branch of the Malet Family* (1885)

Malet, Sir Charles Warre, *Papers on the Subject of Sir Charles Warre Malet's Application for Precedency in the Order of Baronets according to Ancient Patent of Charles the Second* (Salisbury, England 1805)

Mallet, Mathilde, *Our Ancestors* (1933)

Maxwell-Lyte, Sir Henry, 'Historical Notes on Some Somerset Manors Formerly Connected with the Honour of Dunster' *SRS* Extra Series (Taunton 1931)

Maynard, D. C., *The Old Inns of Kent* (1925)

Moir, T. L., *The Addled Parliament of 1614* (Oxford 1958)

Morrill, J. S., *The Revolt of the Provinces* (1976)

Morrill, J. S., *The Cheshire Grand Jury 1625–1659* (Leicester 1976)

Neale, J. E., *The Elizabethan House of Commons* (1949)

Ollard, Richard, *The Escape of Charles II* (1966)

Page, F. M., *History of Hertford* (1959)

Parkes, Joan, *Travel in England in the Seventeenth Century* (Oxford 1925)

Parry, R. H., ed., *The English Civil War and After 1642–1656* (1970)

Pearl, Valerie, *London and the Outbreak of the Puritan Revolution 1625–1643* (Oxford 1961)

Pollard, A. F., *The Evolution of Parliament* (1926)

Powell, J. E. and K. Wallis, *The House of Lords in the Middle Ages* (1968)

[PRO] *Guide to the Contents of the Public Record Office* 2 vols. (1963)

Pulling, A., *The Order of the Coif* (1884)

Rebholz, R. A., *The Life of Fulke Greville, First Lord Brooke* (Oxford 1971)

Rendle, W., *Old Southwark and Its People* (1878)

Rendle, W. and P. Norman, *The Inns of Old Southwark* (1888)

Richardson, R. C., *The Debate on the English Revolution* (1977)

Roberts, Clayton, *The Growth of Responsible Government in Stuart England* (Cambridge 1966)

Rowe, Violet A., *Sir Henry Vane the Younger* (1970)

Rowse, A. L., *The England of Elizabeth* (1961)

Royal Commission on Historical Monuments (England)
  London II *West* (1925)
  Dorset I *West* (1952)

Russell, Conrad, *The Origins of the English Civil War* (1973)

Russell, J. M., *The History of Maidstone* (Maidstone 1881)

Sanford, J. L., *Studies and Illustrations of the Great Rebellion* (1858)

Saunders, Hilary St. George, *Westminster Hall* (1951)

Shaw, W. A., *The Knights of England* 2 vols. (1906)

Siebert, F. S., *Freedom of the Press in England 1476–1776* (Urbana, Illinois 1952)

Stone, Lawrence, *The Causes of the English Revolution 1529–1642* (1972)

Tite, Colin C. G., *Impeachment and Parliamentary Judicature in Early Stuart England* (1974)

Trevelyan, G. M., *England under the Stuarts* (1949)

Underdown, David, *Somerset in the Civil War and Interregnum* (Newton Abbot 1973)

Veall, D., *The Popular Movement for Law Reform 1640–1660* (Oxford 1970)

Verney, Peter, *The Standard Bearer* (1963)

Wade, C. E., *John Pym* (1912)

Weaver, F. W., ed., *Somerset Incumbents from the Hugo MSS* (Bristol 1889)

Wedgwood, C. V., *The Great Rebellion I: The King's Peace 1637–1641* (1955)

Wedgwood, C. V., *The Great Rebellion II: The King's War 1641–1647* (1958)

Wedgwood, C. V., *Thomas Wentworth, First Earl of Strafford 1593–1641* (1964)

Weston, Corinne C., *English Constitutional Theory and the House of Lords 1556–1832* (1965)

Williams, Norman Lloyd, *Sir Walter Raleigh* (1962)

Williamson, J. B., *The History of the Temple, London* (1924)

Willson, D. H., *The Privy Councillors in the House of Commons 1604–1629* (Minneapolis 1940)

Wingfield-Stratford, Esmé, *King Charles and King Pym 1637–1643* (1949)

Wyndham, H. A., *A Family History 1410–1688* (Oxford 1939)

Zagorin, Perez, *The Court and the Country (1969)*

C   *Printed articles*

[Anon], 'ART III 1. "A Journal of the Parliament Begun November 3d Tuesday anno Domini 1640, anno 16 mo Caroli Regis." By Sir Simonds D'Ewes, Bart. Harleian MSS 162 to 166. Brit. Mus. 2. *The Autobiography and Correspondence of Sir Simonds D'Ewes, Bart.* Edited by J. O. Halliwell Esq. Two vols. 8vo London: 1845.' *The Edinburgh Review* LXXXIV 169 (July 1846).

Adair, E. R. and F. M. Greir Evans, 'Writs of Assistance 1558–1700' *EHR* XXXVI 143 (July 1921)

Box, E. G., 'Notes on some West Kent Roads in Early Maps and Road-books' *AC* XLIII (1931)

Colvin, H. M., 'Views of the Old Palace of Westminster' *Architectural History* IX (1966)

Eden, F. S., 'Heraldic Painted Glass at the Law Society's Hall, London' *Law Society's Gazette* XXV (Oct. 1928) 267.

Foster, Elizabeth R., 'Procedure in the House of Lords during the Early Stuart Period' *JBS* V 2 (May 1966)

Glow, Lotte, 'The Manipulation of Committees in the Long Parliament 1641–1642' *JBS* V I (Nov. 1965)

Glow, Lotte, 'The Committee-men in the Long Parliament August 1642–December 1643' *Historical Journal* VIII I (1965)

Glow, Lotte, 'The Committee of Safety' *EHR* LXXX 315 (April 1965)

Havighurst, A. F., 'The Judiciary and Politics in the Reign of Charles II' *LQR* LXVI (1950)

Heale, Rev. J., 'Poyntington' *SANHS* XVI (1870) XX (1874)

Hexter, J. H., 'The Problem of the Presbyterian Independents' *AHR* XLIV (Oct 1938)

Hirst, D., 'The Defection of Sir Edward Dering' *Historical Journal* XV 2 (1972)

Laslett, P., 'The Gentry of Kent in 1640' *CHJ* IX 2 (1948)

Malden, H. E., 'The Civil War in Surrey 1642' *SAC* XXII (1909)

Malet, G. E. G., 'The Origin of the Malets of Enmore' *Genealogists' Magazine* (June 1939)

Malet, Octavius Warre, 'Memoir of Sir Thomas Malet' *SANHS* XX (1874)

Marshall, George W., 'The Malets of St. Audries' *SANHS* XVI (1870)

Onslow, Earl of, 'Sir Richard Onslow 1603–1664' *SAC* XXXVI (1925)

Pennington, D. H., 'A Day in the Life of the Long Parliament' *History Today* III (1953)

[Various], 'Special Issue on the English Civil War' *The Journal of Modern History* XLIX 4 (Dec. 1977)

Chronology

c1582		Thomas Malet born. Place and date not known.
1600		
	29 Feb	Admitted to Middle Temple.
1606		
	7 Nov	Called to the bar.
1614		
	5 Apr	Member of Parliament for Tregony, Cornwall.
1621		
	30 Jan	Member of Parliament for Tregony, Cornwall.
	4 May	Appointed steward and keeper of certain properties belonging to Westminster Abbey.
c1622?		Marries Jane, daughter of Francis Mills.
c1623		Eldest son John born.
1624		
	18 Jan	Acquires long lease of a 'mannour place' at Poyntington.
1625		
	17 May	Member of Parliament for Newtown, Isle of Wight.
1626		
	6 Feb	Member of Parliament for Newtown, Isle of Wight.
	28 Apr	Becomes a bencher of the Middle Temple after his reading.
	4 Sep	Appointed solicitor general to Queen Henrietta Maria.
1633		
	8 Oct	Becomes treasurer of Middle Temple (for one year).
1634		Appointed justice of the peace in Somerset.
1635		
	2 Jan	Created serjeant-at-law.
1641		
	1 Jul	Appointed judge of King's Bench.

1642

25 Mar	Kentish petition agreed at Maidstone during his winter assizes.
28 Mar	Committed to the Tower of London by the House of Lords.
2 May	Released from the Tower of London on bail.
26 Jul	Further Kentish petition agreed at Maidstone during his summer assizes.
6 Aug	Committed once more to the Tower of London by the House of Lords.

1644

6 Nov	Released from the Tower on bail to arrange exchange of prisoners.

1645

3 Feb	Released from his bail on completing his exchange. Remains at Oxford with the King.
24 Jun	Granted a pass by Sir Thomas Fairfax on the capture of Oxford.
24 Nov	Ordinance of Lords and Commons disables him from being a judge.

1648

2 Nov	Ordinance of Lords and Commons absolves him from delinquency.

1660

31 May	Reappointed judge of King's Bench.
9 Oct	Sits in judgement upon the Regicides.
5 Dec	Excused daily attendance in Westminster Hall during term.

1663

Jun	Ceases to sit on the Bench.
19 Jun	Receives a patent of baronetage.

1665

17 Dec	Dies at Poyntington, Somerset, at the age of about eighty-three.

Index

In the Index I have sought to give to names titles and appointments a precision which could be tedious to the reader if he found it in the text. Items in footnotes are indexed (by page number) only when they are a matter for discussion there. The only titles and offices listed are those held in the book. Peers shown as 'summoned by writ' sat in the House of Lords when they had a father still living. References to 'knight' under counties relate to the knight of the shire for that county. Family relationships all refer to Sir Thomas Malet.

J.K.